KNOWLEDGE AND DEVELOPMENT

Volume 1
Advances in Research and Theory

KNOWLEDGE AND DEVELOPMENT

Volume 1
Advances in Research and Theory

Edited by
Willis F. Overton
and
Jeanette McCarthy Gallagher
Temple University
Philadelphia, Pennsylvania

PLENUM PRESS • NEW YORK AND LONDON

Library of Congress Cataloging in Publication Data

Main entry under title:

Knowledge and development.

Includes bibliographies and index.
CONTENTS: v. 1. Advances in research and theory.
1. Cognition. 2. Cognition (Child psychology). 3. Developmental psychology.
I. Overton, Willis F. II. Gallagher, Jeanette McCarthy, 1932-
[DNLM: 1. Cognition. 2. Child development. WS105 K73]
BF311.K6385   153.4   76-26163
ISBN 0-306-33201-9 (v. 1)

© 1977 Plenum Press, New York
A Division of Plenum Publishing Corporation
227 West 17th Street, New York, N.Y. 10011

Printed in the United States of America

Contributors

Michael J. Chandler, *Department of Psychology, University of Rochester, Rochester, New York*

Gerald Gratch, *Department of Psychology, University of Houston, Houston, Texas*

Frank H. Hooper, *Child and Family Studies Program, University of Wisconsin, Madison, Wisconsin*

Bärbel Inhelder, *Faculté de Psychologie et des Sciences de l'Education, Université de Genève, Geneva, Switzerland*

Lynn S. Liben, *The Pennsylvania State University, University Park, Pennsylvania*

Jean Piaget, *Faculté de Psychologie et des Sciences de l'Education, Université de Genève, Geneva, Switzerland*

Nancy W. Sheehan, *Child and Family Studies Program, University of Wisconsin, Madison, Wisconsin*

Foreword

From an informal group of a dozen faculty and graduate students at Temple University, the Jean Piaget Society grew in seven years to 500 members who have interests in the application of genetic epistemology to their own disciplines and professions. At the outset Piaget endorsed the concept of a society which bore his name and presented a major address on equilibration at the society's first symposium in May, 1971. Had he not done so the society would no doubt have remained a small parochial group, like so many others throughout the country, interested in Piaget and his theory. With the encouragement of Genevans and the leadership of its first four presidents, Lois Macomber, Barbara Presseisen, Marilyn Appel, and John Mickelson, the society undertook a number of programs to collect and disseminate the results of scholarly work in genetic epistemology. Particular emphasis was placed upon applications of Piaget's theory to developmental psychology, philosophy, and education.

One of these programs was the publication of an annual series on the development of knowing, of which this volume is the first. In 1973, the society asked Hans Furth with the assistance of Willis Overton and Jeanette Gallagher to initiate and plan a series of yearbooks with the result that in addition to this volume, a second volume on education was commissioned, and a third one on the *décalage* issue was planned. The subsequent volumes in this series will include not only contributions by psychologists on the nature of knowing and its development but contributions by philosophers, historians, anthropologists, linguists, and others who have adopted perspectives, whether critical or supportive, of a genetic epistemological interpretation of what constitutes knowledge and what it means to know something.

The topics of future volumes, while not limited to the particular views of any single person, will be devoted to the explication and extension of the position that our understanding of knowing and knowledge is advanced by an analysis of their development and history, their structural organizations, and their construction by active human minds.

December, 1976

FRANK B. MURRAY
President, The Jean Piaget Society

Preface

The present volume includes two theoretical contributions by Piaget and five reviews of current research in the areas of the development of concepts of chance and probability, infancy, social cognition, memory, and aging.

In the first chapter Piaget addresses the question of how we are to explain the order and novelty found in biological and cognitive development. The traditional popular mechanical answer to these questions has been given by the neo-Darwinian model of chance variation and selection. Monod has argued that the selection of one form or another is not a chance occurrence but an active choice that results from teleonomic or regulative activity. Piaget supports this position but argues that it should be extended to include "chance" variations or novel forms as well as selection. Piaget maintains that variation is not a mere trial and error with selection following. Rather, variations are the products of directed activity of the whole, "which controls at the same time the performances as 'trials' and their selection as 'choices'" (p. 6).

In his second chapter Piaget examines the role of action in the development of thinking. In the first part of the chapter he discusses the relation between two types of knowing activity: *figurative*, which aims at describing the world, and *operative*, which is transformational in nature. Piaget explores various types of figurative aspects of knowing, including perception and imagery, in order to demonstrate that these are not sufficient to account for thought processes or concepts (operative aspect). This provides the basis for the second part of the chapter in which Piaget argues that the operations of thought derive from the organism's actions upon objects, and he summarizes the course of this development. In this discussion he elaborates the distinction between physical experience and logical–mathematical experience.

A theme that runs through Piaget's chapters and through his work in general is that knowledge is not a copy of some independent reality imposed upon the subject, but rather, it is an active construction of the subject in interaction with the world. This theme is continued through the present volume particularly in the chapters by Inhelder, Gratch, Chandler, and Liben.

Bärbel Inhelder raises the constructionist theme by addressing the question of whether the child's concepts of chance and probability could derive directly from his observations. Through a series of research studies she answers this question in the negative and suggests that chance and probability are understood by the child in the context of his logical–mathematical operations.

Gerald Gratch's chapter on the development of the object concept during infancy highlights the controversy between those who maintain that the young infant is aware of a world of permanent objects and Piaget's view that the infant must construct such permanent objects, in stages, through sensorimotor activity. Gratch analyzes the research literature in two parts. The first part examines studies of infants less than six months of age. These studies have generally been motivated by the assumption that the infant already has a world of object permanence. The second part explores studies of infants older than six months. These studies have been generated either by efforts to support Piaget's position or to criticize it from an empiricist perspective.

In his review of research in the field of social cognition Michael Chandler begins from the constructionist theme and goes on to an important holistic aspect of Piaget's theory. This aspect maintains that affect and thought, social and physical, subject and object, are not discrete components but points of special emphasis within the realm of knowing. Chandler employs this perspective to analyze the work of researchers who have generally oriented themselves toward either the objective pole (person perception and social sensitivity studies) or the subjective pole (egocentrism and decentering studies) of the whole of subject–object interaction.

Lynn Liben's chapter on research in memory development also starts from a constructionist position. She reviews studies which bear upon the hypothesis, originally put forth by Piaget and Inhelder, that memory is dependent on the status of the child's cognitive structures. Included are some of the issues related to memory improvement versus memory regressions. Liben also explores the question of the locus during the encoding, storage, retrieval process that structures may influence memory. The chapter concludes with a comparison of Piaget and Inhelder's cognitive approach and other theories of memory.

The final chapter by Frank Hooper and Nancy Sheehan examines research on the status of logical concepts during the aging years. Hooper and Sheehan are particularly concerned with the question of the type of model which will best handle the cognitive changes of the adult and aging years. One suggestion the authors find promising is a competence–performance distinction which in essence asserts that logical–mathematical structures or competence maintain a relative stability across the later years while specific task behaviors become increasingly susceptible to socio-cultural and situational determinants.

The preparation for the series and the production of this volume were facilitated by a number of people. The board of directors of the Jean Piaget Society and particularly past presidents Marilyn Appel and John Mickelson were a source of continuing support. Carolyn Hegeler and Gail Mickelson provided important typing assistance. Judy Hornblum gave valuable editorial help and compiled the index. Finally, the authors who, in addition to being respected scholars, also proved to be sensitive to issues of time schedules and open to suggestions for revision made the task of preparation a pleasurable one.

Contents

Chapter 3

The Development of the Concepts of Chance and Probability in Children

Bärbel Inhelder

Chapter 4

**Review of Piagetian Infancy Research: Object Concept
Development**
Gerald Gratch

Chapter 5

Social Cognition: A Selective Review of Current Research
Michael J. Chandler

Chapter 6

**Memory from a Cognitive-Developmental Perspective:
A Theoretical and Empirical Review**

Lynn S. Liben

Chapter 7

Logical Concept Attainment during the Aging Years:
Issues in the Neo-Piagetian Research Literature

Frank H. Hooper and *Nancy W. Sheehan*

Chance and Dialectic in Biological Epistemology

A Critical Analysis of Jacques Monod's Theses*

JEAN PIAGET

The outstanding work that Jacques Monod (1971) has devoted to the subject of chance and necessity in human evolution merits a full discussion, for it is characterized by two qualities that are rarely encountered: an undeniable originality in the interpretation of his theses, even those that are quite common, such as the role of natural selection; and a great flexibility of thinking with regard to fashionable tendencies, such as the dialectic in nature. If the following remarks on certain points go counter to the explanatory models of the author, this is certainly not done merely for the sake of a critical reaction. On the contrary, these remarks are to suggest certain further developments that seem to be in the spirit of Monod's work (for instance, the relation between chance and selection), and to support a dialectic which does not belong to any school—a dialectic which I have used spontaneously in my own work and which appears to me to be implicated in the ideas of Monod on the necessary role of self-regulation. [Several Marxists have been able to discover a convergence between my thinking and their theses, but they recognize that this was a simple coincidence (Goldman, 1970).]

JEAN PIAGET • Faculté de Psychologie et des Sciences de l'Education, Université de Genève, Geneva, Switzerland.
*Translated from the French by Hans Furth.

1. Discriminative Properties

To begin with a point of agreement, I have in fact written an entire work (Piaget, 1971a) to show the continuity between biological self-regulation and those mechanisms that underlie the development of intelligence or cognitive functions in general. If Monod's book (1971) had appeared before mine, I would have quoted it in great detail; his manner of interpreting "cognitively" the role of regulatory proteins as "detectors of chemical signals" appears to me most clarifying:

> All these teleonomic performances rest, in the final analysis, upon the proteins' so-called 'stereospecific' properties, that is to say, upon their ability to 'recognize' other molecules (including other proteins) by their *shape*, this shape being determined by their molecular structure. At work here is, quite literally, a microscopic discriminative (if not 'cognitive') faculty.

For me the word "discriminative" would suffice, but I am glad that "cognitive" has been added since these two terms are practically synonomous.

As an aside I would like to say a few words first about the important problem of the relation between organic and cognitive functioning, a problem that Monod did not directly address. One can assert that instinctive knowing with its hereditary program implies a "logic" (Tinbergen, 1971) and I have attempted to show (Piaget, 1971b) that its structure is analogous to that of the logic underlying sensorimotor intelligence, except that the schemes and their coordinations are innate in one case and acquired in another. A simple example can illustrate the point. If *helix pomatia*, as other snails in our country, instinctively buries its eggs under the ground, this behavior can be under the control of a coordination, either at the level of the genome or the epigenotype, between a scheme tending to ensure for its eggs the same protection as for itself and another scheme making the animal bury itself to avoid dryness and cold and construct an epiphragm of dry mucous. But how can the material particles (genes or products of their synthetic activity) underlying these particular behaviors become coordinated in a manner similar to sensorimotor schemes if the coordination of the latter proceeds by relations of analogy while the coordination between representative physical particles is merely spatial? The concept of "stereospecific" connections with their discriminative properties, halfway between chemical and cognitive properties, suggests the possibility of an analogous interpretation. In this way one avoids purely verbal solutions of the problem in which a sort of anticipatory intelligence is projected into those remarkable coordinations, characteristic of instinct, which are at the same time hereditary and cognitive. The general principle of solution would be the following: to schemes that, at the level of behavior, have a logical relation between them would correspond—at the level of genetic transmission or epigenetic synthesis—material elements whose dynamo-geometry would imply analogies of "forms."

2. A Hereditary Linguistic Nucleus?

But why go to all the trouble when it would be so simple with Descartes and Chomsky to admit the existence of "innate ideas"? In fact, it must be said in these introductory remarks that Monod's unreserved approval of the "innate fixed nucleus," which Chomsky postulates at the base of his transformational grammar, appears ill founded even from a strictly biological perspective. The formation of a hereditary language center in the course of man's evolution, which would make language acquisition possible, would raise tremendous genetic problems, if there were nothing but chance and natural selection to explain the event. One could conceivably comprehend how chance could be responsible for variations of an already existing or developing organ; however, the considerable gap between the incapacity and the capacity of learning an articulated language makes the transition appear even more mysterious. But beyond that, to admit the almost instantaneous formation of a center whose function would be, not merely to make learning possible, but to furnish structures such as the relation between subject and predicate, poses even more unsolvable problems. It would mean, if indeed we were dealing here with a chance mutation, the subordination of logic to chance, since Chomsky's fixed nucleus contains the essential of logic. It would also mean to justify by natural selection (whose outcome ordinarily is merely an increased probability of survival) the better adaptation of those subjects who used the subject–predicate relation. Yet the results of this achievement would only occur much later and on a level of reflection since action is concerned only with coordination between sensorimotor schemes.

If, as Chomsky believes, the problem were to choose between innateness or a simple empiricistic associationism, one would have to accept these difficulties. But it so happens that the first of these solutions is really quite useless, even though the second is totally unacceptable— and here Chomsky has done great service by his brilliant and incisive criticism of Skinner's interpretations. First, the formation of language is

certainly a later development than sensorimotor intelligence, the remarkable functioning of which can be observed in, among others, chim-
panzees and the human baby before any semiotic function. This type of
intelligence includes precisely everything that Chomsky needs to furnish his so-called innate fixed nucleus with a logic of actions. Second,
the construction and progress of sensorimotor intelligence from the first
schemes of habit (which are obviously acquired) can be explained by a
continual and self-constructive interplay of regulations—without forgetting the maturation of the nervous system which participates in all behavior but which is limited to the opening up of possibilities and does
not impose ready-made structures and itself depends partly on exercise.
In sensorimotor development one can follow and explain step by step
the elaboration, not programmed by heredity, of a series of active constructions. In sum, the hypothesis of an innate language appears to be at
the same time useless and void of any psychological justification.

3. A Cybernetic Perspective

To turn now to the essential theses of Monod's work on biological
causality, he develops in a most suggestive and convincing manner
conceptions deriving from a contemporary cybernetic perspective and
from experimental knowledge regarding regulatory mechanisms.
Monod himself has made substantial contributions to this knowledge.
Moreover, these theses have a strong tendency toward interpretations
which are only implicitly developed. I refer here particularly to the role
and meaning of chance, a central point on which the author seems to be
pulled in different directions: his tendency toward originality and his
loyalty to traditional conceptions of mutationism and neo-Darwinism.

One of the chief concepts of Monod's (1971) models is the teleonomic character of internal reactions of the organism which permits,
among other things, its self-construction by an "autonomous
morphogenesis." This teleonomy is explained as due to cybernetic
pathways; where Marie Brazier has searched for "mechanical equiva-
lents of finality," Monod finds "an *oriented, coherent,* and constructive
activity." But the strikingly clarifying point is to find in these notions an
action similar to that of the "demon of Maxwell" whose powers lost their
mystery when Szilard and L. Brillouin succeeded in working out the
energy exchanges without contradicting the second principle of
thermodynamics.

We have, therefore, a feasible solution of the irritating problem of
the relation between Carnot's principle—increasing probability of dis-

order or entropy—and biological evolution, which leads in similarly irreversible fashion to an increase of order. Monod (1971) puts it as follows:

> The second law, formulating only a statistical prediction, of course does not deny any macroscopic system the possibility of facing about and, with a motion of very small amplitude and for a very brief space, reascending the slope of entropy—taking, as it were, a short step backward in time. In living beings it is precisely these fugitive stirrings which, snapped up and reproduced by the replicative mechanism, have been retained by selections. (Monod, 1971.)

4. An Active Choice

This important passage furnishes a good example of Monod's concept of selection: with good reason Monod thinks of selection no longer as an automatic lottery based on simple probabilities of encounter or nonencounter with elements of the external environment, but rather as an active choice which is the outcome of teleonomic, that is, regulatory activities. This activity can be conceived as a final generalization of the principle of choice which was already active in the above-mentioned stereospecific discrimination.

Further, on the relations between the selective mechanisms and the actions of the environment—Monod (1971) justly states that these factors are by no means the only agents of selection—one can find the thesis developed by several great contemporary biologists, particularly clearly by Waddington (1962). If a certain environment imposes on a given species a totality of selective constraints, it is frequently the case that the environment has been first chosen by representatives of the particular species:

> Different organisms inhabiting the same ecological niche interact in very different and specific ways with outside conditions (among which one must include other organisms). These specific interactions, which the organism itself "elects," at least in part, determine the nature and orientation of the selective pressure the organism sustains. Let us say that the "initial conditions" of selection encountered by a new mutation simultaneously and inseparably include both the environment surrounding the organism and the total structures and performances of the teleonomic apparatus belonging to it. (Waddington, 1962.)

In general, selection is, therefore, no longer to be conceived as a simple lottery which can bring either life or death and which acts in an automatic fashion like a sieve. On the contrary, selection consists of a probabilistic process directed in good part by the choices of the organism; essentially it leads to a modification of the proportions in the composition of the genome and the genetic pool as well as in the coefficient of multiplication, of recombination or variation, and so on.

5. The Role of Chance

If one accepts with Monod these very remarkable contemporary interpretations of the concept of selection and the original form which on many points he gives to them, one can justifiably wonder whether an analogous revision would not be fitting concerning the role of chance which he seems to interpret in a somewhat monolithic fashion. First, obviously two mutations or other chance events do not occur with the same probability; the possible differences in their corresponding classes of frequency (the "mutation rates") should be justified by appealing to reasons that subordinate chance to other factors. Second, compelling motives of symmetry seem to impose this logical consequence; if one admits that selection proceeds in the direction of "choices," then the apparently fortuitous performances must be interpreted according to models that proceed in the direction of "trial and error." In other words, to the extent that one appeals to a teleonomy within the process of selection, one approaches the processes of behavior as "trial and error" or "gropings." It is well known that at the level of behavior the apparently most fortuitous gropings are not the effect of pure chance, with selection taking place afterward, but are more or less directed by an exploratory mechanism of the whole which controls at the same time the performances as "trials" and their selection as "choices." Moreover, to consider the appearance of certain mutations—apart from the most accidental mutations—as due to a sort of "scanning" is close to the idea of L. L. Whyte. Inspired by mathematical analyses, he stated the hypothesis of a potential regulation of mutations with the possibility of "silencing" some and reinforcing others or making them compatible with the totality of the system.

6. An Ordered Series

We believe that the notion of variations distributed according to a mode of "scanning," or of multiple trials more or less controlled in their general direction, is in accord with certain facts of systematics. Detailed studies of the *limnaea* in zoology or the *sedum* in botany demonstrate that the variations of the different species in these genera are not distributed haphazardly but according to an ordered series of a total number that is actually quite limited. One can observe this in the variations in stature which obey certain laws of proportion between surface and volume, in colors—again within certain limits, in the expansion or contraction of the helix or the leaves, in the entire range of possibilities between a maximum cutting off or maintaining of sterile branches, and so on. True enough, these are variations already selected by the environment, but it is remarkable that, with certain limited directions being open, the entire range of possible modification is being tested.

7. The Role of the Environment

We turn now to the important problem of the relations between the organism and the environment in the evolution of variations. Concerning the Lamarckian hypothesis of a hereditary fixation of characteristics acquired under the double influence of the environment and of "habits" imposed by it, Monod (1971) states with reason:

> This is of course today an unacceptable hypothesis; yet one sees that pure selection, operating upon elements of behavior, leads to the result Lamarck sought to explain: the close interconnection of anatomical adaptations and specific performances. (Monod, 1971.)

In general, one can hold that where Lamarck posited an elementary causal action (via the intermediary of behavior) of environmental elements on genetic entities, contemporary biology has replaced this direct action by a probabilistic causal action (selection), performed by the environment on a system of plurality–unity. This action modifies the proportion or the coefficients but requires nonetheless the intermediary function of behavior. From the perspective of causality, there is a great difference between these two positions since a system of plurality–unity has its regulations and a teleonomy—in short it is an active internal organization; but from the perspective of its outcome, the action of the environment is equivalent to that which it would be in a Lamarckian perspective. Waddington (1962) even employs the taboo expression of the "heredity of acquired characteristics" to designate the hereditary fixation of novelties that were at first phenotypic, when a "genetic assimilation" (as he calls it) confirms these acquisitions by natural selection.

Why then is it necessary to reexamine this problem? Because from an epistemological and psychogenetic perspective there remain a series of essential questions that have in no way been resolved by the neo-Darwinian model of fortuitous variations, solely controlled by selection. If, for example, one holds that mathematics and logic originate only from the gropings of chance of which selection has retained the best ones, this would deprive these disciplines of their fundamental characteristic, namely their deductive necessity. Thus they would be reduced to the rank of disciplines of mere approximations—an entirely unacceptable situation. It is, therefore, of utmost importance for the epistemology of those disciplines to analyze more profoundly the relations or the interactions between the subject and the object, that is, from a biological perspective, between the organism and the environment. Only in this manner can one hope to attain a solution that is adequate to the problem of knowledge.

8. The Sources of Knowledge

Although Monod excels in interpreting important biological questions, his explanations of the various forms of human knowledge appear somewhat fragile. This would not be of much consequence in view of the more general aim of his book. However, in the particular case where he discusses biological concepts, it raises an interesting problem: it gives us all the necessary means from which to extract an epistemology that is better and more in tune with his initial positions. In short, Monod considers only two possible sources of knowledge, innateness and experience, while he holds at the same time that all novel hereditary variations are fortuitous and all experience is approximate. Paradoxically he seems to forget as a possible third source of knowledge the very mechanisms of self-regulation of which he has made so much use on other occasions. We refer here, not to their variable contents, but to their general form, which consists of a combinatory system of anticipations and retractions. This formal mechanism, found at all levels from the regulations of the genome to those of behavior, seems to be the source of the logical–mathematical operations. The regulations, originally directed merely toward the results of external acts, become "perfect" in the sense of Ashby, that is, sufficiently anticipatory to bring with them the precorrection of errors. The semireversibility of feedback becomes thus a perfect operatory reversibility.

In the following we shall examine first the role of experience of the environment. This role appears to us at the same time to be more direct, but also requiring a greater activity on the part of the subject than in the hypothesis of pure-chance variations without any "scanning." Subsequently, we shall discuss the concepts of preformation and of a constructive rather than nonconstructive interpretation of evolution.

9. Logical–Mathematical Experience

Monod provides two distinct interpretations regarding the concept of experience; they are in no way incompatible, but he has the tendency to regard them as an entity whereas a clear distinction seems to be called for. First, there is experience in the empiricistic sense: gropings controlled by the properties of the external objects, followed by selection as a function of success or failure. This form of experience exists of course but to attribute to it, as does Monod (1971), the possibility of a hereditary fixation would simply be a return to pure Lamarckism: It would be the transmission of characteristics that in the last analysis are imprints imposed on the subject or on the organism by the objects and the external environment. But there is another form of experience which we have called logical–mathematical. There the information derives, not from the objects as such, but from the actions that are performed on the objects and from the general coordination (order, classes, correspondences, etc.) between the actions. This is no longer an Aristotelian abstraction, but a "reflecting" abstraction that extracts certain operations from the active coordinations themselves. When one applies to physical knowledge (experience in the first sense) or to the properties of objects the results of these logical–mathematical experiences, this is then no longer an exogenous process since it means to reconstruct the object by means of an operatory composition or an internal deduction. In these situations Monod (1971) introduces aptly the second type of experience, in speaking of "simulations" as distinct from visual imagery and of "imaginary experiences," when he "identifies himself by motoric mimicry with a molecule of protein." Einstein, too, remarked on the role of motoric sketches rather than visual or figurative imagery in connection with his discoveries. These situations are, therefore, far from an empiricistic experience, since we are dealing here with an operatory reconstruction of the object by the subject.

10. Phenocopies

One can assume (with the imprudent speculation of a psychological epistemologist who loves to return to his original biological interests) that the relations between the organism and the environment are comparable to those between the subject and the object in logical–mathematical experience. When, as frequently happens, a phenotypic variation is produced under the influence of the environment—this would correspond to an empirical experience originating from the object—and subsequently becomes a hereditary variation of the same form, we would not say with Lamarck that there is strict continuity between these two situations. Rather we would hold that there is a relation between the two and we would present the case in the following form: The genotype reconstructs the phenotypic structure in an endogenous manner. (We believe that we have demonstrated this relation in the case of the lake-dwelling *limnaea stagnalis* where the contracted form is hereditary only in regions that are agitated by waves.) In this connection one often speaks of "phenocopies" but the organism is here without doubt as active as in the act of knowledge where the subject reconstructs the object. The phenotype may well be conceived as a type of mold, but the molding is dependent on genotypic or epigenotypic syntheses and is not a simple action of the mold as it might act on soft pastry. This brings to mind the stereospecific activity so well described by Monod (1971):

> And so it may be that the 'cognitive' properties of cells are not the direct but rather an exceedingly indirect expression of the discriminatory faculties of certain proteins. Nevertheless the construction of a tissue or the differentiation of an organ—macroscopic phenomena—must be viewed as integrated results of multiple microscopic interactions due to proteins, and as deriving from the stereo-specific recognition properties belonging to those proteins, by way of the *spontaneous* forming of noncovalent complexes. (Monod, 1971.)

Such mechanisms could very well play a role in the case of phenocopies.

Are these "speculations" (a term Waddington uses) not contradictory to the "dogma" of action in one direction only of the DNA on the RNA? (The "speculations" of this great scientist have already threatened this dogma: see Figure 36, p. 181, of his *Strategy of the Genes*). Admittedly, whenever I am faced with a dogma, I wait impatiently for the heretics and this expectation was fulfilled with the article of H. W. Temin and Satoshi-Mizutani in the June, 1970, issue of *Nature*. These authors state that they have identified in the virus of a chicken sarcoma an enzyme which makes copies of DNA by means of particles of RNA. In the same issue there was an article by D. Baltimore indicating the discovery of enzymes that are similar to other analogous viruses.

In fact, the logic of a system where cybernetic loops intervene at all levels makes one suspicious of actions in one direction. Even if one excludes all direct causal influence of the environment on the genome, it is difficult to comprehend that the genome would adapt itself to the environment if it did not have some information concerning the outcome of its "responses" (in the sense of Dobzhansky or Waddington) to environmental tensions. It is characteristic of all regulation to furnish feedback information during the course of the actions which it is about to regulate. Selection is, of course, a type of information but it comes much too late if the actions are already finished and all that remains is to correct errors. The biological teleonomic organization constantly takes account of errors in the programming of future actions. Why then should just the genome alone remain ignorant as to what is transmitted, when one provides it with a highly organized synthetized activity and with a generous share of self-regulation?

11. The Problems of Innateness

On the questions of innateness, already discussed above, it must be unfortunately admitted that Monod, partly influenced by Lorenz, concedes here to the fashion of today: He believes, as do numerous biologists, that one can furnish a solution to the most difficult problem of knowledge by simply appealing to innateness; at the same time he affirms the chance nature of each novel mutation, whether it is a simple morphogenetic variation or implies a change in a cognitive instrument.

Lorenz himself has shown the limits of such a perspective, which is rather disastrous for epistemology: Since the content of heredity varies from one species to another, the reduction of Kantian categories to simple innateness does conserve their a priori character relative to experience but it takes away their internal necessity. Consequently the fundamental structures of knowledge, including mathematics and logic, are reduced by Lorenz to simple "innate working hypotheses"; such a solution is totally unacceptable, for this is an a priorism diluted into a pure conventionalism. Monod (1971) is somewhat more cautious: He reduces these structures to a simple *"program* that is innate, that is to say, genetically determined." Regarding biological structures in general Monod (1971) states:

> No performed and complete structure pre-existed anywhere; but the architectural plan for it was present in its very constituents. . . . The necessary information was present, but unexpressed, in the constituents. The epigenetic building of a structure is not a *creation;* it is a *revelation.* (Monod, 1971.)

In short, with regard to human, cognitive structures a distinction is mandatory: Heredity furnishes merely a range of possibilities of actions, not a program. It remains that some of these actions are actualized and this is the work of self-regulatory activities—a literal self-construction.

12. A Negation of Constructivism

We touch here the heart of the matter: the entire work of Monod (1971) is centered on teleonomy, self-regulation, and autonomous morphogenesis. But restrained by his conceptions on the radically for-tuitious character of novel variations, Monod ends up somehow in spite of himself in negating constructivism. His conception logically implies that all cognitive novelty is pure chance and the sole remedy ensuring its adaptation would be found through natural selection. However, as said before, all that is implied by a formal mechanism of self-regulation, from the genome to behavior, would lead one to stress general self-constructions at all levels.

The evolution of the entire life cycle is reduced for Monod (1971) to an uninterrupted series of accidents which in general have a happy outcome because the organism with a maximum of "intelligence" (after the manner of the demon of Maxwell) makes the best of the blows of chance which fall on and around him. But they remain nevertheless external accidents. Surely science was not made by simply looking at the fall of apples, for Newton asked himself some problematic questions when he looked at the apples. Can one hold that the evolution of life (which prefigures the progress of science) takes place without "trials" of any sort? How could one explain the transition from the limited number of genes in the bacteria to a number a thousand times bigger in higher animals? What is the source of this progress if not the evolution of the "genetic system" (in the sense of Darlington)? However, Monod (1971) asserts: "... *Evolution is not a property of living beings,* since it stems from the very *imperfections* of the conservative mechanism which in-deed constitutes their unique privilege." Thus we have this paradox that the genome, the conservative organism *par excellence* is being sub-jected to a continual series of internal revolutions that as such have nothing to do with its development. We prefer to hold with Waddington that the genome is not so ignorant and that its essential evolutionary mechanisms are but one aspect of its otherwise brilliant capacities for "strategies" or reorganizations in the form of "continuous responses" to the "tensions" of the environment.

13. Monod and Meyerson

In fact, we believe that one finds in Monod's book an echo of a past epistemology which was introduced by the "philosophic courage" of E. Meyerson: Reason can do nothing more than observe and identify, whereas the real is irreducibly diverse and consequently irrational. Hence, there is an increasing separation between reason and the real where the increasing number of identifications which make up the richness of science finally leads only to failures or to a retreat from real problems. Similarly for Monod the genome's primary task is to conserve, but internal or external chance events impose on it a constantly changing series of modifications of its program. Consequently there is the obvious profusion of evolutionary forms, but those should be considered from the viewpoint of its tendency toward identity, the outcome of an accumulation of unfortunate "imperfections."

14. The Dialectic of Nature

Fortunately the true spirit of Monod is not found in the abstract thesis of the above interpretations but in the richness of his concrete analyses, which provide abundant support for constructivism. Those data could permit the author by means of a dialectic mental process to "pass beyond" the well-founded antithesis of conservation and variation—yet he prefers to reduce this antithesis to an idealized model of a genome that is completely closed upon itself and of chance events that are totally uncontrolled by the genome.

Concerning the "dialectic of nature," there is no contradiction in pairs of opposite words, such as direct and inverse operations in kinematics or actions and reactions in physics. These terms are the equivalent of thesis and antithesis in a dialectic process. They are not contradictory, because they are part of a coherent total system: a "group" for geometric operations, a stellar system interrelated by actions and reactions, and so forth. If a particular physical system is disturbed by an external action (an additional particle projected into an atom, a chemical combination imposed on a molecule, etc.), it is then modified or may even disintegrate to give birth to a new system, but there is the potential for a return to the original system in accord with pre-existing laws or regulatory relations so that the totality of the situation is itself a coherent system. Thus the negation of the first system would actually be in conformity with coherent operatory compositions and there would be no contradiction. In short, what the dialectic of nature calls contradiction is reduced at the physical level to a totality of related direct and inverse operations that play a fundamental role within the "operators" characteristic of the object. To use the term contradictory in this connection would show a curious neglect of an essential aspect of all dialectic, namely, the "totality." Within their respective total systems these operations are not contradictory since, on the contrary, it is their coherent composition that constitutes these systems.

15. Death Is Not the Inverse of Life

At the level of biological systems this situation changes, for the death of an organism is not the inverse operation of life and one cannot combine these two processes. Moreover, vis-à-vis a biological system, a series of perturbations may occur of which some are tolerated and are compensated for to varying extents—the system making the best of these perturbations—while others lead to deficiencies or pathological states. In this case there is the specific notion of "normal" and "abnormal," a notion that is meaningless in a physical system. Hence, if one considers a contradiction as being relative to the "normal" activities of a subject—without application to physical–chemical systems—it becomes clear that the concept of "the normal" is situated halfway between physical causality and the "epistemic nominative." This should not be surprising if one considers the organism as the departure point in the formation of the subject. Without exaggeration or equivocation one can, therefore, posit a contradiction right within the biological system, between the [epistemic] laws that ensure its normal functioning and the [physical] perturbations that are liable to modify the organism in an abnormal and more or less lethal direction.

16. An Ordered System of the Whole?

Moreover, if a physical system is transformed into another, this occurs in conformity to a totality of laws and causes which itself constitutes a coherent and stable system—so stable that one is able to consider these laws as permanent and independent of time. However, in biology one can admit that, apart from general laws, each taxonomic group comprises in addition certain regulatory relations that are more or less particular to a certain group. It would seem that this is not so different from chemical "species" where specific properties and laws also vary from one category to another. But this diversity of chemical elements remains compatible with a rational system of the whole, expressed in the table of Mendeleev, together with the electromagnetic relations implied in the system; thus the diversity in the chemical realm is the final outcome of a combinatory process within a deductible system of the whole. The diversity of the biological species is quite different and has its historical reasons. There is a mixture of contingency and necessity in every history: The plasticity of biological structures is such that none of the innumerable novel forms that became established in the course of evolution is strictly deductible from preceding forms. Even in the case of change in the environment or sufficiently powerful perturbations, the phenotypic reactions of a genotype imply the establishment of relations that were not contained in previous connections. This explains the variability of "reaction norms."

17. Compensatory Regulations

Consider any modification, the formation of a biological class or a new species in the course of evolution or even the reorganization of the functioning of an individual organism, such as the equilibration of the nerve paths in a crab that has lost one of its pincers. In all these cases compensatory regulation responds to external perturbations in a manner comparable to the "passing beyond" that surmounts contradictions. One has here on a material level the equivalent of a dialectic because in every case these overtakings are the occasions of forming structures and relations not contained in pre-existing programs.

Monod may claim that his theoretical position is antidialectic, but one can see that he quite definitely uses dialectic processes in many places. He subordinates the "autonomous morphogenesis" of the organism to epigenetic mechanisms which are essentially based on self-regulation, and, while denying the existence of an internal dynamism within evolution (since for him this would be a constitutive property of life), he considers evolution as an uninterrupted series of responses to chance perturbations, which is equivalent to a series of overtakings overcoming the contradictions—even though his formulation does not make manifest these conceptions. One must go to the limits of the theses and consider the responses and the multiple activities of the demon of

Maxwell, so aptly indicated by Monod, as being precisely the vital activity that tends toward evolution. In other words, they express an internal requirement of equilibrations and re-equilibrations and "go beyond" in a ceaseless process, because they are never sufficiently perfect, given the imperfections of behavior and the limits of the usable environment—even though the imperfections can always be corrected and the limits can always be extended. In this perspective the dialectic of life is identical to the evolution of life. Even if one stays with the restrictions of Monod with his antithesis of internal regulation and of disintegrating chance events, he has provided in his fine book the wherewithal to satisfy the needs of those who hold that the behavior of the cognitive functions is an endogenous process with a continual overtaking due to the intrinsic necessities of self-regulation. If life is indeed, as Monod thinks, the outcome of a compromise between conservation and variation, it suffices to admit the primacy of regulations in their general mechanisms over the content of invariably specific hereditary transmissions so that the compromise becomes an operatory composition. This composition of invariance and transformation becomes, then, increasingly similar to the operatory combinations over which the adult human intelligence finally achieves mastery.

References

Goldman, L., 1970, "Marxisme et Sciences Humaines," Gallimard, Paris.
Monod, J., 1971, "Chance and Necessity: An Essay on the Natural Philosophy of Modern Biology," Alfred A. Knopf, New York.
Piaget, J., 1971a, "Biology and Knowledge," University of Chicago Press, Chicago.
Piaget, J., 1971b, Hasard et dialectique en épistemologie biologique, *Sciences, revue de la civilisation scientifique* 71:29–36.
Waddington, C. H., "New Patterns in Genetics and Development," 1962, New York, Columbia University Press.

The Role of Action in the Development of Thinking*

JEAN PIAGET

We should like to set forth, without delving into otherwise well-known theoretical considerations, a number of facts and experiments which might be of interest to those who have a practical concern with the study of thinking. We have in mind, not only child psychologists, but also educators whose aim is to translate this psychology into effective teaching processes.

The following discussion will be divided into two parts: one devoted to the general problem of the two aspects of the cognitive functions, that is, the figurative and the operative aspects, and the other devoted to the more particular problem of the relation between action and the operations of thought.

1. The Figurative and Operative Aspects of the Cognitive Functions

To better understand the leading role played by action in the development of thinking, it is important first to classify the cognitive

JEAN PIAGET ● Faculté de Psychologie et des Sciences de l'Education, Université de Genève, Geneva, Switzerland.
*Translated from the French by Hans Furth.

functions into two categories, according to whether they depend directly or indirectly on action. It is important above all to study the relation between these two categories: Are they independent of one another or is one increasingly subordinated to the other?

1.1 Proposed Classification and Statement of the Problems

The physical, mathematical, and other realities which the mind strives to know appear in two forms: as states or as transformations. Each transformation sets out from one state to end in another state, so that it is impossible to understand transformations without knowing states; conversely, it is impossible to understand states without knowing the transformations from which they result, as well as those to which they can give rise. From the logical viewpoint, knowledge therefore presumes two types of instruments: descriptors that furnish the characteristics of the states or transformations, and operators or combiners that enable the transformations to be reproduced and manipulated, inclusive of their initial and final states. A further conclusion follows: Although it is necessary to describe in order to comprehend, description is not sufficient for comprehension. Hence, from the viewpoint of logical comprehension states are subordinate to transformations.

From the psychological viewpoint—the viewpoint from which our investigation started—a similar classification can be made. First, there are cognitive functions, or aspects of these functions, which correspond to descriptors. These are the aspects that have to do mainly with the configurations of reality; for this reason they can be called the *figurative* aspects. Essentially, these are (1) perception, (2) imitation, and (3) the mental image, which can be called a sort of internalized imitation—an attempt to reproduce in schematic fashion the perceptual models. These figurative functions essentially refer to states, and, when they deal with transformations, they translate them (more or less) in terms of figures or of states (as in the perception of a movement in terms of a well-formed *Gestalt*). But on the other hand, there are the cognitive functions, or aspects of these functions, which essentially relate to transformations: They are (1) action, in its sensorimotor mechanisms (the sensorimotor schemes, including the dynamic instinctual mechanisms); (2) interiorized actions in their general forms, reversible and coordinated into coherent overall structures. These operative aspects of the cognitive functions (whose operatory form is the particular case No. 3) are indispensable to the reproduction, manipulation, and consequent comprehension of transformations. Unless the subject acts on the object and transforms it, he will not comprehend its nature and would remain at the level of mere description.

The three great problems, then, which this classification raises are the following: (1) Are the elements of thinking (concepts, etc.) drawn exclusively from the figurative aspects (as maintained by positivism, which sees in concepts the product of perceptions, abstracted, generalized, and formulated by means of language), or are the operative mechanisms indispensable to the development and structuration of concepts? (2) Do the operative mechanisms establish themselves independently or are they themselves drawn from figurative structures (perception or images, etc., as the Gestaltists hold when with Wertheimer they attempt to reduce operations to Gestalt structures)? (3) Do the figurative structures themselves develop independently, or is their progress due in part to outside contributions drawn from operative mechanisms, and hence from action in general or operations?

It is on the answer to these three types of questions that the solution of our general problem of the role of action in the development of thinking depends.

1.2. Perceptions, Concepts, and Operations

We have studied on a broad scale (Piaget, 1969) the development of certain concepts and of the corresponding perceptions, so as to determine the relation between these two groups of phenomena. A variety of situations are found in this regard and we shall recall the principal ones.

1.2.1. Divergent Evolution of a Perception and a Corresponding Concept

First, a partially divergent evolution is sometimes observed in the case of concepts and in that of the corresponding perceptions. For example, the concepts proper to projective geometry (perspective, etc.) do not start until at about 7 years of age, i.e., representation or anticipation of the shape of an object (watch, crayon, etc.) according to the position it occupies with respect to the observer; or anticipation of the shape of a shadow on a screen according to the position of the object with respect to the light source (Piaget and Inhelder, 1956). Perspective in drawing is not generally very definite until at about 8 or 9 years. Lastly, the correct representation of the respective positions of a scene of

three mountains or three houses according to the position of the observer (in relation to the scene) is not acquired until at about age 10.
There is, therefore, a development of projective concepts beginning at
age 7, with a first plateau at about age 10 to 11.

On the other hand, projective perceptions are much more preco-
cious, because the perceptual constancy of shape, which entails a projective aspect, begins at the end of the first year. We undertook with Lam-
bercier (Piaget, 1969) perceptual measurements of apparent or projective
size. For example, a child is shown a vertical rod 10 cm long placed 1
meter away from him and a rod of variable length is placed 4 meters
away, and he is asked to tell when the latter has an apparent size equal
to the 10 cm rod (in this case it should be actually 40 cm long). In this
situation the average adult (as distinct from artists and draftsmen)
makes appreciable mistakes, the rod chosen being generally 20 cm or
less in length, because constancy of size (real) prevails over projective
size. The young child, however, has great difficulty in understanding
the question—one has to explain the task to him by having him paint on
a flat glass the apparent size of a distant doll seen through this glass—
but when he has understood, he gives much better answers at 6 to 7
years than the adult: the child's answers range from 25 to 40 cm. As the
child gets older, perceptual projection deteriorates while conceptual
projection develops.

It is evident that in this first example the concept contains much
more than perception alone. The projective perception, in fact, merely
supplies the knowledge that corresponds to one particular viewing point
(one position in relation to the object, then another which erases the
previous perception, etc.) Projective concepts (perspective, etc.), however, presuppose two kinds of properties which perception by itself
does not provide: (1) An interrelation or coordination of the various
viewing points, such that the subject understands *why* the object has
apparently changed shape because of a change in position with regard to
the subject; (2) a possibility for deductive reasoning enabling the child to
anticipate what the shape will be when he is in a position he does not
presently occupy. It can thus be seen that both comprehension and
deductive reasoning or anticipation result from actions or operations on
the part of the subject. To understand these changes in apparent shape
the subject has to move about or move the object in relation to himself,
and these are actions; he must interiorize these actions as reversible
operations so that these transformations can be deduced or reproduced
in thought. These actions and operations are the starting point of one of
the "groups of transformations" on which projective geometry is based.

1.2.2. Prefiguration of Concepts by Perception

At the other extreme from the situations of which we have just given an example are those in which perception prefigures the concept, and the concept or the operations act in return upon the organization of perception. The term "prefigure" simply means that perception develops in a manner similar to ("partially isomorphous" with) the concept; the problem of the relation between these remains open and will be discussed later.

An example of this situation is that of systems of references or natural axes of coordinates (orientation with respect to the horizontal and the vertical, and the development of these two privileged directions). From the point of view of the concept, it is necessary to make a careful distinction between the sensorimotor schematism and the concepts or representational operations. At the sensorimotor level, the infant very quickly succeeds in distinguishing the horizontal from the vertical, but only in his own body (lying or sitting-up positions) and by an exclusively tonic or postural means. It might then be thought that such an early experience would be translated into thought by an equally early concept, but this is not the case. One must wait for the age of 9 or 10 years for a child viewing a bottle of colored water to be able to draw the horizontal level in advance by anticipating what will happen when the bottle is tilted to different positions. The trouble is that he is looking for points of reference within the jar, whereas to judge the horizontal he has to refer to the exterior of the jar, that is, to the stand on which the jar is placed, to the table, etc. The difficulty is the same for the vertical (a mast on a boat floating on water or a plumb line suspended from the end of an inclined rod).

From the viewpoint of perception, the evolution is as follows. From his early years the child can judge the horizontal and the vertical with respect to the line of regard which corresponds and is tied to a postural evaluation (hence the sensoritonic theory of H. Werner and S. Wapner). He does not know how to evaluate the horizontality or the verticality of a straight line with respect to other points of reference than his own body. We have performed, for example, the following experiment with P. Dadsetan (Piaget, 1969). A variable line, but one varying slightly from the horizontal, is drawn inside of a right-angle triangle the base of which is inclined; since the line is close to this inclined base it is hard to judge its horizontality without looking for reference points outside of the triangle, such as the edges of the sheet where a frame is drawn in black lines for this purpose. The results were striking: (1) The youngest subjects were not overly misled by the triangle, which they did not look at; (2) then the errors increased up to about age 9 to 10 because of the triangle and because of failing to look at the exterior frame of the figure; (3) around 9 to 10 years the errors diminished abruptly and greatly, because the subjects were taking account of the frame; (4) when the operatory or conceptual test for the anticipation of the horizontality of the water level in tilted jars was applied to the older subjects, a good correlation was found between the conceptual judgment and perception, but with the former in the lead.

It is therefore evident that, in this situation, although perception prefigures concept, the concept acts back on perception again beginning at age 9 to 10; up to this age the child does not have the "idea" of looking at the external frame to use it as a reference, while at the operatory level, where he begins to construct and generalize the systems of reference (by generalization of two- and three-dimensional measurement), the habits which he acquires orient his perceptual exploration and therefore indirectly modify his perception.

1.2.3. Relation of Perception to Concept

There is no point in giving examples of other situations where perception and concept are related: they are either cases of interaction, or cases of perceptual prefiguration but without any known return action by the conceptual judgment on the perception. This is the case, for example, with perceptual constancies and operatory conservations, where there is an analogous mode of formation with an interval of 6 to 7 years between the beginning of the perceptive constancies and the beginning of the operatory conservations; but the conservations are by no means derived from the constancies.

The conclusion to be drawn from these and other facts is the following: While a concept obviously obtains indispensable information from the corresponding perception, the concept is not, however, extracted from the perception by simple abstractions and generalizations, as Aristotle believed, and as contemporary positivists still think. If this were the case, the concept, while more general, would be poorer than the corresponding perceptions because it would only have abstracted some of the perceptual aspects and neglected others. Actually, a concept such as that of perspective or that of a system of references or coordinates is a good deal richer than the projective perceptions or the perceptual coordinates, because it always entails a system of operations or transformations (classifications, seriations, correspondences, measurements, etc.). This operative aspect of concept is not reducible to the perceptual structures and derives from the sensorimotor structures or from the structures of action in general. We are now going to establish this fact by comparing the operatory structures to the perceptual "Gestalt" structures.

1.2.4. The Gestalt Position

The Gestalt psychologists have described the Gestalt as being the more general structure of the perception. They are no doubt right, except that a structure is not an explanation but only the result of a functional and dialectical process which alone is explanatory. All we wish to do for the present is to compare the Gestalt structure, characteristic of perception, with the operatory structures characteristic of intelligence, to see if the latter are reducible to the former. A Gestalt is defined by Kohler and by Wertheimer by means of two characteristics: (1) It is a totality which has its own laws as a totality, distinct from the laws of its components (perception and sensations); (2) it is a nonadditive totality, that is, the whole is different from the sum of its parts. These two characteristics are conceived by the Gestaltists as integral, and this is why, when Wertheimer attempted to explain the operatory structures of mathematical forms or logical forms (the syllogism for example), he tried to reduce them to *Gestalten*.

Now, if we compare this Gestalt structure to an operatory structure such as the whole-number series, we see that the latter has the first but not the second characteristic. The whole-number series shows laws of totality: "set" laws, "body" laws, "ring" laws, "lattice" laws, etc., which mathematicians have described and which have a deep psychological meaning. But on the other hand it is a strictly additive totality, because 2 + 2 equals precisely 4, not a little bit more or a little bit less, as in perceptual illusions.

For this reason alone it is impossible to draw from perceptual structures the operatory or conceptual structures. The reason is that the former, being nonadditive, are irreversible and of a probabilistic nature, like all figurative functions. An operatory structure, however, like that of the whole number, derives from a certain form of action (here the action of gathering together) that has become reversible (gather together and break up → add and subtract) and consequently susceptible to precise or necessary deduction, in contrast to irreversible and probabilistic structures.

1.2.5. Perception and Thinking

As far as relations between perceptions and thought are concerned, we can therefore conclude by responding as follows to the three questions posed at the end of Section 1.1.

1.2.5.1. Causal Thinking. In all cases where an attempt has been made to derive a concept from the corresponding perceptions alone, it has been forgotten that it is not these two terms alone that are involved. There is a third term that is fundamental and constitutes the common origin: it is the complex of the sensorimotor structures, the reflex, the sensorimotor intelligence itself (which is established in the second half of the first year).

For example, Michotte sought to explain the formation of the concept of cause by a phenomenon peculiar to perceptual causality, which he studied in detail as launching and pulling. But there exists a sensorimotor causality whose initial feature is its exclusive tie to one's own action, such as actions of pushing, pulling, swinging suspended objects, etc., regardless of spatial contacts. For example, an infant may shake the crib by various movements in attempting to act on objects situated two or three meters away. Not until around 10 to 12 months of age does the infant begin to recognize spatial constraints (need for contacts) and to objectivize (assign the causality of the action to relations between the objects themselves). On the other hand, the visual perceptual causality of Michotte derives from a tactile-kinesthetic perceptual causality which is prior to it, because if the subject did not have the muscles and motricity, he would not "see" any impacts, thrusts, resistances, etc., in Michotte's little figures, but only successive and regular movements. Tactile–kinesthetic causality depends, of course, on the action itself as a whole, which therefore constitutes the common origin of perceptual causality and of conceptual causality.

1.2.5.2. Reasoning. Likewise, the operations of thought do not derive from Gestalts, as we have seen, and their genesis can be followed beginning from the sensorimotor actions. From the sensorimotor level of the first year, we witness the formation of schemes of action which comprise general coordinations of *combinations* (coordination of vision and grasping with the hand, or of two movements in one, etc.), of *ordination* (making use of a means, such as pulling a blanket, before aiming directly at the purpose, which is to reach the remote object placed thereon), etc., of *correspondence* (the learning of imitation), etc. These general coordinations constitute, prior to language, a sort of logic of action which is fundamental for the further development of operations. For example, the coordination of movements (of one's own body or of objects manipulated in the action) ultimately results, at about 12 to 18 months, in the acquiring of a "group" structure (in the sense of the geometries). The possibility of "returns" to the point of departure (reversibility of the set) and of "detours" (associative compositions making it possible to reach the same point by different routes) already confers on this structure the reversible mobility properties which will characterize future operations. Furthermore, the actions of this quasi-operatory structure (these are successive actions with no simultaneous representation of events) lead to the constitution of an "invariant of a group" in the form of the scheme of the permanent object: the infant becomes capable toward the end of the first year of looking for an object (which he did not do at all between 4 and 9 to 10 months) by taking into account successive movements and positions (Gruber *et al.*, 1971). Therefore, we have here the germ, not only of future operations, but also of schemes of conservation; and conservation characterizes all operations once they are established.

1.2.5.3. Perception and Development. Perception, therefore, is by no means sufficient to account for these developments, which involve action as a whole. Nor does perception itself develop with age in an autonomous or independent manner, for it is increasingly subordinated to intelligence and to the operations which are active and participate as schemes of action. We have seen an example of this in connection with the perceptual coordinates. Many others could be mentioned, but there is no need to dwell on this.

1.3. Relations between Mental Images and Operations

Perception is a first example of a figurative function which does not explain the operative aspects of thought but is increasingly subordinated to it. A second, equally convincing example is that of the mental image.

Associationist psychology considers the mental image to be a prolongation of perception and an element of thought, as if reasoning consists of associating images with one another and with perceptions. From the viewpoint of the development of the child, the mental image does not appear to play any part just after birth, as perceptions do, and it does not manifest itself until after 1½ to 2 years, at the time of the appearance of the symbolic function (that is, imaginative or functional play, deferred imitation, language acquisition, etc.) The image, therefore, essentially plays a symbolic role, but under an internalized form (neurologically the representation of a movement produces similar waves in electromyograms or in electroencephalograms as the performance of the movement itself).

We might wonder, therefore, what the relations are between images and the operations of thought: Do the former prepare the latter or do they only serve as symbolic aids? And do images develop independently of the operations of thought or under their increasing influence?

First, two classes of images must be distinguished: *reproductive* images, which evoke already known events or objects, and *anticipatory* images which depict events not yet observed.

1.3.1. Reproductive Images

As far as reproductive images are concerned, two kinds of facts are of interest here. The first is that the retention of these memory images in the memory is better when they are tied to action than when they have been recorded as the effect of perception alone. For example, we have performed some experiments (Piaget and Inhelder, 1971) with designs of little buttons. Three conditions were compared:

1. The child simply looks at the design and has to reconstruct it from memory.

2. The child copies the design with other buttons and has to reconstruct it from memory.

3. The child watches an adult who is making the design and has to reconstruct it from memory.

Different groups of subjects were examined following the order 1→2 or 2→1, etc., 1 week or 2 weeks apart.

Clear results were obtained when the designs had a clear-cut pattern (but not when the designs were just arbitrary arrays of elements or pictures): (a) The results were better when the child acted than when he only watched. (b) In the 2→1 order there was a definite influence of the previous action on the later perception (even if the design had been altered slightly from one experiment to the next), whereas in the 1→2 order the previous perception had no influence on the results of the later action. (c) The fact that an adult was observed in action (situation 3) added nothing to the simple perception (1) and was by no means equivalent to the action of the child himself (2). This last point contains a little pedagogical suggestion, though it is in agreement with what has long been known: The pupil learns much less by watching something being done than by doing it himself.

The second revealing fact concerns the different varieties of reproductive images and their frequency in relation to the daily scenes or events which give rise to their formation. Three types of images can be distinguished: static (representing immobile objects), kinetic (changes of position), or transformational (changes of forms). In everyday life there are as many movements and transformations as there are static objects. However, when one studies the image representation of elementary movements or transformations in children younger than 7 or 8, some very curious difficulties are encountered. For example, children are made to draw from memory, without showing them the model, a rod that turns 90° or 180° like the hands of a watch, or a tube with colored ends that flips 180° end over end in falling from the edge of a box onto a table, or simply the four differently colored sides of a revolving square (rotating in a plane or in space); they have all kinds of unexpected difficulty in drawing the intermediate positions. Similarly in the case of the transformation of an arc of flexible wire to a straight line, the child does a poor job of representing the intermediate positions, and draws the straight line no longer than the chord of the arc, even though he is aware that the latter is being stretched.

In short, images reproducing movements or transformations are very infrequent or very inaccurate before age 7 or 8. Clearly, they do not consist of mere passive evocations but involve active anticipations or re-anticipations. As for anticipative images relating to movements or transformations that are still unknown (such as folding and the subsequent cutting of a corner of the sheet), it is obvious that their production occurs even later. This suggests the hypothesis that the progress of the image, beginning with the primitive static images, is due to the first operations, which begin precisely at 7 to 8 years, and that the image is then more and more subordinated to the operations, instead of constituting their source.

1.3.2. Images of Operations

To verify this hypothesis, we have repeated a number of former experiments of an operatory nature relating to the concepts of conservation, but we caused the result of the transformations to be anticipated by the image before the child actually performs them, and before he is made to study the actual result. One of these experiments (Piaget and Inhelder, 1971) consisted of asking the children to find as many red counters as there are blue counters in a horizontal row of 10 blue counters spaced slightly apart. The youngest made a row of the same length without bothering about whether there was correspondence between the rows. During a second stage, the child makes the rows correspond optically on a one-for-one basis, and states the number (how many?), but if the counters in one of the rows are closed up or spread a little more apart, he says this no longer makes the same number and that one or two counters have to be added at one end to make them equal again. During a third stage, if the length of one of the rows is altered, the child agrees that the number is the same, but not the quantity: "It's 10 and 10, but there's more here." (So the whole is not yet equal to the sum of the parts!) Lastly, in a fourth stage, at about age 7, number and quantity are conserved if the spatial arrangement of the counters is altered, "because they can be put back the way they were before." Here we deal with an operation, therefore, with reversibility and conservation.

The reaction of the little ones is astounding from the point of view of the image: They reason as though they did not imagine that the spread-out counters could be put back in place by moving them only 1 cm or ½ cm from their new position, or as if they did not imagine their identity in the course of the movement. We then constructed an apparatus in the form of an open fan: The red counters at the lower part were close together and the blue counters at the top were spread out, but a lane with cardboard barriers connected each red to each blue and the counters could not get out of their lanes. Here the image of the paths posed no problem, and it was evident that a red corresponded only to a blue and vice versa. So we asked the child to imagine the paths, and nothing was easier. But amazingly this image made no change in the preoperatory reactions: "When they go up there are more and when they come down there are less." Finally, we transformed the image to perception by moving all the red counters at once by a mechanical device; the children were delighted to see this and simply concluded again that the reds increase or diminish according to whether they are raised or lowered.

Another earlier experiment was repeated to study the image (Piaget and Inhelder, 1971), namely, the conservation-of-liquids experiment in which the liquid is poured from a medium-size glass A into a thinner glass B or into a wider glass C. Up to around seven years the liquid is considered by the average subject to increase or diminish in quantity according to the levels, independently of the width of the glasses. To study the part played by the image, we next asked the child to foresee what was going to happen when the transfers were made, to point to the levels and to say in advance whether or not the liquid would be conserved. We then found three kinds of reactions: (1) For most of the young subjects, everything "will be the same," including the levels. But when they saw that the liquid rises higher in B than in A and drops lower in C, they said they had been deceived and denied any conservation of the quantity itself. (2) A second group of subjects (23%) correctly foresaw the levels and concluded that there would be more to drink in B than in A and less in C. Indeed, when they were given the glasses A, B, and C empty and asked to pour the liquid themselves so that each of the participants (the experimenter, the assistant, and the child) would have the same amount to drink (a matter of moral justice!), they poured exactly the same levels regardless of the width. (3) Lastly, there were the subjects (averaging 7 years or older) who correctly foresaw the levels and accepted the conservation. It can therefore be seen that, prior to the operatory level (Stage 3), the image may be incorrect (Stage 1) or it may be correct (Stage 2); however, it is a simple reproductive image that translates the subject's previous experience (transfers can be performed in daily life) but does not lead to conservation because the child lacks understanding of the compensation of changes in height and in width. Even the correct image, therefore, does not suffice to bring on the operation.

Other experiments of conservation of quantities (a clay ball is made into a loaf-shaped roll) and in the conservation of lengths (a rod that is initially congruent with another is slightly shifted) have produced similar results.

1.3.3. Conclusion

In short, the image is useful to the operation to the extent that it symbolizes an exact knowledge of states, but it is by no means sufficient to furnish an understanding of transformations. To understand those, it is necessary to act on the object and coordinate the modifications into a coherent whole. Only operations, which prolong actions by interiorizing them and rendering their coordinations reversible, lead to this understanding: Transformations do not transform everything but always imply an invariant element, hence a conservation.

The results of this research into the development of images converge with those concerning perceptions. This enables us to confirm conclusions about the general relation of the figurative and operative aspects of the cognitive functions. It is now possible to maintain the following:

1. The image is no more sufficient than perception to account for the elements or concepts of thought, which arise out of operative activities that are not reducible to figurative data.

2. The image is no more sufficient than perception to engender operations as such, even though, on the basis of the experience acquired, the image makes it possible to foresee the result of certain transformations. What the figurative aspect lacks is the comprehension of the transformation itself, which is a change of state, not a configuration.

3. The image, like perception, does not develop independently, but its progress is due to a necessary intervention of operations, which alone permit the change from reproductive images to anticipative images of movement and of transformations.

2. Action and the Operations of Thought

The figurative aspects of the cognitive functions, though obviously useful and necessary to the knowledge of states, are incapable of accounting for thought, because by themselves they cannot succeed in assimilating the transformations of reality. The reason is that knowledge is not a static copy of reality. To know an object is not to furnish a simple copy of it: It is to act on it so as to transform it and grasp within these transformations the mechanism by which they are produced. To know, therefore, is to produce or reproduce the object dynamically; but to reproduce it is necessary to know how to produce, and this is why knowledge derives from the entire action, not merely from its figurative aspects.

2.1. The Subject and the Object

From the primacy of action and the insufficiency of the figurative aspects follows a first consequence regarding the analysis of the relations between the subject and the object: The analysis must look for a dialectic, not a static relation, between these two concepts.

Any static relation between the subject and the object consists in dissociating them, and this dissociation is the source of inextricable difficulties. To set out from the subject to comprehend the object is to assume an aprioristic or idealistic perspective which prevents attaining the object. If one considers the subject as an assemblage of ready-made structures, one forgets that the subject does not exist in a given form once and for all time. The subject is none other than the assemblage of the actions which he exercises on the objects, and these actions are unceasingly transformed in accordance with the objects and modify the subject. To set out from the object independently of the actions of the subject is to assume an empiricistic or positivistic perspective which forgets that the object is attained only by successive approximations. The whole history of the sciences shows that objectivity is not a starting datum, but is constructed and acquired by a continuous and laborious effort. These successive approximations relate to the actions of the subject in his conquest and reconstruction of the object.

The subject S and the objects O are therefore indissociable, and it is from this indissociable interaction S⇄O that action, the source of knowledge, originates. The point of departure of this knowledge, therefore, is neither S nor O but the interaction proper to the action itself. It is from this dialectic interaction ⇄ that the object is bit by bit discovered in its objective properties by a "decentration" which frees knowledge of its subjective illusions. It is from this same interaction ⇄ that the subject, by discovering and conquering the object, organizes his actions into a coherent system that constitutes the operations of his intelligence and his thought.

Let us give two examples of this decentration to show the necessary role of actions and operations in the conquest of the object, and especially to show how the operation, founded on general coordinations of action, frees the action of its individual and subjective aspects and permits a decentered objectivity of the ego or self.

The first of these examples is a familiar event (Piaget, 1930). Many children questioned before age 7 believed that the moon followed them at night, and I saw some who seemed to be checking on this. One child went into a store and looked out the door to see if the moon was still waiting, another ran along a block of houses from one corner to find that there again was the moon at the next intersection. So here we have a pseudoknowledge due to one's own immediate action, without any decentration. The children I questioned were quite amazed when I asked them whether the moon follows me too (response: "Of course!"), and what would it do, then, if I went from A to B and the child from B to A (response: "It will go with you first, maybe, but then it will catch up with me again."). At about 7 or 8 years of age this belief vanishes. I have seen children who remembered why it did (or at least explained it nicely). A boy of 7 said, for example, "When I got friends in school I knew that the moon can't follow everybody at once and that it only seemed to follow us but it didn't really." So in this case a decentration by reciprocity of actions sufficed to correct the initial error.

The second example is more subtle and shows the influence of additive operations on a representation of conservation. It will be recalled that the child begins with no conservation of number for lack of additive operations, and that he acquires this conservation when he coordinates the actions of combination $(1 + 1)$ into a coherent form, such that the whole equals the sum of the parts. Now, this decentration of the additive operation which thus frees itself from figurative appearances (perception or image) furnishes us with a good example of decentration in connection with the conservation of physical quantities: the conservation of sugar dissolved in water.

The experiment (Piaget and Inhelder, 1962) which I performed with Bärbel Inhelder consists of putting a glass of water on a scale, and showing how the weight increases when two or three lumps of sugar are added, and how the water level rises when they enter the water (then marking the new level). The questions are: (1) What becomes of the sugar after it dissolves? (2) Does it retain its weight? (3) Does the water level remain high or does it go down again (conservation of volume)? During the preoperatory stages when there is still no additive operatory composition, there is no conservation in this physical domain either: The dissolved sugar is presumed to be annihilated (and the sweet taste of the water to disappear the way an odor goes away), the weight of the glass to decrease after the sugar dissolves, and the water level to fall again to where it was before the lumps were immersed. But beginning with the formation of additive compositions, the child acquires the conservation of substance first, then weight, and finally volume. He begins by stating that the sugar in dissolving divides into increasingly smaller grains. He then supposes that, when the sugar seems to have vanished, all that is left are grains so small that they can no longer be seen, but—and this is where the importance of additive composition is noted—all these grains together are equivalent in their sum to the initial visible lumps, so that the substance of the sugar is conserved. But at first the child thinks that these grains are too small to weigh anything, least of all to take up space; afterward, however, he will admit that each little grain has a little weight and finally a little volume, the sum of these weights or of these volumes then being equal to the total weight of the lumps before they were dissolved and to their total volume measured by the level of the water.

We see from this example how the coordination of the actions of combining or adding, once they have been interiorized as coherent operations, leads to a decentration and an objectivity sufficient to overcome the figurative appearances. Thus children acquire those difficult forms of conservation of the substance, weight, and volume of a body that during transformation had become invisible. This conquest of objectivity is all the more interesting because it is achieved at about the same ages as transformations during which everything can be seen, such as rolling a ball of clay into a stick and seeing the quantity of matter, the weight, and the volume remain the same. With the sugar as with the clay, conservation of the quantity of matter is observed at from 7 to 8 years on the average, conservation of weight from 9 to 10 years, and conservation of volume from 11 to 12 years.

2.2. The Development of Operations

Operations are interiorized, reversible actions grouped into overall systems having their laws of composition as systems or totalities. For example, an action which a child performs at a very early age consists of combining objects that are similar to one another into a pile or collection A. Likewise he can combine other objects similar to one another in another pile A', and if he brings these two collections A and A' together to make one whole B, he is engaging in a new action consisting of combining, not individual objects, but collections or piles, and we shall write this simply as $A + A' = B$. These are material actions, but actions already endowed with general signification; it can be seen right away that these actions are at the starting point of operations of combining or of addition. But a long road still separates these actions from the corresponding operations, because they still have to be interiorized, rendered reversible, and grouped into a system of the whole.

The interiorization of actions raises all sorts of neurological and psychological problems which have been studied, particularly in the USSR. I shall not dwell upon interiorization, except to note that it is supported by the symbolic function. At the sensorimotor level, from birth to 1½ or 2 years, actions cannot as yet be internalized as outlines. With language, symbolic play (pretense), deferred imitation, and the mental image, interiorization becomes possible through two factors: figurative outlines of actions originating in the nervous system and operative signification deriving from higher levels of coordination of actions. But we note especially that an interiorized action is still an action: To combine two pebbles or put together two abstract units $1 + 1 = 2$ is still adding elements to form a whole, and, if the object of the action seems to disappear in "pure" mathematics, it is always present in the form of "some-object-in-general."

Reversibility presents a problem that is just as complex. When the child has combined the two collections A and A' into a whole B, one might think that this is already a reversible action, because he can dissociate the whole B to regain the subcollection A, in the form of $B - A' = A$. This is, indeed, a beginning of reversibility but it is still very incomplete, because the child is inclined to forget the whole B; when he thinks of collection A he will forget that $A = B - A'$, that is, that A is a remainder relative to the whole B. This comment seems artificial, but the following experiment (Inhelder and Piaget, 1969) will show that it is not at all artificial.

Children aged 5 and 6 were given pictures of flowers, such as seven primroses, two roses, and one violet, and they were asked, "Are all the primroses flowers" "Yes, sure." "Are all these flowers primroses?" "No, there are also some roses and one violet." "So, in this bouquet are there more primroses or more flowers?" "But if the flowers are taken away will the primroses be left?" "No, they are flowers too." "Then are there more flowers there or more primroses?" "More primroses, because there are only three flowers," and so on. In other words, the child may very well be thinking of the whole as "all the flowers" and of a part as "the primroses." But when he thinks of a part A, he destroys the whole B, and all that is left is the other part A'. He then answers that $A > A'$ when he asked if $A < B$, because the whole B no longer exists for him when he has dissociated it in thought. To understand the inclusion $A < B$, it is therefore necessary to conserve the whole and think reversibly: $A + A' = B$, therefore $A = B - A'$, and therefore $A < B$.

It is this absence of reversibility which explains the nonconservations about which we spoke. When the child pours water from one bottle X into a narrower bottle Y and says there is more because the water rises higher, he is neglecting the fact that Y can be put back into X. Above all, he neglects the fact that, if the water column is higher, it is at the same time thinner, and that if one adds to a whole a quantity Q in height and takes away the same quantity Q in width, $+Q -Q = 0$; that is, nothing has changed. Now, it is precisely this that the child of 7 to 8 years says when he acquires conservation: "It is higher, but it is narrower, so it is the same."

To pass from action to operation, it is clearly necessary that the action become reversible. This is what happens when the child no longer bases his reasoning on particular and isolated actions, such as "pouring," "adding," etc., but on the general coordination of the actions. We have already seen that, beginning at the sensorimotor level, actions are coordinated with one another under general forms of combination, seriation, correspondences, and intersections. To the extent to which these general coordinations apply also to particular interiorized actions they become reversible. More precisely, any coordination of actions, like any biological coordination, tends to maintain equilibration by a series of regulations and self-regulations. Now, equilibration through self-regulation consists of compensatory mechanisms acting by retroactive or anticipatory corrections. This equilibration therefore tends toward a reversibility. When the coordinations are fully achieved, as in the case of coordinations of actions, by combinations, seriations, correspondences, this reversibility can become entire through an intentional regulation of thought.

But operations are not merely interiorized and reversible actions. They are also, by their very nature, grouped into systems of totality; they can repeat themselves indefinitely in the sense of direct compositions, and they can be inverted so that compositions between direct and inverse operations yield still further combinations. In the case of the combinations of which we have been speaking up to now, as soon as the infant can combine two classes in the form $A + A' = B$, he can continue in the form $B + B' = C$, $C + C' = D$, etc., and thus construct a classification, for isolated classes do not exist. As soon as a class is constructed, it is opposed to other classes and thus it involves the construction of a classification of some form or other.

Likewise, a transitive asymmetrical relationship $A < B$ does not exist in an isolated state, and it entails the seriation of other relations $B < C$, $C < D$, etc. A number does not exist in isolation but participates in the operatory series of the whole (or natural) numbers. A family relationship likewise participates in a family tree. Two classifications form a multiplication table or double-entry matrix. Two seriations can be made to correspond. In short, as soon as there are reversible operations, there is a constitution of structures of the whole having their laws of totalities as structures or systems. But these structures do not constitute, a priori, a point of departure which would characterize the "subject's" thought once and for all time: They are the end point of an uninterrupted succession of actions on the objects which are finally coordinated into reversible operations. And by "finally" we refer simply to a certain stage of development, this stage itself being followed by a series of others in a dialectic without any definite end.

2.3. Physical Experience and Logical–Mathematical Experience

Thus the operations of thought derive from action on objects, and every action on the object starts with an indissociable interaction $S \rightleftarrows O$ between a subject S which acts and object O which reacts. Two types of knowledge need to be distinguished: On the one hand, physical knowledge in the broadest sense, i.e., knowledge which concerns the properties of particular objects; and, on the other hand, logical or mathematical knowledge, which is always applied to objects-in-general. Beginning at a certain level, this knowledge proceeds alone in a deductive manner without further need for experimental verification.

2.3.1. Two Types of Experience

It has often been claimed, and the entire Anglo-Saxon school of logical positivism still claims, that only physical knowledge derives from experience. In contrast, logical–mathematical knowledge remains alien and constitutes a pure deductive mechanism or a simple "language" whose syntax and semantics do not originate in experiences but merely serve to describe them. Such an interpretation seems to me to be incorrect, historically and psychologically. As I have unceasingly repeated, logical and mathematical operations derive from action, and, like physical knowledge, they presuppose experience in the true sense of the word, at least in their initial phases.

Historically we know very well that, prior to the axiomatic mathematics of the Greeks, there existed in Egypt and elsewhere empirical and utilitarian mathematics which served for computations and surveying. There existed, therefore, a stage in which mathematics originated from experience prior to the occurrence of a deductive construction. Here, as is often the case, engineering preceded science and material action preceded the operations of the intellect.

On the other hand, in the field of child psychology, it is quite apparent that at the preoperatory levels where deduction is not yet possible in a controlled manner and at the beginning of the operatory levels themselves, the child discovers by experience some logical and mathematical truths which he still is unable to deduce. A first example is the example of transitivity. When the child of 7 to 8 years knows how to construct a seriation by arranging in an operatory manner a set of 10 sticks measuring 10 to 14.5 cm, he knows deductively that $A < C$ if $A < B$ and $B < C$. His operatory construction consists in searching first for the smallest of the sticks, then the smallest of those remaining, etc., so that he understands in advance that an element E is both larger than the ones before ($E > D, C, B, A$) and smaller than the ones coming after ($E < F, G,$ etc.). This reversibility leads to systematic seriation and then brings on the immediate understanding of the transitivity $A < C$, etc. But before he acts in this operatory manner, the child is unable to construct his seriation except by trial and error: He gets $B < E$, then $B < C < E$, then $A < B$, etc., unsystematically, for lack of advance coordination of his successive actions. In this case, if he is shown two sticks $A < B$ and A is concealed, and if he finds that B < C, he is unable to deduce that A < C and he needs to be shown A in order to compare it with C. Experience is therefore necessary in order to gain this logical truth!

In arithmetic, too, a commutative equation such as $2 + 3 = 3 + 2$ is by no means evident at the preoperatory levels prior to experimental verification with objects. Furthermore, any concrete teaching of arithmetic by computation with objects demonstrates the need for continual action and verification by experiment before such computation becomes deductive. Moreover, at every level of teaching and even of mathematical invention, it is found that verification through concrete examples is necessary before we can get to general and abstract demonstrations. What mathematicians call "intuitions" (which can never prove anything but play a useful role in the discovery of new perspectives) seem to be a residue of these levels of action and experimentation.

It is nevertheless true that, in the course of its development, mathematics attains a purely deductive level at which experimental verification becomes useless. Deductive demonstration suffices and, in some cases, even becomes impossible because experience is finite and cannot lead to the infinite. This freedom from experience poses a problem, and so it remains to be explained whether mathematical operations derive from particular actions or from general coordinations of actions.

Before such a problem can be discussed, however, it has to be properly stated. To say that the operatory reasoning peculiar to mathematics has no need of experimental verification after a certain level of abstraction is attained means neither that mathematics is contradictory to experience nor that mathematics loses all contact with the object. On the contrary, one of the most surprising facts of the history of the sciences is that very often mathematicians build structures without any reference to experience. These same structures are then applied to physical experience afterward, sometimes long afterward. An outstanding example is the case of the non-Euclidean geometries which were developed by pure occupation with abstract generalization and which served afterward as frames of reference for a number of physical phenomena. Contemporary nuclear physics is constantly using "operators" constructed by mathematicians long before these "operators" could be applied.

So it must be said that any physical phenomenon is capable of mathematical analysis but that mathematics goes beyond physical experience, either by preceding it in time or by achieving a higher degree of abstract generalization. There is a relation, therefore, between logical–mathematical operations and the physical object, but it is not a direct relation; hence the difficult psychological problem.

2.3.2. The Time Lag of Physical Knowledge

The problem is apparently complicated—but actually made more precise—when we find that, in history and in the development of the child himself, logical–mathematical operations give rise to knowledge, properly so called, long before physical knowledge attains the same degree of precision.

In the history of science, the Greeks were the founders of logic and mathematics, but they never arrived at experimental physics save for a few rare exceptions in the static field (the statics of Archimedes). They did some astronomy, but the physics of Aristotle remained at a very inferior level with respect to his logic or to the mathematics of the period. We had to wait for Galileo and the 17th century to supply us with a theory of inertial movement and to make possible a properly experimental physics as distinct from a roughly empirical physics.

One reason for this is that, in the logical–mathematical domain, the commonest operations are at the same time the simplest: additive composition, serial ordering (concept of order), correspondences, are obvious examples. In the physical domain, however, the common phenomena are the most complex, and to achieve simplicity it is first necessary to dissociate the factors. The fall of a dead leaf, for example, is impossible to express as an equation, and the genius of Galileo, more than 20 centuries after the beginning of deductive mathematics, consisted in sufficiently dissociating the factors to make the time duration an independent variable and attain a "simple" movement.

Bärbel Inhelder has performed a series of experiments on the discovery of elementary physical laws by the child. We have published the results, together attempting to analyze them from the viewpoint of the logical operations involved in such experiments. To us the clearest and most general result of this research has been the difficulty which children and even preadolescents have in dissociating factors; apparently this dissociation assumes a combinatorial system, that is, logical operations of a level higher than simple classification, seriation, correspondence.

One of the experiments (Inhelder and Piaget, 1958) consisted of giving the subjects a set of rods of varying flexibility and asking the subjects (1) to account for the differences in flexibility (length of the rod, thickness, cross-sectional shape, and material of which the rod is made), and (2) to demonstrate how these factors affected the flexibility. A child may quite easily discover all or some of these factors, but it is not until around age 14 to 15 that he manages to furnish systematic proof: varying only one factor at a time while neutralizing the others by making them invariable. A child of 9 or 10, for example, quickly discovers that length has something to do with flexibility; but when he is asked to prove it, he takes a long, thin rod and a short, thick rod. If he is asked why, he says, "So you can see the difference better," and he hasn't the faintest suspicion that he is not proving anything.

In other words, young children resort directly to action, then they classify and do seriations, coordinations but in a global fashion, without trying to dissociate the underlying factors. Older children, after some groping, make a list of the hypotheses and study one factor at a time, then two at a time, three at a time (this is indispensable in other experiments). Furthermore, they do not use merely the elementary or concrete operations of classification, relation and numbers, but operations of propositional logic (implications, disjunctions, conjunctions, incompatibilities), which also presuppose a combinatorial system. To dissociate the factors, it is necessary to have a twofold combinatorial system, the one being applied to ideas or propositions and the other to particular facts or observations.

It can be seen, therefore, that although the child begins at 7 to 8 years of age to handle elementary logical–mathematical operations deductively, he must wait until he is 14 or 15 before he becomes capable of conducting experiments. This gap is reminiscent of the centuries which separate the arithmetic of Pythagoras or Euclid's elements from the physics of Galileo or Descartes.

2.3.3. Experience and Deduction

These different findings (A and B) seem to indicate that experience is indeed necessary for the formation of the logical–mathematical structures as well as for physical knowledge. There is, nevertheless, a difference between these two types of experience, although both, of course, consist of actions exercised by the subject on the objects.

Physical experience consists, as we have just recalled, of acting on objects and modifying them (by varying one factor, for example) so as to discover the properties of the objects and to gain knowledge by abstraction from the object itself. It is in this manner that the child discovers that one rod is more flexible than another or that there is a relation between flexibility and length.

Let us examine, however, an experience of the logical–mathematical type, such as discovering that the numerical sum of a set is independent of order (commutative equation): $2 + 3 = 3 + 2$. A great mathematician told me that as a child he had discovered this with amazement. Counting 10 pebbles in a row, he got the idea of counting them in the other direction, then counting them arranged in a circle, and he was enthusiastic about the fact that he always found 10. What is the nature of this experience?

There is, of course, once again, the acting on objects to modify them (arranging them in a row or in a circle) and discovering from the object the result of these modifications (10 from left to right = 10 from right to left, etc.). But the difference between the physical and the logical–mathematical experience is this: in the case of physical experience, the properties discovered were already present in the object; but, in the case of logical–mathematical experience, they were introduced or added by the subject's action. The rod was flexible before the child bent it, i.e., the bending did not make it flexible; but the linear or circular arrangement of the pebbles did not exist for these pebbles before they were arranged by his action. As for the number, it will be said that there were 10, not 9 or 11 pebbles; but they were simply objects capable of being numbered and, in order to assign the number 10 to them, it was still necessary to coordinate them with the names of numbers 1, 2, 3, . . . , 10, or with the fingers of the hand, etc., because number is a relation, not an absolute property.

In other words, what the subject discovered in the case of the logical–mathematical experience is that the result of the action of counting by the cardinal numbers is independent of the action of ordering. The logical–mathematical experience consists of abstracting from the object characteristics relative to the actions which modified the object, and not merely characteristics made evident by those actions but existing independent from them. It may therefore be said that, even if the action characteristics are discovered as residing in the object, logical–mathematical experience proceeds by abstraction from the actions themselves or from their coordination, not from the object independently of such actions.

Since these actions, exercised on the object, add new characteristics to the object and are the point of departure for the logical–mathematical operations themselves (Section 2.2), it is easy to understand why mathematics can become purely deductive. It is sufficient that the subject, instead of experimenting with the pebbles, can perform the same operations on any objects whatsoever that are symbolically evoked by the signs 1, 2, 3 . . . or x, y, z. . . . In the physical domain, however, if the flexible rod is replaced by some other object, there would be the risk of asserting something utterly false.

2.3.4. Objections

This interpretation of logical–mathematical experience has encountered objections which tend to diminish or eliminate its difference from physical experience. But we believe that these objections arise out of misunderstandings which can be dispelled by the following comments.

1. The two types of experience, physical and logical–mathematical, simply constitute two poles, not two entirely separate types, because they are *in fact* inseparable. In the case of the commutativity verified with the pebbles, a physical exprience is added to the logical–mathematical experience, because the pebbles have been arranged and counted. It can therefore be concluded that the pebbles have been conserved during the manipulations, that they have not merged into one like drops of water. This is the physical aspect that is inseparable from the logical–mathematical aspect. Conversely, the actions that intervene in a physical experience are always inseparable from general coordinations whose nature is logical–mathematical (combining, seriating, relating). These two types of experiences are, therefore, actually two poles or two orientations, in a manner similar to the relation between the subject and the object which are both inseparable ($S \rightleftarrows O$). The physical pole, therefore, in various proportions according to the situation, corresponds to the $\leftarrow$ arrow and the logical–mathematical pole to the $\rightarrow$ arrow.

2. Logical–mathematical experience still bears upon the object, but upon the object modified by the action. The subject, of course, has no awareness of the difference between an abstraction from the object discovered by the action and an abstraction from the object modified by the action.

3. Logic and mathematics always bear upon objects, even in the case of "pure" mathematics, but these objects may remain indeterminate because general coordinations are involved, not particular and differentiated actions as in physical experience.

4. Lastly, and above all, connecting the logical–mathematical operations to the actions of the subject consists, not in neglecting physical reality, but in finding it inside of the organism on which the subject depends. The general coordinations of action are, indeed, linked to the coordinations of the nervous system. It is known that McCulloch and Pitts in studying the various types of neuronic or synaptic connections have found structures isomorphic with those of propositional logic. The nervous coordinations themselves depend on the organic coordinations in general, which are of a physical–chemical nature. The problem of the adaptation of mathematics to physical reality, if it is not abstracted from physical experience but from the general coordinations of action, can

therefore be given a biological solution. This problem touches the very foundations of our knowledge. Doubtless the biology of variability and evolution rather than child psychology will give the answer to this question. This does not mean, of course, that mathematics and logic are recorded in advance in the organism. It means that the actions and the operations by means of which they are constructed are not arbitrary but derive their laws from those of an organism that is one object among others, while still constituting the source of the subject.

References

Gruber, H., Girgus, J., and Banuazizi, A., 1971, The development of object permanence in the cat, *Developmental Psychology* 4:9–15.

Inhelder, B., and Piaget, J., 1958, "The Growth of Logical Thinking From Childhood to Adolescence," Basic Books, New York, Chapter 3.

Inhelder, B., and Piaget, J., 1969, "The Early Growth of Logic in the Child," Norton, New York, pp. 94–97, 101–110.

Piaget, J., 1930, "The Child's Conception of Physical Causality," Routledge and Kegan Paul, London.

Piaget, J., 1969, "The Mechanisms of Perception," Basic Books, New York, pp. 173–176, 219–222.

Piaget, J., and Inhelder, B., 1956, "The Child's Conception of Space," Routledge and Kegan Paul, London.

Piaget, J., and Inhelder, B., 1962, "Le Développement des Quantités Physiques chez L'Enfant," Delachaux et Niestlé, Neuchâtel, Chapter 4.

Piaget, J., and Inhelder, B., 1971, "Mental Imagery in the Child," Basic Books, New York, pp. 231–239, 276–290, 259, 270.

The Development of the Concepts of Chance and Probability in Children*

BÄRBEL INHELDER

1. Introduction

It is both stimulating and gratifying to see great physicists and mathematicians interested in the developmental psychology of certain basic concepts of their subject. Einstein was the first to suggest to Piaget the analysis of the relation between the concepts of speed and time in children. Now it is particularly Rosenfeld, in the Niels Bohr Institute in Copenhagen, who through his original insights as theoretician and historian of physics is giving new incentives to the Genevan research in the genetic epistemology of causality. We feel honored by this current interest in our past studies on the concept of random events in children. This research was done by Piaget and myself with a team of colleagues some time ago. If we had to do it today with all the knowledge we have acquired on cognitive development in general, we could do so from a

BÄRBEL INHELDER ● Faculté de Psychologie et des Sciences de l'Education, Université de Genève, Geneva, Switzerland.

*This article summarizes research described in greater detail in J. Piaget and B. Inhelder, *La genèse de l'idée de hasard chez l'enfant*, Presses Universitaires de France, 1951, particularly Chapter 1 (Section 2) and Chapters 3 to 6 (Sections 3 to 6). Another reference to the research of Section 7 is found in B. Inhelder, "Developmental theory and diagnostic procedures" in D.R. Green, M.P. Ford, and G.B. Flamer (Eds.), *Measurement and Piaget*, New York: McGraw-Hill, 1971, pp. 163–167.

more sophisticated conceptual and methodological standpoint. In any case, a specialist on probability theory generated our research on random situations by asking us whether in every "normal" person (i.e., neither a scientist nor mental patient) there is an intuition of probability just as there is an intuition of primary numbers.

In epistemological terms this problem may be expressed as follows: Are the concepts of chance and probability the result of mere registering of everyday observation, and therefore essentially empirical in origin? At first, one might be tempted to say that this is the case. Indeed, most of our actions imply a spontaneous estimation of the more or less probable nature of the expected or perhaps dreaded events. An observer watching an adult crossing a road will see that he behaves as if he is continuously evaluating the probability of an encounter in terms of the frequency and speed of the traffic; young children appear to have become adapted to such a situation practically, although the psychological mechanisms behind this adaptation are still unknown. In everyday life we are continually involved in an inextricable mixture of causal factors and sequences. Objectively, daily life consists mainly of complex situations and events: the fanciful trajectory of a falling leaf is a more common observation than a rectilinear movement. Subjectively, of course, our interpretation of these situations and events can either simplify or complicate them. During our life we are forced to guess or to make our decisions on the basis of empirical frequencies and stochastic functions. For the young child also, life is full of unexpected events, frustrated expectations, and whims.

It is necessary, however, to distinguish between adaptive behavior at the practical level and systems of conceptualization. This distinction is essential, not only for probabilistic behavior, but also for other aspects of the development of knowledge. The current research of Piaget and his team on children's solution of problems of practical intelligence confirms the existence of a very clear gap between two developmental levels: the elementary level of the action itself, and the growing awareness of this action as an expression of its conceptualization. One of our collaborators asked logicians, physicists, and mathematicians to walk on all fours and then to recall the movements they had made. While the eminent physicists were quite successful at this, the no less eminent logicians and mathematicians were not.

Concerning the problem of this talk, we can state the hypothesis that reasoning about frequency and probability and concepts of random situations are distinct from forms of practical behavior without conceptual awareness and do not simply reflect or duplicate the observable events. They require as a frame of reference the construction of logical–mathematical operations which are then attributed to physical events in terms of causal explanations. If this hypothesis turns out to be true, probability and chance thinking would occur relatively late in cognitive development.

This general trend that has emerged from our work in Geneva indicates that the operations of thought (logical, mathematical, spatial, temporal operations) have their origin in the child's sensorimotor activity and end up as closed systems. In the psychology of knowledge we consider a system of operations to be closed when the outcomes of these operations (singly or in combinations) remain elements within the original system. These systems, as Piaget has shown, are isomorphic first with semilattices and then later on in development with lattices, group structures, and Boolean algebra. The outstanding feature of this constructive process is the progressive reversibility of interiorized actions which, through self-regulating mechanisms, can compensate for disturbances. These disturbances result from the continual confrontation between the subject's schemes of interiorized actions and the resistance of physical reality. This process of progressive construction reaches two levels of equilibration which Piaget defines as maximal stability with low entropy. The first level of equilibration is formed by the structures of so-called "concrete" operations; we call them "concrete" since their application is restricted to objects actually present in the field of the subjects' action. These operations may be found in class relations and number systems, and in our culture are attained around the age of 7. The second level is constituted by the structures of formal logic, such as propositional logic, implying the existence of combinatorial systems.

Recent research of the Genevan Epistemological Center has shown that causal explanations develop in close connection with the operations of thought and consist in attributing the subjects' operations to physical reality. But the problem of how the developing child assimilates and understands that which at first glance appears to resist physical causality (including random phenomena) remains open. This problem was the subject of the research about which I am about to discuss.

2. The Intuition of an Increasing Mixture in a Collection of Discrete Elements

2.1. Problem

The notion of a progressive and decreasingly reversible mixing is perhaps the starting point of a naive intuition of the concept of random collections. A mixing of elements seems to provide a good illustration of Cournot's definition of random collections as "causal series both interfering and initially independent." The developmental problem is therefore to find out whether, when confronted with an observable mixing of elements, the child imagines that this will result in an increasing mixture of the elements, or whether, on the other hand, he thinks these are interconnected by invisible forces. In other words, does the intuition of mixture (as an expression of the concept of random collections) occur at an early developmental stage or is it brought about by a specific developmental process, the steps of which we must discover?

2.2. Method

The child is presented with an open rectangular box (a cigar box) resting along its width axis on a device which enables it to be tilted back and forth. From this stationary position, the box is tilted toward one of its short sides along which are aligned eight red beads and eight white beads, separated from each other by a short midline separator. Each time the box is tilted and then returned to its original position, the beads run to the opposite short side and then return to their starting point, having undergone a certain number of possible permutations. Thus one creates a progressive mixture: at first, three or two red beads join the white beads and vice versa, and slowly this number increases. Initially, before any tilting, the child is asked to forecast in what order the beads will return to their original places, and whether each color will remain on its original side, or if not, how they will mix. The box is then tilted for the first time and the child notes the changed positions of a few beads. He is then asked to predict the result of a second tilt of the box, which is then carried out, and so on. Next, he is asked to predict the result of a large number of such tilts so that we can see whether he expects a progressive mixture, a to-and-fro pattern (i.e., an exchange pattern in which the red and white beads gradually change places), or a return to the original alignments. In addition the child is asked to draw his ideas of the final situation and of the various stages leading to it. These drawings are very revealing.

2.3. The Developmental Pattern

During a first stage, between 4 and 7 years of age, the child neither predicts a progressive mixture nor shows signs of an intuition of the concept of random collections. His behavior reveals a very significant conflict between his observation of the progressive mixing and the inability of his thought processes to accept this. The child cannot but see the mixing of the beads, but he refuses to acknowledge the random nature of the mixture and, above all, he predicts a return to their original places—a sort of "unmixing." He thinks the beads will "go back to their own places" and therefore seems to consider the mixing unnatural. Thus, initially, the children predict a straightforward return of the beads to their original positions. Those few who say that the beads will mix are clearly not convinced, and it seems that the idea that the beads should return to their proper places remains predominant. When questioned about progressive steps in the mixing, these children think that "it can't mix more, it will remain the same." Some expect a to-and-fro, red taking the place of white and vice versa, until, as they say, "the beads go back to their own places." The mixing seems to be interpreted as the result of a temporary disorder from which the elements seek to free themselves. The apparent reversibility which the children thus attribute to the mixing is in fact the very opposite of operational reversibility.

The second stage is characterized by a first intuition of the concept of random collections, as is shown by the child's own scepticism: "You can't tell, each bead can go to either side." The child predicts that "the beads will mix little by little, they go to a different place" and thinks that the to-and-fro exchange pattern is very unlikely: "It's difficult for that to happen." The child now starts to understand the random character of the beads' trajectories. The concept of mixing is therefore acquired without being clearly analyzed. But because he cannot imagine the multiple possibilities resulting from the interference of the trajectories (collisions) and does not understand permutations, the child has difficulty deciding what the final state will be.

During the third stage, the final positions of the beads after mixing are pictured on the basis of an exchange system. Initially, the child imagines the path of each bead according to a general and regular pattern of movement, as if the beads never collided. Subsequently, however, he regards the final mixture as the chance result of a number of different possible random encounters. Instead of ascribing to the mixture an unpredictable and incomprehensible nature, preadolescent thinking translates this phenomenon into thought operations that are realized even without regularity. The mixture seems at last to be understood as being due to the interference of independent causal sequences, a concept which corresponds to Cournot's definition.

3. The Notion of a Random Distribution and of the Experimental Method

3.1. Problem

In order to analyze the formation of the concept of random distribution in a concrete situation, we have to find out how the child becomes able to dissociate what is due to chance and what can be determined and predicted by simple applications of deterministic laws. We have chosen a situation where the elements are distributed uniformly or concentrated for reasons unknown to the child. It is a grasp of this distinction between what is random and what is not so that constitutes the most important intuition of probabilities.

3.2. Method

The experiment is conducted in a most simple form. A pin is put into a central hole in a brass disk and then fixed onto a board which is divided into equal segments (a reference point is marked on the rim of the disk). Each segment of the board is painted a different color. The disk is made to rotate continuously and the child is asked several questions, for example: "Can you tell where the disk will stop, on which color the little marker will stop, and could it stop on a different color?" Each time the disk stops the child puts a match on the spot. "If we continue to rotate the disk a great number of times, 10 times, 20 times, will there be more, fewer, or the same number of matches on each segment, or will there be many on one segment and none on the others?" This first part of the experiment was devised only to examine the development of the concepts of random distribution. Once a child has noted the regular and random distribution, the experimenter introduces a constant relation by placing small magnets capable of attracting an iron bar on the bottom of the disk. On each segment is placed a box of matches, two (of a different color) weighing 20 gm (a, a'); two weighing 50 gm and containing a magnet (b, b'); also two weighing 50 gm without a magnet (c, c'); and two weighing 100 gm (d, d'). We want to know what the child's reaction will be. Will he be struck by the miracle? By which mental operations of exclusive disjunction will he confirm or refute this hypothesis?

3.3. The Developmental Pattern

At the first stage, the children did not grasp the idea either of chance in terms of random distribution or of a constant nonrandom relation. They thought they could foresee and explain it all. If they were wrong, then they thought this was a whim of nature: "The disk stopped, it's a little tired." For many years the child thinks one can aim for a particular color, the one not yet hit. No doubt he has the idea that something like moral justice underlies the physical phenomenon. The impossibility of conceiving of either random or lawful processes corresponds, from the logical point of view, to the child's incapacity to comprehend the disjunction "A or B." At this stage, everything is constituted as a mixture of whim and moral determination. Hence, the child is impervious to any experimental evidence to the contrary. Some children attribute the stopping of the disk to the weight of the box. It is quite fruitless to show them that the disk never stops opposite the heaviest boxes. The child simply answers: "It's the middle weight that attracts," without thinking of verifying that of the two boxes with equal weights, one not the other stops the disk.

During the second stage, one can see the beginnings of a grasp of the concept of random distribution and the gradual interrelating of the successive random results. The child puts forward several possibilities which indicate a trace of doubt, and he begins to dissociate *certainty* from *possibility*. To the question, "Can you tell where the disk will stop?" a child answers: "It turns and the speed becomes smaller, smaller, and you can't tell where it's going to stop." However, he thinks that it will stop on a different color each time: "It's more just"—meaning correct and fairer—"as it cannot stop each time on the same." But he does not take a stand on the increasingly regular distribution as the number of trials increases, and to the question, "If you play a great number of times, is there a chance that the disk will have stopped on each color?" the child replies: "I can't say in advance, we'll see." Nevertheless, he thinks it is more probable "that it's more regular [both in the moral and statistical senses] when you do it less often," adding, "I can't explain, but I understand it well." So it seems as if the child is capable of anticipating possible compensations between successive trials, but this only for small numbers, hence a Genevan physicist referred to "the law of small and large numbers." It is clear that the child is amazed at the constant stopping due to the magnet and thinks that "it isn't natural, there's a trick" without, on the other hand, being as yet able to proceed systematically to the exclusion of the different possible factors which could cause the constant stopping. Later research on the inductive reasoning processes and experimental strategies has shown that these methods imply formal logical operations.

During the third stage, the preadolescent discovers formal operations of exclusive disjunction, and starts thinking in terms of relative frequencies in long-run sequences of trials. He says, for instance, "The greater the number of trials, the greater the chance of it being regular; the more you do, the more it evens out, because it stops once here, once there, and after a certain number of trials they're all equal." Underlying these still clumsy explanations resides the growing understanding of compensation between series of successive events. At the same time he can draw up a set of formal operations of exclusive disjunction and in this experiment says: "Why does the disk always stop on this same segment? If there was nothing to stop it, it would be as likely to stop on another segment, let's have a look. It stops either because of the boxes or because of something else. I take off the boxes, the disk stops somewhere else. If that happens only once, it doesn't mean anything, it may be due to chance." He repeats the experiment. "Without the boxes, it doesn't stop, therefore there's something in the boxes making it stop. I'll see whether all the boxes do the same thing." He eliminates all save b and b'. "Here we are, it may be due to the weight of the boxes." He compares b and b' to c and c'. "These two stop the disk, the other two have the same weight, it's therefore something else that makes it stop, etc. etc. . . ." To avoid misunderstandings, we must stress that even in this third stage the child does not grasp the idea of the expected frequencies that would be obtained in a long-run sequence of trials. We see from this example that the progress in probabilistic reasoning is closely connected to progress in formal thought operations, which underlie the experimental method of systematically varying the various factors involved.

4. Chance and Miracle in the Game of "Heads or Tails"

4.1. Problem

Having studied the development of the concept of random distribution in terms of physical events, it seemed equally important to analyze this same concept in the games of chance that children know so well. These games, as it is well known, were at the basis of Pascal's early probability theories long before their development in the realm of physics. Of course, these games, of "heads or tails" or drawing of beads out of a bag imply a physical aspect; but it is essential here that the player himself intervenes (rather than being a mere observer of a random distribution) by actually doing the drawing and placing the bets. It is precisely these operations effected by the subject himself that create the emotive appeal of games based on chance and were the basis of the mathematization of probability. As the Genevan studies on number and geometry have shown, mathematical concepts are acquired by means of a special process of abstraction applied, not only to the objects, but primarily to coordinations of actions. It is thus to be expected that when the subject's action intervenes in a random event or situation, he is more likely to grasp the concept earlier. To understand better the contribution of this operational concept of random situations, we introduced into the game a sort of miracle in the form of a series of exclusively heads or tails, in contrast to the random distribution of either type in the normal game.

Chance is indeed, for the subject, the negation of miracle. To understand the nature of a random distribution is for the child, as for us, to admit the very low probability of a long sequence of either heads or tails. So we occasionally introduced a trick into the chance game to find out whether children of different ages are in any way aware of this low probability, surprised at this astonishing fact or miracle, or even realize the impossibility of the situation which then leads them to discover the trick.

4.2. Method

One of the experiments proceeded as follows: about 20 white counters showing on one side a cross and on the other a circle were used. Heads or tails was played and the child was asked to observe 20 tosses. Then without the child's knowledge, 20 loaded counters having a cross on each side were substituted. The experiment was repeated and the trick explained should the child not have discovered it for himself. Then, one further experiment was conducted. Again without the child's knowledge of whether or not they were marked with crosses on both sides, the counters were tossed one by one to observe the child's reasoning underlying his assessment of whether or not the counters were loaded.

4.3. The Developmental Pattern

At the first stage, the child was sometimes surprised by the exclusive appearance of the crosses but he did not deem this impossible in terms of probability. Even after he had been shown the "trick" he thought he could achieve the same result, i.e., the miracle with counters that were not loaded. Three types of responses can be noted. The first may be called phenomenistic: the child thinks that "if you haven't seen them you can't tell." Here everything is considered perfectly natural and reality is not dissociated from appearances. There is, therefore, no miracle, only new facts. The case of the trick counters seems quite natural or simply amusing because rare. As one child said: "They turn upward."

A second response is compensatory in nature. The child seems halfway between a feeling of justice and of sufficient reason. He thinks that "next time there will be more crosses because last time there were more circles."

The third response is one of "personal power." As a child said, "It's a trick you did with your hands. You throw them like that," and he thinks he himself can re-create the phenomenon with the nonloaded counters. The child can see the shaking up of the counters and their spinning during their fall. He says, "They're spinning and falling," yet he still feels one needs only to throw them in a certain way to obtain only crosses.

The second stage is characterized more by the appearance of a qualitative notion of randomness coupled with a lack of understanding of long-run frequencies. The most striking fact is the refusal to accept a miracle. We ask, "How will they fall?" "Face up and face down," says the child, and when he uses the trick counters, he ponders for a moment and discovers that "they're [the crosses] on both sides." "Could that happen with the other counters?" "No, because they fall on one side or the other, they can't all fall on the same side because they spin while falling." Or "Could one have all the counters fall on the side with crosses?" "No, because there are too many; they are too well mixed." However, the children still refuse to estimate the relative frequencies of the crosses and the circles in terms of probability and they clearly think that to know whether or not the game is tricked, one is no more certain after one hundred than after ten trials.

A true estimation of probabilities is characteristic of the third stage. As a child of 12 says: "For one counter it is chance that is the deciding factor, but the more there are, the more one is likely to know whether they are mixed." "With the ordinary games and many counters, there will be a good half on each side" (he means exactly half). Finally, to find out if the game is rigged, the child reasons: "If you go on throwing them, you can become more and more sure. With 5 counters, all the crosses would turn up say once out of 25 tosses, but with 6 counters you would need 40 tosses, and with 7 counters, it's impossible." However arbitrary these estimates may be, they show a remarkable and growing awareness of probability as a function of long-run frequencies. The most likely result is half and half, and it becomes even more likely as the number of tosses is increased (the same child thinks that with a million tosses one can be sure). Similarly, the same child understands that the least likely situation is either all crosses or all circles, an outcome that becomes increasingly unlikely as the number of tosses increases.

5. Random Selection of Pairs

5.1. Problem

The quantification of probabilities and random selections is founded on combinatorial operations and in certain cases on the results of combination and permutation.

5.2. Method

The child is shown 40 marbles, 20 red and 20 blue, which are all put into a bag. He is then asked to draw out pairs of marbles in succession. We wondered in particular if the child would understand that the most likely distribution would yield 5 red pairs, 5 blue pairs, and 10 mixed pairs according to the laws of distribution a–a, a–b, b–a, b–b. In other words, would he have an intuition of probability corresponding to Mendel's law?

5.3. The Developmental Pattern

The developmental trend can be rapidly outlined: During a first stage, the child does not foresee the appearance of any mixed pairs, and he refuses to make any estimate of frequency: "I don't know anything, I'm guessing, there will be both red and blue ones." "Which will come out easiest?" The child answers: "Perhaps the red because they're not as mixed," but after a few draws he changes his mind and thinks that "the red and the blue together go quicker, because the marbles are mixed better." "And what if we keep on starting all over again? Will there be the same number of marbles of one color or of mixed marbles, or more of any one kind?" The child answers: "You can't tell, it's luck, maybe it will be the same."

During the second stage he predicts quite well the three types of pairs, but only during the third stage does the preadolescent think there will be more mixed pairs than pairs of one particular color. When the experimenter suggests "What if we play a great number of times?" the child thinks that there will be 10 mixed draws, 5 all red draws and 5 all blue. At this point in their development, the children are able to draw up a table of all possible two-element pairings.

6. The Quantification of Probabilities

6.1. Problem

Progress in the interpretation of the concept of chance depends both on the child's capacity to perform combinatorial operations and on his gradual interrelating of individual cases with the expected general distribution. This interrelating itself requires the performance of logical operations (class inclusion and disjunction) and mathematical quantifications. It was therefore important to study these underlying operations. We thus devised a lottery game.

6.2. Method

We used two series of white counters, of which some had a cross on the back. The child examined the composition of each series; the crosses represent what we call favorable cases, while the total number of counters in each series constitutes the number of possible cases. Both series are then laid on the table and the child was asked to evaluate in which of the two series he was more likely to find a cross on the first draw. The composition of the two series can be as follows: same number of favorable and possible cases in each; a different number of favorable, but the same number of possible cases; etc.

An easier version of the problem of relating favorable to possible outcomes can be studied with a simple sequence: If two black and one white counter are mixed in the palm of a closed hand, which color is more likely to be drawn?

6.3. The Developmental Pattern

Let us note only the particularly interesting fact about the first stage, namely, that the children think they will draw the single white counter more often. This, we think, is explained by the lack of understanding the logical relation between part and whole. The children are incapable of executing the inclusive addition $A + A' = B$, and never say that B could be either A or A' and that A' is more probable in this case because it stands for two units against only one for A. It is quite clear, therefore, that there can be no probabilistic reasoning at this point since the child cannot as yet conceive the relation between favorable and possible cases.

During the second stage, however, the children begin to be able to quantify these probabilities thanks to a grasp of the relation between disjunctive and inclusive operations. The child understands that if the unknown $x = B$, then it must be either A or A', but it is just as likely to be A as A'. The disjunction operation thus reveals the dependency of probabilistic quantification on the basic logical operations. Finally, during the third stage, the preadolescent is able to link favorable draws with the total number of possible draws, and henceforth interprets probability as a degree of rational expectation that can be mathematically assessed.

7. The Concept of Random Situations in Psychotic Children

We thought it would be interesting to examine a group of psychotic children, between 10 and 15 years of age, at different levels of operational development and deterioration. It is well known that the reasoning processes of such children are more or less deeply disturbed. All of them, even those who were still functioning on a high intellectual level, betrayed an incapacity to understand and assimilate random phenomena and refused to reason in probabilistic terms. They judged all events as though the universe were perfectly rational and predictable or as if it were governed by magical causes. In the experiment with magnetic disks a typical but very gifted and intellectually oriented psychotic boy of 13 said, despite repeatedly unsuccessful predictions: "It will always stop on the same color, you can do that very easily if you've got speed in your fingers; if you haven't got it, you give it again each time. There will always be the same braking strength, it stops at the same place, only you've got to start from the same place." When I objected that this precision in the fingers is very difficult to obtain, he insisted: "You start learning in the fingers, if you get the red once, you always get it ... it depends what you want." As soon as physical reality resists and cannot be fitted into clear causal sequences, psychotic children object to predicting or judging in probabilistic terms. We have seen that it is not the capacity to perform the underlying logical and mathematical operations that is lacking. The psychotic child of this type cannot consider chance phenomena, because he attributes to these phenomena hidden causes or external interventions in the form of tricks. He regards the world as animistic and his thinking often betrays forms of primitive dualism. The general reason seems to be, on the one hand, his systematic attribution of meanings to everything and, on the other, the feeling that his own reasoning powers are unlimited. These are two reasons for refusing to admit that anything is beyond his comprehension and for minimizing the chance factor which can be upsetting both intellectually and emotionally.

8. Conclusions

Our psychological experiments, of which we have been able to mention only a few examples, leave no doubt as to the fact that the first qualitative notion of randomness, even when limited to concrete contexts, only appears at about the age of 6 or 7, and is dependent upon the ability to perform concrete logical operations. Furthermore, the gradual nature of the elaboration of reasoning about probability could account for its late acquisition. To interpret these results, we must situate them within the larger framework of our knowledge of the development of the child's mental operations.

Logical and mathematical operations are structured systems of interconnected operations resulting in total reversibility and rigorous deduction. However, where the most probable composition of forces favors random events, each single random event is irreversible. Between these two extremes, we see the inductive procedures of the child as he seeks to sort out in any given event what is random and what is deductible.

During a first period, from about 4 to 7 years of age, a child's reasoning does not distinguish between possible and necessary events and evolves within a sphere of activity as remote from the idea of chance as it is from operational deductions. In fact, the child's thinking often oscillates between the predictable and the unpredictable, but nothing is predictable or unpredictable in principle. One might, therefore, say that it is the lack of a system of reference consisting of a series of deductive operations which prevents the child of this stage from understanding the true nature of random events. The strangest fact is certainly the children's difficulty in grasping the irreversibility underlying the random process of progressive intermixture (at a given moment) when their thought processes are still dominated by preoperational irreversibility (not being able in one's thinking to cancel or mentally compensate a perceived transformation). It is precisely the lack of this system of reference that explains why the child at this stage cannot apprehend the irreversibility inherent in random events.

It is also because of lack of operational reasoning that the child, like some of his famous historical predecessors, accepts miracles as natural, and this because he cannot conceive of the rare event with a very low probability, relative to both natural regularities and random fluctuations.

During the second period, from about 7 to 11 years of age, the child discovers random events in their most unsophisticated form, i.e., conceiving undetermined events as unpredictable, which contrasts with that which is determined or predictable in the domain of facts that can be organized by means of concrete logical operations. This discovery takes place at a time when the concrete operations on classes, relations, number, as well as causal and spatiotemporal operations are being progressively elaborated. In consequence, the child reacts very skeptically: "You can't tell, this might happen or that might happen." During this period, children become aware of random situations by antithesis to deductive necessity, as they are now capable of deductive reasoning and therefore can note the distinction between what is deductive and what is not.

During the third period, when he elaborates formal and more particularly combinatorial operations, the preadolescent becomes capable of assessing the total number of possibilities and of conceiving of the relation between those cases selected as favorable and the whole, seen as the sum of the combination of all possible cases. The assessment of probability is thus the product of a comparison between combinable and reversible events and irreversible random events, since only a small fraction of the totality of possible events is actualized.

The discovery of the random distribution as a function of "large numbers in the long run" is, psychologically speaking, the true basis of probability. During the preceding second period, the child reflects only on particular events and behaves as if he were naively applying Joseph Bertrand's dictum: Chance has neither conscience nor memory. He now seems to behave in accordance with the principle that "frequency of occurrence tends toward probability." It is, therefore, clearly within the framework of an operational system that the concepts of randomness and probabilistic reasoning are developed. Rational operations gradually confer their degree of intelligibility on random events.

I hope that our research may help to shed light on the psychological and developmental mechanisms at work in the elaboration of the most elementary forms of probabilistic thinking.

4

Review of Piagetian Infancy Research

Object Concept Development*

GERALD GRATCH

1. Introduction

This review primarily is addressed to research published in the English language on Piaget's notions of the object concept. The infant's achievement of the concept of the object can be viewed as the cardinal achievement of the sensorimotor period. To have the idea that the world is populated with enduring, independent objects, including persons and events, implies that the infant has a scheme of cause, space, and time within a coherent framework. Further, Piaget has argued that the conceptions of cause, space, and time develop consistently with an invariant reference point, which is nothing else but the concept of the object. As we shall discuss below, Piaget's theory of what is object awareness and how it is achieved contrasts strongly with empiricistic views. The infant does not become increasingly aware of the nature of objects through repeated exposure to them. Rather, the infant constructs, in stages, a scheme of the object of his knowledge through his sensorimotor activity in the physical and social world of things and persons.

GERALD GRATCH● Department of Psychology, University of Houston, Houston, Texas.

*I wish to give special thanks to M. Keith Moore. I acknowledge a heavy debt for his inspiration and ideas about the work contained in this review. Also, I am very appreciative of the considerable help Hans Furth has provided on both substantive and editorial issues.

Piaget (1954) diagnoses the stages from the infant's responses to hidden objects. He describes six stages. In the first two, the infant shows no special behavior related to objects. In the next two stages, the infant's orientation to hidden objects is determined by how he acted on them while they were in view. In the fifth stage, the infant's search is free of prior activity; he need only see where the object disappears to find it. But it is only in the sixth stage that the infant can consistently imagine and identify the location of objects, even when their place of disappearance is subsequently obscured.

While a good deal of research has been done bearing on other facets of Piaget's theory of infant development, it has not developed as clear a set of issues as the research on the object concept. Given spatial limitations, only brief mention will be made of aspects of this literature. Taking off in part from Piaget's observations, Bruner and his co-workers (1969, 1973) have conducted a number of studies of the development of skills which they interpret from a vantage closely related to the thinking of Bartlett (1958). Some investigators (Brunet and Lezine, 1965; Casati and Lezine, 1968; Corman and Escalona, 1969; Decarie, 1965, 1974; Lezine et al., 1969; Uzgiris and Hunt, 1974) have constructed batteries of scales to assess various facets of the themes Piaget developed in his three infancy books, and various attempts have been made to examine such issues as attachment and the bearing of social class on intelligence in the light of performance on the scales (see Gratch, 1975, for a review of much of this work). The psychometric work has provided support for many of Piaget's observations, but its relevance to his theory is still open to question at this point. The development of the scales has not been guided by a clear analysis of the relations between the notion of "action schemes" presented in The Origins (1952) and the "categories" of knowledge presented in The Construction (1954). In the former volume, Piaget focused on the development of adaptive mechanisms, tracing a course from reflex adjustments through intentional sensorimotor adaptation. In the latter, Piaget accounts for the development of the concepts of object, space, cause, and time. The scales consist of task series extracted from the books and are given labels from the books such as "the development of means" and "of causality." These comments are not made to denigrate this work—it is to be applauded—but rather to point out that the scales suffer from a lack of conceptual analysis and methodological clarity in the sense that such complex notions as causality are identified with a particular task series. There have been no efforts to "triangulate" in the sense suggested by Campbell and Fiske (1959). In other words, no attempt is made to identify the existence of a concept through several convergent methods.

An example of the difficulty of determining whether the scales get at infants' concepts and adaptive mechanisms or only at performance on particular tasks is provided by Uzgiris and Hunt scales (1973). Their thoughtful efforts have not yet proved successful because, we believe, the scales are focused on particular tasks rather than general notions. Decarie (1974) has made this point in a more substantive manner as she has attempted to account for the general failure to find correlates of Piagetian infancy-scale performance; we will describe her views and the work of her associates later on.

The methodological caveat we have raised is also relevant to the work on object concept development. The study of the development of such a notion is tied to a relatively simple paradigm, hiding objects in various manners and places. Whether such studies exemplify merely infants' strategies with relatively restricted hiding games or get at levels of object conception is a sometimes manifest and sometimes latent issue in the literature.

2. Introduction to Research on Object Concepts

Some 30 odd years passed before Piaget's (1954) account of object concept development in infancy captured the attention of empirical investigators. Prior generations saw the problem as an important one but construed it in a narrow way. Their primary focus was on the delayed response problem. It was assumed that search for an object hidden in a place occurred because search was guided by a representation of the absent object. Investigators addressed themselves to such questions as which species are capable of such thought, when in ontogeny does such thought emerge, and what structures in the central nervous system are responsible for representation (Fletcher, 1965; Munn, 1955). These lines of investigation ceased to command attention, perhaps because it became clear that neither success nor failure in delayed-response situations directly implicated presence or absence of representational abilities. Thus, it was found that prefrontal-lobotomized monkeys failed to search, not because they lacked the structure responsible for thought; rather, because they had difficulty in focusing their attention (Fletcher, 1965). It was recognized that such "nonthoughtful" creatures as wasps were capable of prodigious feats of delayed recall.

In his formulation of the problem, Piaget has retained the theme of search for an absent object, but he has posited that the basis for search and what is searched for change in a systematic way with development.

When, in early infancy, search occurs, it is as a result of extensions of actions already in progress, and the infant is unaware of the distinction between himself and object. In late infancy, the infant searches for objects as such because he has developed a framework which enables him to both perceive them as "disappearables" and to imagine their possible locations and states when they are out of view.

Piaget came to this conclusion through posing a dilemma. On the one hand, he empirically documented that in the first six months of life infants become increasingly able to deal with objects, e.g., they make increasingly subtle discriminations among them, they track movements of objects over increasingly diverse and wide-ranging trajectories, they react to them as polysensory events, they increasingly appear to anticipate event sequences, they come to be able to reach out and grasp for objects in a skilled manner. On the other hand, at about 6 months of age, such a seemingly competent creature will not recover a desirable object that is hidden directly within his view.

Piaget resolved the dilemma by asserting that they are not aware of things as "objects." In other words, they are only aware of "pictures," confounded resultants of their own sensorimotor activities with the objects of those activities. As such, infants may reinstitute the actions that were "responsible" for the "interesting spectacles" but they do not search in the sense in which search implies the independent existence of an object. Search for objects occurs only when the infant develops a conception or theory of objects in terms of which the "pictures" are interpreted and object conception derives from the coordination of the schemes underlying the activities with objects.

The literature to be reviewed, on both an empirical and a theoretical level, is closely related to the dilemma Piaget posed. Empirically, there are two relatively disparate literatures. One addresses itself to infants under 6 months of age and examines and extends Piaget's focus on the ability of such infants to track visually the movement of objects. The other addresses itself to infants over 6 months of age and examines and extends Piaget's focus on the ability of such infants to find stationary objects which are hidden in various places. One major way in which both literatures extend Piaget's empirical work is by making explicit a theme Piaget stated but did not elaborate empirically. That theme is the problem of object identity—namely, how does the infant know that the object that disappears and the one that reappears is the same object rather than two similar objects? One major way in which the two literatures do not adequately confront the dilemma Piaget posed is in terms of study of the transition period at about 6 months. While this period is studied, its critical significance has only recently been clearly sensed.

The empirical state of affairs is largely reflected in the theorizing. The work on infants under 6 months of age primarily is motivated by an attempt to show that Piaget is in error, that such infants do live in a world of permanent objects, objects which are known to exist when not in view. The difficulties older infants have with disappearing objects is explained in terms of their need to develop more adequate motor and information processing skills or spatial conceptions. The work on infants older than 6 months of age primarily is motivated by either an attempt to support Piaget's theory or to criticize it from a nondevelopmental, empiricist point of view.

3. Studies of Infants under Six Months of Age

Bower has been the principal investigator and theorist of this domain. He has conducted many studies in an attempt to show that very young infants live in a world of objects rather than sensations or action-dominated events (see Moore, 1974, for a review of his work and that of others). A particularly impressive example of his findings is that infants within the first 2 weeks of life both manifest intentional reaching for objects and are aware of their substantiality (Bower, 1970, 1972a). In this series of studies, Bower and his associates have reported that when objects are suspended at various compass points close to an upright supported infant, the infant's extended hand was not only directed toward the object but the molding of the hand conformed to the size and shape of the object. Further, as evidence that the infant is reaching for a solid object, they have reported that the infant was very distressed when its hand reached the area where a virtual image of an object was projected—the infant was not distressed when he contacted an actual object but was distressed when he failed to contact the expected, the virtual object.

Given various evidence that very young infants operate in a visual world of objects, Bower hypothesized that they were aware of the permanence of objects as well. Following Michotte (1955), he argued that information about the persistence of absent objects was present in the object-disappearance and object-reappearance transitions, and he set out to demonstrate that very young infants registered such information (1967). He reported that infants as young as 50 days of age would respond to a slow screening of an object in an alleyway as if the object continued to exist behind the screen, but they would not show such awareness when the covering was very rapid. With increasing age, he reported infants could take account of ever more rapid screenings, and, surprisingly, 50-week-old infants responded to an instantaneous disappearance as if the object continued to exist behind the screen, the instantaneous disappearance being a transition that should not specify object existence. He interpreted these results as indicating that very early in life, if not at birth, infants are aware of the permanence of objects on a perceptual basis; the ability to process such information improves with age and a conceptual basis for judging the permanence of objects develops around a year of age as a means of dealing with cases such as an instantaneous disappearance which are not covered by perceptual mechanisms.

These studies have been criticized on methodological (Gratch, 1975; Piaget cited in Bower *et al.*, 1971) and on theoretical grounds (Moore, 1974). The thrust of the methodological criticism is the likelihood that the infants were responding to changing scenes rather than to the screening of an object. Nevertheless, these studies certainly warrant careful replication and extension. Moreover, as a consequence of this first series of studies by Bower, attention has been directed to the importance of analyzing the types of visual displays which do and do not contain information about object permanence. Further, Bower was led to pursue the problem more deeply and to formulate a developmental account of object permanence as opposed to his intial nativistic theory.

Bower *et al.* (1971) studied visual tracking and took as their cue Piaget's argument about what it means when a young infant is observed to track an object in view and then follows it beyond the screen behind which it disappears. Piaget argued that, when 4- and 5-month-olds behave in this fashion, they only *appear* to be tracking an object as such. In fact, he claimed the infant only knows the object in the context of looking and does not know that the object continues to exist behind the screen. Instead, the infants are only extending their act of following the moving object; they make an inertial response because it often is "crowned with success."

Bower *et al.* (1971) exposed 8-week-old infants to a series of trials in which the object moved behind a screen and then reappeared and moved on to a stop in view. They introduced two types of control to show that "inertia" was not involved. First, the object moved on either a circular trajectory or a linear one, the former demanding a mode of following that precluded following because of poor head control. Second, their test for the presence of object permanence, looking beyond the screen on those occasional trials where the object stopped *behind* the screen, was balanced by a comparable number of trials where the object stopped *in front* of the screen. The results were striking. When the object went behind the screen and remained there, the infants looked beyond the screen, as if anticipating the reappearance of the object. But when the object stopped in front of the screen, the infants looked beyond the screen as well! Thus, the study nicely confirmed Piaget's argument: young infants are not anticipating object reappearances, rather they are following trajectories or are continuing action paths which result in "interesting spectacles."

Bower *et al.* (1971) interpreted their findings in a somewhat different manner, in part inspired by Piaget's hypothesis that for young infants objects do not remain identical to themselves in various action contexts. They hypothesized that the infants' behavior was a result of believing that an object in motion is *not* the *same* object as that object stopped. To explore whether the paradoxical effect was due to the aforementioned identity confusion, the investigators presented 8-, 12-, 16-, and 20-week-old infants with one of four situations designed to pit reliance on the object's features to guide tracking against reliance on the object's trajectory. The four conditions presented an object disappearing on one side of a screen with either: (a) the same object coming out on the same trajectory; (b) a different object coming out on the same trajectory; (c) the same object coming out at the same moment that it disappeared, a trajectory clearly different from the original one; or (d) a different object coming out beyond the screen in the (c) manner. The infants in each condition experienced a series of such trials, and, at specified times in the trial series, the object would either stop behind the screen or in front of it.

The results of this study were inconclusive. The authors did not report what the infants did on the initial trials, when the object behaved in either a "normal" or an "abnormal" manner. These are the trials of interest because they provide a basis for determining whether the infants entered the situation with ideas about how objects "should" behave. Unfortunately, the authors reported on what the infants did when the object stopped out of view or in view. These trials are ambiguous because one cannot know whether behavior on them is a function of the infants' ideas about objects or is a function of their having learned, somehow, to cope with the strange circumstances represented by conditions (b), (c), and (d). For example, in the instantaneous disappearance–reappearance conditions, (c) and (d), the 8- and 12-week old infants tended to either refuse to look or checked back and forth at the termini of the screen when the object stopped behind the screen. It is unclear whether this behavior indicates that they can only follow movement and become disrupted when another movement is introduced, as the authors argue, or that having learned, during the trial series to expect the object(s) to reappear instantaneously, the failure of the object's reappearance disrupted their conduct.

The authors viewed their data as indicating that 8- and 12-week old infants react to objects as though they have stationary and moving forms; according to this more elaborated version of their identity hypothesis, the forms are uncoordinated and in the specification of these forms motion and place are more important than features. However, by 20 weeks of age, the infant coordinates the two ways of identifying objects, place and trajectory, so he can identify the stationary and moving object as one. In other words, by 20 weeks of age, the infant is seen as tracking objects as such and his notion of the object includes featural identity as well.

While the initial evidence for this intriguing idea is somewhat ambiguous, a number of subsequent studies provide some support for the hypothesis. Gardner (1971) more adequately examined one feature of the Bower *et al.* (1971) study. In her first study, 3- to 21-week-old infants traced an object which moved behind a screen. She varied the size of the screens and found, like Piaget and the previous authors, that infants looked beyond ever wider screens with increasing age. To assess whether the infants were just tracking or were looking for objects, she presented them with a trial series in which the same object reappeared on half of the trials and a different object reappeared on the other trials. Younger infants simply tracked the object, irrespective of whether it was the same one or not. The 12- and 15-week-olds showed a variety of reactions, indicative of disruption, e.g., look around the room, stare intensely at the new object. On the other hand, 18- and 20-week-olds seemed to be tracking objects as such, seemed to be aware of specific objects in their absence, because when the different object appeared they would look back at the screen as if seeking to find the other object.

Bower and Paterson (1973), in two interesting ways, examined the thesis that very young infants perceive the stationary and the moving object to be two different objects. If the hypothesis is correct, then infants should continue tracking a moving object which stops and look back for a stationary object which moves in situations where *no screens* are present. In the first study, infants between 12 and 23 weeks watched the slow sweep of an object through a 180° arc.

Bower and Paterson then investigated whether analogous results would be found when a stationary object began to move. They studied 11-, 16-, and 21-week-old infants in two situations. In one, the infants saw, for 5 seconds, a carrier with three flashing lights located at the center of a track. Then the carrier slowly moved for 5 seconds to a second position on the right side of the track. The carrier remained there for 5 seconds and then slowly moved back to the center. This cycle was repeated four times, followed by a catch trial when the carrier moved from the center to a third position on the left. The other situation differed mainly in that the catch trial consisted of a stop of twice the normal duration rather than a move in an opposite direction. Again, while infants at all ages tracked the object on the non-catch trials, only at 21 weeks did the great majority of the infants do so on the catch trials. Bower and Paterson speculated that the younger infants follow the rule ". . . when the object at A disappears, an object at B will appear."

Thus, the Gardner and the Bower and Paterson studies seem to suggest that by about 21 weeks of age infants clearly have their "mind's eye" on permanent objects. The fact that younger infants do not keep their gaze fixed on the object but seem to focus on trajectories or particular places is a striking phenomenon. It may indicate that they identify the successive moments of objects as distinct entities and that object knowledge is a result of coordinating the initially disparate cues of place and trajectory. On the other hand, while the results certainly indicate that the infants are not perceiving the events as adults do, they may only reflect that the infants have developed situation-specific expectancies about where and how "interesting spectacles" are to be seen. We would like to emphasize this later point because Bower and his associates give the impression that these young infants are rather efficient trackers and that it is relatively easy to observe when the infants are in touch with stable objects as opposed to visual scenes. However, there is good reason to doubt whether this is so, in part deriving from studies of older infants reported in the next section, in part deriving from studies of tracking. Nelson (1971) carefully studied the responses of 3- to 9-month-old infants to a train engine which moved around an oval track with a tunnel positioned over one portion of the track. While he found that both infants under and over 5 months of age came to orient with increasing efficiency to the disappearing and reappearing train over an extended trial series, the most impressive finding of his well-documented report is an implicit one, namely, that the infants of all ages never developed a precise expectant way of orienting to the train in the tunnel and its emergence. In a pilot study, Muriel Meicler, a student of mine, has made comparable observations with 6-month-olds.

Bower (1972a) conducted another study which bears upon both later development and the question of what it is that is developing. Perhaps the empirical sequence which Piaget has described may only nominally be characterized as "object concept development." It is possible that the empirical sequence involves manifold responses and manifold situations with only a superficially unifying aspect of disappearing objects. In an effort to assess whether there is a concept developing, Bower and Paterson (1972) and Moore (1969) made the bold conjecture that such a view would be supported if acceleration of one behavior in the sequence speeds quite different behavior in another portion of the sequence. They exposed one group of infants at 12 weeks of age to 4 weekly sessions in a tracking task designed to provide a conflict between place and trajectory ways of structuring a situation in which an object disappears and reappears. They reasoned that feedback concerning the inadequacy of both hypotheses would lead the infants to develop a more mature rule, and this greater maturity would lead the infants to more ably cope with the task demands of situations they confront as they grow older.

The training group was exposed to the tracking task employed in Bower and Paterson (1973). A control group was brought to the laboratory weekly during the training period and was provided with no special experience. After training, at the age of 16 weeks, both groups were tested on the tracking task, and the training group performed without error whereas the control group tended to err on the catch trials, the trials where the object stopped at the 90° point of the 180° arc. Both groups of infants than had weekly reaching experience for 10 weeks and then were tested weekly on object-permanence tasks. One task was intended to assess whether the infants were performing at the Stage 4 or the State 5 level in Piaget's theory. The toy was hidden under a cloth at one place, A. If the infant found it, it was again hidden at A. If the infant succeeded, the toy was hidden at a second place, B. Following these trials, a different toy and different covers were introduced and the sequence was repeated. Six such cycles of 3 trials occurred in each session, and an infant was considered to have succeeded when he did not err on 6 successive B trials. The mean age of success for the training group was 39.3 weeks whereas the mean age of success for the control group was 48.6 weeks, a striking difference. When the infants succeeded, they then were given the following task. Two cloths were placed on the table, a toy was placed under one of them, and then the positions of the two cloths were transposed. There were 6 such trials in a session. The criterion of success was 2 successive errorless sessions. Testing had to be discontinued before all infants succeeded, but 80% of the training group succeeded and the mean age of these children was 43.7 weeks whereas only 60% of the control group succeeded and their mean age was 59.5 weeks.

The study is indeed impressive and tends to confirm the unity of the object concept. The differential treatment was a visual tracking task involving no manual search, and the criterial tasks were manual search tasks administered some 20 weeks later.

A problem implicit in the discussion so far is why 6-month-olds fail to recover a toy placed in front of them. If, at 20 weeks of age, they know that the object is behind a screen, why don't they simply remove the cover? Bower and Wishart (1972) addressed this issue in two experiments. In the first, they raised the question of whether the failure at 6 months is due to manual difficulties. Sixteen 20-week-old infants saw a toy placed on a table; the toy was then covered with an opaque cup and the infants were given the opportunity to search. Subsequently, the toy was covered with a transparent cup, and then it was once again covered with the opaque cup. The transparent cup was picked up by 14 of the 16 infants, and 10 of the 14 went on to pick up the toy, whereas only 2 infants got the toy when it was covered by the opaque cup and this occurred on their second trial. Thus, the infant's difficulty clearly is not a manual one.

In the second experiment, the experimenters presented seated 20-week-old infants with a manikin dangling from a string. Before the infants could reach for the toy, room was plunged into darkness and the infants' behavior was recorded through an infrared TV system. Before and after this task, Bower and Wishart assessed whether the infants would remove the cloth from a toy covered in front of them. All infants failed the latter tasks, but all reached out to the direct locus of the toy in the dark, some even after distress that lasted as long as 90 seconds. Bower and Wishart conclude that out of sight is not out of mind, but they are not clear why the infants fail in one situation and not the other.

The answer to the question appears to be supplied by two further studies by Brown and Bower (in press). In one study, infants between 22 and 37 weeks saw a toy covered by a cloth or by an upright vertical screen. The great majority failed to remove the cloth but did get the toy from behind the screen. The authors do not describe how the toy disappeared behind the screen, but apparently finding the toy is attributed to the fact that this screening involved a "behind" relation which these infants comprehend. However, when the cloth was placed over the toy, this created an "inside" relation, and the infants' failure in this condition is attributed to their inability to comprehend such a relation because they see the cloth as a replacement of the object by the cloth. Further support for this interpretation is provided in a second study with infants between 7 and 15 months of age who saw toys hidden in various places and ways under both opaque and transparent cups. The infants' level of object-concept performance was comparable under the two conditions, leading the authors to conclude that the problem for the infant is comprehension of spatial relation and not memory of an object "out of sight."

Moore (1974) has attempted to put these studies in perspective, and the conclusion to this section leans very heavily on his views. On balance, although some of the studies reviewed in this section can be faulted, and some can be interpreted in other ways, the findings are encouraging support for the line of theorizing that Bower is evolving, one that increasingly takes into account developmental changes but, unlike Piaget, has a strong nativist bias about the origins of object knowledge. Smillie (1972), in an interesting paper, has presented a similar, though less articulate, account. However, we would like to state additional reasons for being cautious about Bower's findings and views. The infants' reaching in the dark can be interpreted simply as evidence of Stage 3 secondary-circular reactions. The finding that infants would recover the object from behind vertical screens but not from under covers can be interpreted in similar terms. If Brown and Bower (in press) had moved the object behind a stationary vertical screen, then the infants could have retrieved the object by simply continuing the act of reaching initiated by the disappearing object whereas taking off a cover involves more than the continuation of a reach. The same argument would apply if the screen were placed in front of the toy. That procedure would bring the authors' explanation into question because, given the authors' views, both the screening and the cloth covering should be interpreted by infants as a replacement of the object by the cloth. Moreover, the results of the Brown and Bower studies are at variance with another study reported by Bower (1972b). In the course of the longitudinal study conducted by Bower and Paterson (1972) referred to earlier, infants at 21 weeks succeeded with screens but failed with cups and covers. However, at 25 weeks the infants lost their ability with the vertical screen, and when they regained it at 27 weeks, they could also solve the task with cloths and cups. Why the children should lose their understanding of the "behind" relation and then, simultaneously, rediscover this relation as well as achieve understanding of the "inside" relation is not obvious. Finally, Brown and Bower's account does not explain why 5- or 6-month-old infants ever fail a partial hiding task, where the toy is partly obscured by a cloth (see next section). Bower's (1966) study of amodal completion, where one form is superimposed on another, suggests that far younger infants see the whole object under a screen, and his own work and that of others suggests that the problem poses no manual difficulties for the infant.

4. Studies of Later Infancy

The studies reviewed in this section, while bearing upon Piaget's theory, in no sense attempt to evaluate his theory as a whole. They tend to be addressed to selected aspects of his theorizing about the course of object concept development. In particular, they tend to focus on his account of how infants come to find an object that is hidden in one location and then come to find an object that is hidden in more than one location.

4.1. Search in One Location

As has been repeatedly noted, 5- and 6-month-old infants have great difficulty in recovering a desirable object which is covered by a cloth within their view. In cross-sectional (Uzgiris and Hunt, 1974) and longitudinal studies (Schofield and Uzgiris, 1969), it was found that infants can reliably retrieve a partially hidden object about a month before they retrieve a completely covered object, the ages being about 6 and 7 months, respectively. Comparable trends were found in a longitudinal study by Gratch and Landers (1971) and in a cross-sectional study by Gratch (1972). In the latter study, Piaget's observation of an intermediate step of successful finding if the infant is reaching before the toy is hidden was confirmed. Also, a step prior to the last one was discovered, namely, the ability to gain the toy when the infant grasps it and then has his hand covered with a cloth.

Perhaps even more important in illustrating the complex sequence of steps that infants go through in coming to solve the seemingly trivial problem of finding a completely covered object are the following observations made by Schofield and Uzgiris during their longitudinal study. As the infants solve the partial or total hiding problem, they initially tend to look away when the toy is covered, then they dwell on the cover both visually and tactually but do not remove it, and finally they take the cover in a slow hesitant manner and look toward the toy only after some delay.

Thus there is ample evidence that there is a developmental problem for the infant. Piaget definitely does not imply that its solution is a matter of motor skill development or a matter of getting the visual information about object permanence into the manual system, as Bower sometimes argues. Piaget's explanation of how the infant comes to search for the object in Stage 4 is in terms of the coordination of action schemes. It is not an easy argument to follow, but Moore (1974) seems to have captured it by giving it the following character. When the rudimentary visual permanence derived from anticipation of seeing is coordinated with the rudimentary tactile permanence from anticipation of grasping then the infant expects to grasp what he expects to see. The infant's awareness of the object is more firmly grounded in space and there is a better basis for coping with the delay introduced by total covering of the object. In conjunction with this achievement, the coordination of the secondary circular reactions of reaching and grasping provides the means whereby the obstacle of the cover can be attended to without distracting the infant from expecting to grasp what he expects to see. At this point, the baby hardly has a clear idea of absent objects to guide his search, but he has a basis for keeping after the disappearing object which goes beyond the level of secondary circular reactions, of making "interesting sights last."

Schofield and Uzgiris (1969) examined the assertion that intersensory coordination is a necessary precursor to Stage 4 search by longitudinally assessing infants' coordinated schemes for examining objects and their stage of object permanence. The children shifted, with increasing age, from stereotyped handling of the toys to a coordinated visual and manual inspection of them. The major increase in inspectional activity came at the time the infants were able to retrieve a partially covered object but could not find a totally covered object. Thus, Schofield and Uzgiris, at best, provide only equivocal support for Piaget's hypothesis because one should find that the ability to find a totally covered object occurs shortly after the appearance of such intersensory coordination.

Harris (1971) also attacked the problem of object exploration and search by comparing persistence in search of infants who were only allowed to inspect an object visually and infants who could also manually interact with it. Harris found that 8½-month-old infants in the manual condition searched longer than in the visual condition, but the reverse was true for 12-month-olds. How these results bear upon Piaget's theory is unclear because the results do not permit one to know whether handling affected search structures or only motivation to search. Inspection of Harris' table of means suggests that many of the younger infants may not have reached at all; further, the reversal of the effect for the older infants may indicate that for them handling resulted in satiation with the toy whereas, for the younger ones it increased the motivation.

Gratch (1972) conducted yet another study which is relevant to Piaget's line of argument. Piaget sides with Bishop Berkeley in attributing to touch the means whereby the size–distance constancy problem is solved. The infant is hypothesized to learn about the invariant size of objects in near space by moving them to and fro and noting that their variable visual appearance is associated with their invariant feel in hand. Piaget (1969) places great importance on the information infants can derive about the object from grasping and seems to believe that the achievement of size–distance constancy in near space is related to Stage 4 search. Against this view, Gratch and Landers (1971) were surprised to find that infants who could solve the partial-hiding problem would fail the following task. When the infant reached for and grasped the toy, the experimenter would drop an opaque cover over their hand. The infants tended to either sit with toy in hand or slowly release the toy and remove their hand. Either the covering had disrupted their desire for the toy or they did not appear to be deriving information about the object in hand.

Gratch (1972) followed up this result by comparing the behavior of 6-month-old infants when they grapsed the object and an opaque or transparent cover was placed over their hand. In the case of the transparent cover, the infants would remove it, thus demonstrating that they both had the necessary skill and were not so distressed by the covering that they abandoned the situation. In contrast, many of the infants did not remove the opaque cover, and an interesting association was found between success on this task and manner of removing the transparent cover. Infants who simply shook the transparent cover off their hand failed to remove the opaque cover, whereas, infants who removed the transparent cover with their free hand succeeded in removing the opaque cover, doing so by shaking it off. As reported earlier, these infants all could solve a partial-hiding problem and could not solve the total-covering problem. This study suggests that 6-month-olds do not derive information about objects through touch and calls into question Piaget's argument about the development of size constancy and leaves open the question of what relation exists between intersensory coordination and Stage 4 search.

The coordination of sight and sound also has been explored. Freedman et al. (1969), noting that blind infants do not appear to search for a sounding object until about 10 months (Fraiberg et al., 1966), set out to determine whether the phenomenon is peculiar to the blind infant or is consistent with Piaget's (1954) observation that the sound of a hidden object does not facilitate search for it in young infants. They report that it is not until about 10 months that sighted infants will be as likely to search for a sounding object as a nonsounding one, indicating that sighted infants also do not use sound cues to identify objects until late in the first year. However, their study is inconclusive because the infants watched the nonsounding toy disappear behind a screen whereas, their attention was distracted away from the sounding toy as it disappeared. Ginsburg and Wong (1973) report that 6-month-old infants would search for a music box if it sounded continuously through the hiding process but would not search for it if it was not sounding. They conclude that sound served as a cue for search, but given their report, it is impossible to determine whether the differential performance was due to differential interest in the disappearing "objects" or to the sound cue. Moore (1974) believes that a demonstration that sound does facilitate search is crucial to Piaget's theory because coordination of circular reactions between different modalities is a major mechanism for the development of object permanence. He is now conducting a study which, it is hoped, will more conclusively determine the cue value of sound.

Thus, the studies reviewed in this section generally conform to and amplify aspects of Piaget's account of Stage 3, but they also point up the need for a clarification of how the coordination of different modalities of action leads to an isolation of the "object" from action. This issue will again be taken up later.

4.2. Search in Two or More Locations

Piaget observed that when his three infants were *first* able to sit and watch an object being covered at one place, A, and retrieved it, they did a curious thing when he hid the object in a second place, B. They carefully watched it being hidden at B, but when it disappeared, they turned directly to A and searched there. Piaget indexes Stage 4 in terms of this phenomenon, and it has played a key role in his thinking about object concept development. To him it clearly demonstrates that simply being able to search for a hidden object does not signify that infants are aware of the independent existence of objects. He recognizes that one may interpret the phenomenon differently. One may view it as an infantile version of adult "absent-mindedness." The infant may clearly note the place of disappearance, forget that place, and then later search at the place where he is accustomed to find it. But Piaget cannot accept this interpretation because, according to him, A is not a familiar place in that the infant finds the toy there only once or twice, and no opportunity for distraction occurs because the infant turns to A as soon as the toy disappears.

His own explanation of the phenomenon is both interesting and ambiguous. The infant errs because he fails to register the new place of hiding. When the object disappears at B, the infant interprets the event as one where "the object-I-find-at-A is disappearing" and therefore searches at A. As Smillie (1972) has noted, Piaget places special emphasis on the role of the manual searching and finding of the object at A as leading the object to have that special character. This emphasis leads him to speculate that the infant at this stage still lives in a world where objects do not remain identical to themselves under spatiotemporal transformations. Rather, the world contains many similar objects, each identified separately in terms of the context in which the object is acted upon. An important ambiguity in the account of the AB̄ error is why the infant apparently abandons a strategy that allowed him to locate the object at A. In Stage 4 the infant searches for the object where it disappears at A, but not at a subsequent B, whereas in Stage 5 the infant searches for it wherever it is seen to disappear. Clearly, in Stage 4 it is not the disappearance at B that marks the place, rather it is the prior successful search at A that marks the place.

Gratch and Landers (1971) explored this important developmental concordance of the first successful search at A and the failure at B through search at A. They conducted a longitudinal study to replicate Piaget's observation, beginning their biweekly observations at an age where the infants could not find at A. They discovered that AB̄ occurred in the first session in which the infants found the toy at A on two successive trails, and the phenomenon persisted over a number of sessions. They made a number of other observations which were consistent with Piaget's interpretation of the phenomenon. On the B trials in the early sessions, the infants tended to look only to the A side during the 3-second delay period and they did not attempt to correct their errors by searching at B. Moreover, when the infants found the toy twice in succession at B in the later sessions, the toy was hidden at A and the infants then would search at B. They were still learning about *particular* places and were not learning to search out *any* place, wherever the object was disappearing.

In contrast to these findings, Schofield and Uzgiris (1969) in their longitudinal study did not find many babies making the AB̄ error (success at A, failure at B) and the error has seldom been found by investigators who have used object-concept scales (Bell, 1970; Corman and Escalona, 1969; Miller *et al.*, 1970; Uzgiris and Hunt, 1974).

Harris (1973) suggests that failure to find the error may be due to the amount of time that the object is out of view. He noted that Schofield and Uzgiris allowed the infants to reach for the cover as soon as it was placed over the object. Moreover, he argues that the error is due to forgetting. He found that 10-month-old infants on a two-place search task made the AB̄ error when the object was hidden at B with a 5-second delay but not with *no* delay. In a second study, Harris found he could induce the error by covering the hidden object in a particular sequence, at B first and then covering the empty hiding place but not with the reverse sequence. Harris interpreted both effects as proactive interferences from the last successful search at A: (1) delay produces the AB̄ error by allowing the infant time to resample the situational cues after the disappearance and become confused with his last search, thus forgetting the hiding at B; (2) the covering sequence produces the effect by distracting the infant back to the location of his last search, inducing confusion and forgetting of the new location at B.

Harris appears to have demonstrated that 10-month-old infants err because they register and then forget the new hiding place, but it is not clear that he has shown that Piaget's argument is incorrect. Because 10-month-olds are less likely to make the error than 9-month-olds (Gratch and Landers, 1971), they therefore may err for different reasons than 9-month-olds. Gratch and his associates regularly use a sequence of covering that did not lead to error in Harris' study and found, nevertheless, that 9-month-old infants make the AB̄ error (Evans, 1973; Evans and Gratch, 1972; Gratch and Landers, 1971; Landers, 1971). Finally, Gratch *et al.* (1974) conducted a study with 9-month-olds in which the delay interval was varied. The infants waited either 0, 1, 3, and 7 seconds before the tray was moved within their reach following the covering of the toy. The great majority of the infants in the 1-, 3-, and 7-second conditions erred. These results are not consistent with Harris' view. However, almost none of the no-delay infants erred. The infants tended to reach toward the toy as it was being hidden. To rule out the possibility that such a reach in combination with the movement of the tray could have "frozen" the infants at B and led them to succeed, a number of infants were studied where the tray was not moved. Instead, the infants were restrained, in some cases only their bodies, in some cases both their arms and their bodies. Almost none of these infants erred, so there appears to be evidence that the infants are registering the new place of hiding, a result that is not quite consistent with Piaget's argument.

The issue is unresolved. However, analysis of the delay behavior on the first B trial of the 1-, 3-, and 7-second infants provides some support for Piaget's interpretation. Infants who were highly attentive to the tray during the delay and erred were very likely to look only at the A side during the delay period. Moreover, these infants tended to be the younger infants. On the other hand, infants who were not highly attentive to the tray during the delay and erred did not show a particular pattern of gazing either at the A or B wells and tended to be older. Thus, there is some direct support for the argument that early in Stage 4 infants do not register that the toy is being hidden at B. Further, one can argue that success in the no-delay condition is due to an extension of an overt or incipient act of reaching, a secondary circular reaction, and does not indicate registration of the new place.

Harris (1974) has reconsidered his claim that the AB̄ error can be explained as a matter of forgetting and now feels that the spirit of Piaget's account is correct. Impressed by the observation of Butterworth (1974) that such errors occur even when transparent covers are used, he focused his attention on the relevance of what Piaget has called "residual" reactions. Piaget noted that, even when infants solve the AB̄ problem in Stage 5, they will return to a previous location if they fail to immediately find the object at a new location. He interpreted such behavior as a sign that the infant in Stage 5 is still not clear about the relation between an object and its place of disappearance. Harris investigated the limits of infants' understanding of this relation by presenting 12-month-old infants with a situation in which a car moved into one of two transparent boxes. On the first three trials, the car moved into box A and the infant could push open a door to get the car. The next two trials were tests in that the doors could not be opened and the car moved into the B box and once into the A box. While the great majority of the infants initially approached the door where the car was located, several approached the A door when the car moved to B. Moreover, the infants then vacillated between the two doors, persisting far longer at the A door when the car was at B than at B when the car was at A. To check on the possibility that the search at the empty door was simply an attempt to find an alternative route to the car, Harris did the same experiment with 10- and 12-month-old infants, the only change being that a single test trial was given at door B, which was opaque. Both the A and B doors could be pushed open, and the great majority of the older infants initially approached the A door. The picture was less clear among the younger subjects, approximately the same number approaching the A or B or approaching neither door. Thus, Harris found further support for Piaget's contention that infants confound their awareness of where objects disappear with their prior actions on them.

Landers (1971) focused on the ambiguity in Piaget's account that was alluded to earlier, namely, that the infant localizes the hiding of the toy at B in terms of his successful manual search at A but somehow localizes the hiding of the toy at A on the basis of visual observation. He speculated that the manual search at A was not the critical factor, that simple observation of the toy's disappearance and reappearance at A might lead infants to make the AB̄ error. Further, in line with a learning theory analysis of such behavior, he examined the influence of the number of the preceding trials at A upon the subsequent B error. He compared three groups of 9-month-olds: Group 1 searched for the toy 2 times at A, Group 2, 8 or 10 times, and Group 3 observed the toy hidden and uncovered 6 or 8 times at A and then searched for it twice at A. The great majority of the infants in each condition searched at A on the first B trial, but the Group 2 infants made a longer run of consecutive errors than the other two groups. He concluded that the error was determined by the number of searches at A and that observation was not a factor in specifying A as a special place. However, his study is inconclusive on several grounds. For one, all three groups searched at A, none simply observed. Second, on the critical first B trial, all three groups were equally likely to err. Third, when the infants erred, they were handed the toy. This may have functioned as a reinforcer for subsequent B trials, leading Group 2 to persist longer in their more well-established habit of A search.

Evans (1973) addressed these issues in a much more direct way. He composed four groups of 9-month-old infants in terms of whether they simply observed the disappearance–reappearance of the toy at A or searched for it and whether they did this on two or five A trials. Further, when the infants erred on the B trials, they were not given the toy. He found that the four groups did not differ in terms of either likelihood of searching at A on the first B trial or the length of the run of trials of erroneous A search. Thus, somewhat surprisingly, the amount of experience at A did not affect the AB̄ error; clearly overt search at A is not a necessary cause of the error. Rather, observation of the disappearance–reappearance at A suffices to mark A as a special place.

Of course, this finding does not contradict the spirit of Piaget's analysis, but it does point to ambiguities in it. While Piaget is talking about action schemes and not motor responses, his emphasis on the importance of manual activity and its relatively late developmental coordination with visual activity leads him to single out the overt manual act of finding the object at A as crucial in the AB̄ phenomenon. The difficulty that this emphasis leads him into is perhaps even more dramatically illustrated by Decarie's (1969) finding that even severely deformed thalidomide babies come to be able to localize and remove the covers from hidden objects. In their case, it is not easy to see how the coordination of looking, reaching, and grasping played a role in their achievement. These phenomena seem to be more easily interpreted within the frameworks proposed by Bower (1972b) and Moore (1969, 1974), which place more emphasis on the object information that infants take in visually.

Finally, Evans and Gratch (1972) considered one more aspect of Piaget's discussion of the AB̄ error. It will be recalled that Piaget suggests that the phenomenon indicates that such infants identify each object in terms of its action context, they do not yet appreciate that the same object may exist in various contexts. Evans and Gratch reasoned that if the infant searches at A because he sees "the toy-I-find-at-A" being hidden at B, he should not err if a distinctively different toy is hidden at B, a toy he has never handled at A. They found that 9-month-olds were equally likely to err when the same toy was hidden at A and B and when different toys were hidden in each place, even though the infants gave clear signs that they were aware that a different toy was being hidden.

Thus, the infants appeared to be treating A as a special place, a kind of "toy box," rather than erring because of difficulties in conceptualizing the identity of objects. Of course, from both the point of view of Bower, Broughton, and Moore and of Piaget, it can be argued that identity was always the issue. It is possible that the infants searched at A because they were looking for the A-toy. That argument has been made to account for strange antics in a number of previously reported studies of infants under 6 months of age (e.g., Moore, 1974), and we have sometimes observed 9- and 10-month-old infants find the toy at B and then, with toy in hand, search at A. However, this line of argument has the problem of accounting for why the infant seeks the old toy when a new one is at hand. This view is particularly hard to accept in the light of the fact that Evans (1973) and Landers (1971) did not find that the likelihood of the AB̄ error declined with increasing numbers of trials at A, an increase that should satiate the infants on the "old" toy.

The observations Piaget uses to infer stages of object concept development have been well confirmed within the framework of Piagetian object-concept scales, though Uzgiris (1973) believes that the ability to find an object that is seen to disappear at A or B should be classified as Stage 4 rather than Stage 5. However, Moore (1974) has proposed that Piaget's sampling of the developmental tasks involved in the achievement of the object concept is insufficient. He argues that there are too few data points to permit the discovery of the mechanism for stage change, and he proposes that the transitions cannot be explained in terms of the enrichment of action schemes by the feedback from the consequences of actions upon things. Instead, he proposes "that the structures which account for the task sequence and the development of object permanence are successive reorganizations of spatial rules for the essential identity of hidden objects" (Moore, 1973). He reports on a longitudinal study which revealed a number of new steps which form a Guttman scale order with the typical Piagetian series and which fit better into his interpretive framework than that of Piaget. For example, he finds the AB̄ task proves to be considerably harder if a seemingly minor change in procedure is made. If the examiner shows the toy in his hand between the two covers, moves his hand under one of the covers and brings his empty hand from under that cover and positions it between the two covers, then infants who no longer commit the AB̄ error will do so.

4.3. Do Infants Really Search and for What?

In the previous discussion and in the presentation of Bower's views, the question of what kind of an object is searched for has been raised. Piaget also has addressed himself to the issue in the framework of arguing that in Stage 4 infants become aware of the three-dimensional nature of objects, e.g., objects have a back side, and have a measure of shape and size constancy. We now present a number of studies which have taken up this question.

Charlesworth (1966) studied what happens when 4- to 12-month-old infants see a toy hidden, search, and then either find it or discover there is no toy. By 8 months, almost all the infants studied showed concern over finding no toy, displaying such reactions as distress and active visual or manual search. Thus they appear to be expecting to find an object and, significantly, this is around the age that infants begin to make the AB error (Gratch and Landers, 1971). Further, it is interesting to note the discrepancy between the age of these infants and the age of 18 to 20 weeks at which Gardner (1971) found such reactions when a moving object disappeared behind a screen and a different one appeared beyond the screen.

Charlesworth's study, however, does not indicate whether the infants are searching for an object that has disappeared or whether they are expecting to find a particular object. It is possible that the infants are not so much searching as that they are engaged in operant, or secondary circular, reactions. The expectation may refer to the consequences of their action and not to the disappearing object. Appel (1971) wondered whether the infants only treated the disappearing object and the cover as diffuse cues to deploy a well-practiced cover-pulling operant. To assess this possibility, he studied 9-month-olds in a one-position hiding game. For half the infants, he hid a toy on five trials. For the other infants, he hid "no-toy" on five trials. "No-toy" consisted of the examiner going through the hiding motions with an empty hand for half the infants and simply rapping on the front of the covered tray for the other infants. The "toy" infants searched and the "no-toy" infants refused to search on all trials, indicating that the disappearance of the toy was the cue for cover-pulling; the infants could be said to be searching. The conditions then were reversed. The new group of toy infants proceeded to search, providing further support for the hypothesis. But to the surprise of the investigator, the majority of the new group of no-toy infants persevered in their previous habit and searched on the first no-toy trial and some searched on a second and a third trial, doing so even though they were attentive to the "no-hiding."

To deal with the difficulties posed by the latter result, two more studies were conducted. In the first, 12-month-old infants were studied under the same conditions to see whether, with increasing age, there would be evidence that infants would still persevere in the no-toy condition or would be more clearly oriented to the cue of toy disappearance. The latter hypothesis was supported; 12-month-olds searched only when the toy was hidden and did not search when no toy was hidden, irrespective of condition order. The second study took up the implication of the 9-month results for the AB̄ error. From the search in the no-toy condition one could argue that the AB̄ is not an erroneous search for the toy hidden at B, but simply a redeploying of the A habit, the activity of the examiner at B being only a diffuse signal to pull off the A cover. Half the infants saw a toy hidden at B and half simply observed the examiner rap in front of the covered but empty B well. Significantly more 9-month-olds searched at A when the toy was hidden at B than in the no-toy condition, indicating that the hiding of the toy at B is somehow implicated in the AB̄ error. Twelve-month-old infants were also studied. In the toy condition, they did not err. But interestingly in the no-toy condition, very few infants refused to search, thus indicating that the introduction of a second position raised a difficulty that one position did not. The great majority of these infants searched at A, B, or at A and B in a pattern. As Harris' study (1974) indicated it seems clear that even 12-month-old infants have a poorly articulated sense of the relation between thing, place, and their prior action.

The previous studies demonstrate that 9- and even 12-month-olds have a diffuse sense of what is going on when a toy is being hidden and that they are searching because a toy is hidden. But neither the Appel nor the Charlesworth studies answer the question of what the infants expect to find when they search. Will any toy do? Piaget made one observation that suggested to him that by Stage 5 infants expect particular objects to appear because Laurent refused to accept a number of objects which were different from the one that was covered (1954, Obs. 54, p. 67).

LeCompte and Gratch (1972) took up this question. Nine-, 12-, and 18-month-old infants saw a toy being hidden and retrieved it on three trials. On the fourth trial, the same toy was hidden, but the infants found a grossly different toy, and then the cycle was repeated with the new toy, the next trick involving the original toy. In recording the infants' behavior, LeCompte and Gratch used a line of analysis similar to that proposed by Charlesworth (1966). They hypothesized that an infant who had a concept of object permanence would orient to the disappearance and the reappearance of the object as a unitary event, one describable by the rule "what goes into a hiding place will remain there in the same form." Therefore, they expected that such an infant's reaction to the first sight of the new toy would be surprise, a sudden intense reaction to the fact that the first phases of the event were not followed by the later phases of the event. They expected to find lesser reactions, i.e., puzzlement, in infants who had a contingent, an "empirical," sense of the connection between the toy that disappeared and the toy that reappeared. Such an infant would initially stare at the new toy and slowly begin to be bothered by what he was seeing. Further, some infants would react to the "novelty" and appreciate that there was a new toy but show no distress over the violation of the rule or contingency. To further assess the infants' level of awareness, infants who had a concept of object permanence would ignore the toy they found and would search, here and there, for the expected toy and perhaps might "question" the experimenter about what happened. Infants who had an "empirical" sense of the hiding situation were expected to focus on the new toy in a confused manner, neither being able to accept it or reject it. They were not expected, however, to search for the missing toy because they would lack an object concept, i.e., a notion of an enduring, independent object located in a spatiotemporal framework. Infants who were reacting to a "novel" event were expected to take and examine the toy.

LeCompte and Gratch found that 18-month-olds tended to react initially with surprise or deep puzzlement and then search for the missing toy, sometimes also "questioning" the examiner. Nine-month-olds tended to react as if a novel object was present or tended to show an initial mild puzzlement and then repeatedly picked up and dropped the toy they found. The reactions of the 12-month-olds were intermediate. The investigators interpreted their findings as being consistent with Piaget's theory.

Saal (1974) extended the LeCompte and Gratch study in two ways. She studied 6-month-old as well as 9-, 12-, and 18-month-old infants and also she began to examine the role of object features in determining reactions to the trick of presenting a new object. One condition, like that of the previous study, involved a gross transformation, two clearly different objects. The other involved a color change in one of the objects. Preliminary analyses of her data indicate she found that both the initial and the subsequent reactions to the new toy increased with age, supporting the findings of the LeCompte and Gratch study. Further, there were no appreciable differences in the infants' reactions to the two types of tricks. The latter results do not support Kagan's (1972) information-processing hypothesis that predicts a greater reaction to a subtle than to a gross change. Further, the age trends for the initial visually based reaction and the subsequent manually related reaction to the tricks were different in suggestive ways. For the initial reactions, there were statistically significant differences between all age groups save the 6- and 9-month-olds. The older infants reacted with puzzlement or surprise at the sight of the new toy. However, the majority of the younger infants reacted only as if they were observing a novel toy, though a substantial minority did seem to be mildly puzzled over the new toy. For the subsequent reactions, a different trend was found. Now, the 9-month-old infants did not differ from the 12-month-olds, and all other groups did differ from one another to a statistically significant degree. Almost all the 6-month-old infants simply inspected the new toy whereas over half the 9-month-old infants showed confusion over the new toy. Thus, while some 6- and 9-month-old infants seemed puzzled over the trick when they saw the new object, having the toy in hand seemed to elicit puzzlement in the 9-month-old but not in the 6-month-old infants. These trends fit nicely with Piaget's emphasis upon the importance of intersensory coordination for giving a new level of meaning to events and with a study by Schaffer et al. (1972) to be discussed below. These results, particularly those of the 6-month-old infants, heightens the need to reconcile the discrepancy between the behavior of children 6 months of age in the present search situation and the behavior of children less than 6 months of age in tracking situations. Finally, at the end of the trial series, there was a trial in which the children searched for the hidden toy and found nothing. While the infants' performance might be affected by fatigue, boredom, or the prior tricks, it is interesting to note that the levels of reaction to this trick were comparable to their reactions to the tricks involving object changes. The results of this last trick also are consistent with those of Charlesworth (1966).

Schaffer et al. (1972) point out that there is an important difference in what an object means to a baby as a function of whether he has a well-coordinated sense of the relation between vision and touch or not. They studied infants on a monthly basis between the time they were 6 and 12 months of age. In each session, infants were given nine 30-second opportunities to see and then handle objects. In the first seven and the ninth trial, the same object was presented, but on the eighth trial, a different-colored copy of the object was presented. At each age, the length of the initial visual fixation decreased over the first seven trials, increased when the change was introduced, and decreased when the original object was presented again. The size of the change in gazing on the eighth trial tended to vary directly with age, there being a substantial difference between the reactions at ages 8 and 9 months. This difference also seems to imply that a new level of seeing the object was present at 9 months because, when the latency to first touch of the new object was examined, it was found that up through the first 8 months of age the infants tended to grasp the object even more quickly than they had on the previous trial. However, at 9 months and at older ages, the infants tended to reach more slowly for the new object.

LeCompte (personal communication) has conducted an exploratory study, one which bears on aspects of the identity hypothesis discussed earlier. In dwelling on how infants come to know that the object that disappears is the same as, and not just similar to, the object that reappears, she pointed out that featural information probably is insufficient to supply an answer. She noted that, at least in the modern industrial world, there are many objects that are almost indistinguishable on a featural level but they can be distinguished from one another in terms of such canons as "one object cannot be in two places at the same time" and "two objects cannot occupy the same space at one time." She explored the relevance of the latter canon to the development of object permanence by studying 9-, 12-, and 18-month-old infants within the same framework she used in her previously reported study. In this case, she tricked the infants by hiding one object and having two identical objects be present when the infant uncovered the well. She compared infants' reactions to this trick with their reaction to a trick where two identical objects were hidden and one was found. An interesting interaction between age and type of trick was found. The age trend conforms to that found in the prior studies—18-month-olds tend to be surprised or deeply puzzled, 9-month-olds tend to treat the new event as novel or mildly puzzling, and 12-month-olds show intermediate reactions. However, 18-month-olds react far more strongly when two objects are hidden and one is found than when the reverse occurs, whereas the opposite is true for 9- and 12-month-olds.

While it is not entirely clear how to interpret the findings of LeCompte, Saal, and Schaffer, it is quite clear that the results point out that far more is going on after 6 months of age qua object knowledge than is implied by the analyses of Bower and Smillie. In fact, Bower (1974) seems now to be backing away from his neonativist competence–performance distinction position and dwells on "repetitions" in a spirit much like that of Piaget's. In this paper, Bower recounts a number of examples of what Piaget has described as vertical decalages, and appears almost ready to think in terms of different levels of conceptualization of the same phenomenon.

Finally, there is a great deal of interest in the relation between the development of attachment and the problem of how infants conceptualize objects. A number of theorists of attachment have argued that the infant cannot be said to "love" his primary caretaker until he knows her as a permanent object (see Ainsworth, 1974, and Schaffer, 1971, for discussions of these and related positions). A number of studies have been conducted in which object-concept indices have been correlated with indices of social development (Decarie, 1965), separation protest (Lester *et al.*, 1974), fear of strangers (Broussard, 1974; Scarr and Salapatek, 1970), and mother–child relationships (Serafica and Uzgiris, 1971). No clear patterns of association have emerged from these studies. Bell (1970, 1971) reports that most children achieve a higher level of object-permanence score when a person is hidden as opposed to a thing and that infants who do not show such a pattern tend to have a poorer relation with their mother in an experimental situation and in general. Her results appear interesting and have led her to introduce a new concept, "person permanence," as essential to explanations of search.

However, these important developments must, at present, be viewed with caution. As Moore (1974) has argued, the emphasis on "person permanence," on degree of affect felt for particular persons, may account for a differential rate of development between search stages, but such an emphasis will not lead to an account of the qualitative form of the stages so long as search for all objects, regardless of affective value, go through the same stages. Schaffer *et al.* (1972) have made a comparable argument. More concretely, it is not clear that the differences in performance toward mother and things reported by Bell reflect more than the greater interest value of persons—mother and stranger are not compared—as opposed to things. For example, there is some evidence that there is no difference between the level of person permanence for mother and total stranger (Meltzoff, 1972).

Decarie (1973, 1974) seems to supply the broadest perspective on the problem. She notes the dangers in simply looking for correlations between indices of such general issues as attachment and object concept. One of her associates, Shaffran (1974), has ably pointed out on a conceptual and empirical level that the usual fear of strangers situation—where the person moves toward the baby in a series of timed steps—is a highly contrived and therefore very specific situation. Moreover, Goulet (1974) and Broussard (1974) failed to find correlations between such an index of fear of strangers and performance on, respectively, a Piagetian scale of causality and a Piagetian person-permanence scale. But interesting and nonlinear relations were found when the data were more carefully explored from a broader Piagetian perspective. The general finding was that infants who were at Stage 4 or beyond changed their reaction as the stranger moved closer whereas infants at lower stages did not.

5. Other Developments

Several important lines of inquiry relevant to Piagetian infancy themes are beginning to develop. One is the relation of phylogeny to ontogeny. Three studies have been published recently which examine the development of object concepts in other mammals: cats (Gruber *et al.*, 1971), squirrel monkeys (Vaughter *et al.*, 1972), and Rhesus monkeys (Wise *et al.*, 1974). While these studies primarily document that the Piagetian sequence holds in the development of these animals, hopefully these studies augur a trend to examine experimentally the relevance of Piagetian themes to the question of the evolution and nature of intelligence.

Others are the recent focus by Schaffer (1971) and Flavell (1971) on studying how the child comes to take the vantage of the other and to reflect on his own perspective, and the role of gesture and language in this process (Bloom, 1973; Huttenlocher, 1974; Inhelder *et al.*, 1972). These emphases should provide an important stimulus to examining the relation between the development of objectivity in infancy and later childhood. Finally, and relevant to this last point, we will briefly describe Bower's (1974) report of a study Mounoud and he did on conservation of weight in infants. Seizing on the observation that young infants' failure to anticipate the weight of objects they grasp can be indexed by the degree to which they drop their arms after grasping the object, they studied infants' reaction to the transformation of a ball of plasticene into a roll. They found that by 12 months of age the infants adjust their arm to the anticipated weight of an object. After adjusting to the weight of the ball, their arms shot upward when they grasped the roll, a sign that they were anticipating a heavier object. By 18 months of age, infants did not make such an overcompensation, implying that they were aware that the weight of plasticene does not vary with its shape.

6. Conclusion

The great value of Piaget's account of infancy lies in the plausible goal toward which the developing child tends: knowledge of a stable world of separately existing objects which includes the infant and other persons. Piaget has been able to present a rich and logically consistent assemblage of natural events and has provided a plausible account of how the infant achieves the goal. Like the British empiricists, Piaget assumes that the infant begins with no knowledge of the external world; but, unlike the empiricists, he believes that the infant develops an idea of the world of objects through constructive activity. The mechanism of development is not association but coordination of limited initial schemes. His theory is under serious study. One thrust is a determined effort to show that the neonate and very young infant are in more direct contact with the world of objects than Piaget assumed. It is not yet clear whether such infants are as aware of objects as some investigators like Bower claim, but the very young infant does appear to have more to build upon than Piaget has believed.

These developments bear upon a second facet of Piaget's theory, namely, the coordination of schemes. While the idea of achieving objectivity through coordinating perspectives has appealed to many theorists in addition to Piaget, the means whereby this occurs has not yet been elucidated, not in the study of infancy, not in the attempts to explain the development of science. For two disparate systems to be coordinated, there must be a fixed point, either internal to one or external to both. Piaget does not appear to have been as articulate on this problem as one would wish. In his solution to the size–distance problem in infancy, he could be interpreted as having adopted, uncharacteristically, a naive empiricistic solution, namely the importance of touch as a reference point. The attempts inspired by Michotte and J. J. Gibson (1966), to identify the natural world invariants to which infants are responsive, hold the promise of permitting investigators to get out of the solipsism of "lookables" and "touchables" and thereby produce a more plausible account of how knowledge is constructed. Gibson has provided an important counterpoint to the traditional cognitive emphasis on the role of subjective set in determining what is perceived. He has pointed out that there are stimulus invariants which correspond to the various sets, that the development of knowledge is as much a change in what is looked at as it is a change in one's ideas. This is a view which G. H. Mead (1938) developed long ago in discussing stages of the act, and this view is part of a constructionist theory much like that of Piaget. From this review, it appears that among investigators there is a growing sense of the need to articulate these two perspectives. In particular, the work of Schaffer (1971) and Saal (1974) seems to provide positive means of elucidating how changes in the development of action schemes lead to changes in what is looked at and what objects mean.

References

Ainsworth, M., 1974, The development of infant–mother attachment, *in* "Review of Child Development Research" B. M. Caldwell and H. N. Ricciuti (eds.), University of Chicago Press, Chicago.

Appel, K. J., 1971, Three studies in object conceptualization: Piaget's sensorimotor Stages four and five. Unpublished dissertation, University of Houston.

Bartlett, F., 1958, "Thinking," Basic Books, New York.

Bell, S. M., 1970, The development of the concept of the object as related to infant–mother attachment. *Child Development* 41:291–311.

Bell, S. M., 1971, Early cognitive development and its relationship to infant–mother attachment: A study of disadvantaged Negro infants. Final report, Project No. 508, U.S. Office of Education.

Bloom, L., 1973, "One Word at a Time," Mouton, The Hague.

Bower, T. G. R., 1966, The visual world of infants, *Scientific American* 215:80–92.

Bower, T. G. R., 1967, The development of object permanence: Some studies of existence constancy, *Perception and Psychophysics* 2:411–418.

Bower, T. G. R., 1972a, Object perception in infants, *Perception* 2:411–418.

Bower, T. G. R., 1972b, Mechanisms of cognitive development in infants. Colloquium, MIT Psychology Department.

Bower, T. G. R.,1974,Repetition in human development,*Merrill-Palmer Quarterly.* 20:303–318.

Bower, T. G. R., and Paterson, J. G., 1972, Stages in the development of the object concept, *Cognition* 1(1).

Bower, T. G. R., and Paterson, J. G., 1973, The separation of place, movement and object in the world of the infant, *Journal of Experimental Child Psychology* 15:161–168.

Bower, T. G. R., and Wishart, J. G., 1972, The effects of motor skill on object permanence, *Cognition* 1:165–172.

Bower, T. G. R., Broughton, J. M., and Moore, M. K., 1970a, Assessment of intention in sensorimotor infants, *Nature* 228:679–681.

Bower, T. G. R., Broughton, J. M., and Moore, M. K., 1970b, The coordination of visual and tactual input in infants, *Perception and Psychophysics* 8:51–53.

Bower, T. G. R., Broughton, J. M., and Moore, M. K., 1971, Development of the object concept as manifested in the tracking behavior of infants between seven and twenty weeks of age, *Journal of Experimental Child Psychology* 11:182–193.

Broussard, M. D., 1974, The infant's conception of object permanence and his reactions to strangers, *in* "The Infant's Reaction to Strangers" T. G. Decarie (ed.), International Universities Press, New York.

Brown, E. E., and Bower, T. G. R., The problem of object permanence, *Cognition*, in press.

Bruner, J. S., 1969, The growth and structure of skill, *in* "Motor Skills in Infancy" K. J. Connally (ed.), CIBA Foundation, Academic Press, New York.

Bruner, J. S., 1973, Organization of early skilled action, *Child Development* 44:1–11.

Brunet, O., et Lezine, I., 1965, "Le Développement psychologique de la première enfance," Presses Universitaires de France, Paris.

Butterworth, G., 1974, Object permanence during infancy, D. Phil. thesis, University of Oxford.

Campbell, D. T., and Fiske, D., 1959, Convergent and discriminant validation by the multitrait-multimethod matrix, *Psychological Bulletin* 56:81–105.

Casati, I., and Lezine, I., 1968, Les étapes de l'intelligence sensori-motrice de l'enfant de la naissance à deux ans, Centre de Psychologie Appliquée, Paris.

Charlesworth, W. R., 1966, Development of the object concept: A methodological study, paper presented at the meetings of the American Psychological Association, New York.

Corman, H. H., and Escalona, S. K., 1969, Stages of sensorimotor development: A replication study, *Merrill-Palmer Quarterly* 15:351–361.

Decarie, T. G., 1965, "Intelligence and Affectivity in Early Childhood," International Universities Press, New York.

Decarie, T. G., 1969, A study of the mental and emotional development of the thalidomide child, *in* "Determinants of Infant Behavior" (Vol. 4) B. M. Foss (ed.), Methuen, London.

Decarie, T. G., 1973, Perceptual constancy and object permanency, paper presented as part of a symposium on Piagetian approaches to infant development, American Psychological Association, Montreal.

Decarie, T. G., 1974, "The Infant's Reaction to Strangers," International Universities Press, New York.

Evans, W. F., 1973, The Stage IV error in Piaget's theory of object concept development: An investigation of the role of activity, Unpublished dissertation, University of Houston.

Evans, W. F., and Gratch, G., 1972, The Stage IV error in Piaget's theory of object concept development: Difficulties in object conceptualization or spatial localization?, *Child Development* 43:682–688.

Flavell, J. H., 1971, The development of inferences about others, Draft of a paper presented at the Interdisciplinary Conference on Our Knowledge of Persons, State University of New York, Binghamton, New York.

Fletcher, H. J., 1965, The delayed response problem, in "Behavior of nonhuman primates," (Vol. 1) A. M. Schrier, H. F. Harlow, and F. Stollnitz (eds.), Academic Press, New York.

Faiberg, S., Siegel, B. L., and Gibson, R., 1966, The role of sound in the search behavior of a blind infant, *Psychoanalytic Study of the Child* 21:327–357.

Freedman, D. A., Fox-Kolenda, B. J., Margileth, D. A., and Miller, D. H., 1969, The development of the use of sound as a guide to affective and cognitive behavior: A two phase process, *Child Development* 40:1099–1105.

Gardner, J. K., 1971, The development of object identity in the first six months of human infancy, paper presented at the meeting of the Society for Research in Child Development, Minneapolis, Minnesota.

Gibson, J. J., 1966, "The Senses Considered as Perceptual Systems," Houghton-Mifflin, New York.

Ginsburg, H. J., and Wong, D. L., 1973, Enhancement of hidden object search in six month old infants presented with a continuously sounding hidden object, *Developmental Psychology* 9:142.

Goulet, J., 1974, The infant's conception of casuality and his reactions to strangers, in "The Infant's Reaction to Strangers" T. G. Decarie (ed.), International Universities Press, New York.

Gratch, G., 1972, A study of the relative dominance of vision and touch in six-month old infants, *Child Development* 43:615–623.

Gratch, G., 1975, Recent studies based on Piaget's view of object concept development, in "Infant Perception" L. Cohen and P. Salapatek (eds.), Academic Press, New York.

Gratch, G., and Landers, W. F., 1971, Stage IV of Piaget's theory of infants' object concepts, *Child Development* 42:359–372.

Gratch, G., Appel, K. J., Evans, W. F., LeCompte, G. K., and Wright, N. A., 1974, Piaget's

Stage 4 object concept error: Evidence of forgetting or object conception?, *Child Development 45*:71–77.

Gruber, H. E., Girgus, J. S., and Banuazizi, A., 1971, The development of object permanence in the cat, *Developmental Psychology 4*:9–15.

Harris, P. L., 1971, Examination and search in infants, *British Journal of Psychology 62*:469–473.

Harris, P. L., 1974, Perseverative search at a visibly empty place by young infants, *Journal of Experimental Psychology, 18*:535–542.

Huttenlocher, J., 1974, The origins of language comprehension, *in* "Theories in cognitive psychology" R. L. Solso (ed.), Lawrence Earlbaum Associates, Potomac, Md.

Huttenlocher, J., 1975, The orogins of language comprehension, *in* "Theories in cognitive psychology" R. L. Solse (ed.), Lawrence Earlbaum Associates.

Inhelder, B., Lezine, I., Sinclair, H., et Stambak, M., 1972, Les debute de la fonction semiotique, *Archives de Psychologie 41*(163):187–243.

Kagan, J., 1972, Do infants think?, *Scientific American 226*:74–82.

Landers, W F., 1971, The effect of differential experience on infants' performance in a Piagetian Stage IV object-concept task, *Developmental Psychology 5*:48–54.

LeCompte, G. K., and Gratch, G., 1972, Violation of a rule as a method of diagnosing infants' level of object concept, *Child Development 43*:385–396.

Lezine, I., Stambak, M., et Casati, I., 1969, "Les étapes de l'intelligence sensori-motrice," Centre de psychologie appliquée, Paris.

Lester, B. M., Kotelchuck, M., Spelke, E., Sellers, M. J., and Klein, R. E., 1974, Separation protest in Guatemalan infants, *Developmental Psychology 10*:79–85.

Mead, G. H., 1938, "The Philosophy of the Act," University of Chicago Press, Chicago.

Meltzoff, Al, 1972, Toward a structural developmental interpretation of separation protest, unpublished honors thesis, Department of Psychology, Harvard University.

Michotte, A., 1955, Perception and cognition, *Acta Psychologica 11*:69–91.

Miller, D. G., Cohen, L., and Hill, K. A., 1970, A methodological investigation of Piaget's theory of object concept development in the sensory motor period, *Journal of Experimental Child Psychology 2*:59–85.

Moore, M. K., 1969, A revision of Piaget's theory of the development of object permanence: A study of infant search for absent objects, unpublished paper, Harvard University.

Moore, M. K., 1973, The genesis of object permanence, paper presented at the meeting of the Society for Research in Child Development, Philadelphia, Pennsylvania.

Moore, M. K., 1974, The genesis of object permanence, Chapter 1 of unpublished dissertation, Harvard University.

Munn, N. L., 1955, "The Evolution and Growth of Behavior," Houghton-Mifflin, Boston.

Nelson, K. E., 1971, Accommodation of visual tracking patterns in human infants to object movement patterns, *Journal of Experimental Child Psychology 12*:182–196.

Piaget, J., 1952, "The Origins of Intelligence in Children," Norton, New York.

Piaget, J., 1954, "The Construction of Reality in the Child," Basic Books, New York.

Piaget, J., 1969, "The Mechanisms of Perception," Basic Books, New York.

Roberts, G., and Black, K. N., 1972, The effect of naming and object permanence on toy preferences, *Child Development 43*:858–868.

Saal, D., 1974, A study of the development of object concept in infancy by varying the degree of discrepancy between the disappearing and reappearing object, unpublished dissertation proposal, University of Houston.

Scarr, S., and Salapatek, P., 1970, Patterns of fear development during infancy, *Merrill-Palmer Quarterly 16*:53–90.

Schaffer, H. R., 1971, "The Growth of Sociability," Penguin, Baltimore.

Schaffer, H. R., Greenwood, A., and Parry, M. H., 1972, The onset of wariness, *Child Development* 43:165–175.

Schofield, L., and Uzgiris, I. C., 1969, Examining behavior and the development of the concept of the object, paper presented at the meetings of the Society for Research in Child Development, Santa Monica, California.

Serifica, P. C., and Uzgiris, I. C., 1971, Infant–mother relationship and object concept, paper presented at the annual meeting of the American Psychological Association, Washington, D.C.

Shaffran, R., 1974, Modes of approach and the infant's reaction to the stranger, *in* "The Infant's Reaction to Strangers" T. G. Decarie (ed.), International Universities Press, New York.

Smillie, D., 1972, Piaget's constructionist theory, *Human Development* 15:171–186.

Uzgiris, I. C., 1973, Patterns of cognitive development in infancy, *Merrill-Palmer Quarterly, 19:* 181–204.

Uzgiris, I. C., and Hunt, J. McV., 1974, "Assessment in Infancy, Ordinal Scales of Psychological Development," University of Illinois Press, Urbana.

Vaughter, R. M., Smotherman, W., and Ordy, J. M., 1972, Development of object permanence in the infant squirrel monkey, *Developmental Psychology* 7:34–38.

Wise, K. L., Wise, L. A., and Zimmerman, R. R., 1974, Piagetian object permanence in the infant Rhesus monkey, *Developmental Psychology* 10:429–437.

5

Social Cognition

A Selective Review of Current Research

MICHAEL J. CHANDLER

1. Introduction

Literature reviews typically begin with some brief justificatory statement defending the particular gerrymandering of conceptual boundaries which led to the inclusion of some studies and the exclusion of others. As a selective summary of research in the area of social cognition the present review similarly requires an explicit statement of its ordering principles and a description of the inclusion rule used to rationalize the walling in and walling out of contending studies. The special difficulties posed by these requirements are that the sharp dichotomy between impersonal and social cognition implicit in this task involves a distinction which is, in the opinion of this writer, both awkward and improper, and that, as a consequence, the research literature dealing with this topic seems to follow no detectable ordering principle. Responsibility for this garbled state of affairs is traceable, in part, to the fact that the collection of studies which together compose the research literature on social cognition includes the efforts of investigators who represent several sharply different psychological traditions. Included in this loose federation are representatives of both Piagetian and Wernerian perspectives, as well as a sizable group of more empirically oriented investigators, operating out

MICHAEL J. CHANDLER • Department of Psychology, University of Rochester, Rochester, New York.

of various information-processing models. Behind these first-rank contenders are smaller groups of more psychodynamically oriented personality theorists, developmentally oriented social psychologists, and a varied assortment of personalogists, psychomotorists, and social philosophers. All these groups proceed from different sets of orienting premises, search for different answers to different questions, and employ often unreconcilable experimental and assessment strategies.

Despite the diversity of background and opinion that divides these various research groups, however, they all share a common responsibility to provide answers to two closely interrelated questions. The first of these concerns the general nature of the relation presumed to exist between human subjects and the world of objects in general. The second concerns the extent to which persons, as opposed to other inanimate or nonsocial objects, are seen as possessing special qualities or characteristics that might substantially alter the nature of the process by which they are understood. While not all research studies to be reviewed include attempts to provide explicit answers to these two questions, the basic epistemological distinctions on which they rest are ubiquitous and cannot be profitably skirted or brushed aside. Whenever one attempts to explore the manner in which people come to know and understand one another, the object of one's study and the process through which such understanding is achieved are one and the same. There is, consequently, no neutral ground which one can occupy in attempting to deal with these important issues, and the only basis on which objectivity can be achieved is through the provision of a clear statement about the particular bias from which one speaks. In the case of the present review, the particular perspective adopted is that version of reality which can be seen most clearly through the window opened by Piaget's cognitive developmental theory.

Piaget's answer to the first of these orienting questions, concerning the nature of the general relationship between human subjects and environmental objects, takes a form which does not fit comfortably into the context of the American psychological tradition. In its effort to achieve some measure of independence from its own philosophical heritage, much American psychology has been quick to disguise its implicit metaphysical assumptions in its methodology, and to dismiss questions about the nature of the subject–object relationship as regressive and outside the proper scope of psychological inquiry. A separate world of stimulus objects was simply posited and the job of psychology was described as one of monitoring the impacts of these supposedly independent stimulus events. In the place of this naive physicalism, Piaget has substituted a constructionistic view which maintains that persons respond to a world which is partially of their own making. All experience, according to this view, is filtered through and assimilated by available cognitive structures which both change and are changed by potential environmental inputs. One important implication of this constructionist position is that the knower and the known are inextricably bound up with one another in a way which makes it impossible to separate environmental objects from the persons observing them. In this view, responsibility for development in general, and the acquisition of knowledge in particular, "neither arises from objects nor from the subject, but from the interaction . . . between the subject and those objects" (Piaget, 1970).

Although the difficulties generated by this interpretation of subjects and objects can be understood and partially compensated for, they cannot be entirely eliminated. As a consequence, neither environmental objects nor the people who try to understand them can be legitimately considered apart from one another. What we choose to identify as the subjects and the objects of knowledge are then, in terms of Piaget's theory, simply convenient, but artifactual, names with which to label different poles of the same nondivisable transaction. Such a view is not entirely foreign to American psychologists who are accustomed to thinking in terms of interactions, and who frequently regard human subjects and environmental objects as generating some third interaction term. As Bowers (1973) has pointed out, however, the emphasis in such views remains on the parts, and the interaction term is thought of as a derivative or by-product. Piaget reverses this ordering of priorities and regards subject and object terms as analytic distillates of a more basic and developmentally prior whole. It is, then, in terms of this interlocking of subject and object, which Furth (1969) has labeled "the knowing circle," that Piaget has attempted to characterize the acquisition of human knowledge and the relationship between subjects and objects.

Piaget's answer to the second of the orienting questions originally posed—concerning possible similarities and differences between the cognition of social and nonsocial objects—builds upon and is perhaps still more foreign and less well understood than his position regarding the relationship between subjects and objects in general. Again, the details of this position are best seen when contrasted against a background of what are, for most American psychologists, more familiar views. From the perspective of theories which do not share Piaget's constructionistic assumption, situations lend themselves to being easily classified as either social or nonsocial. The efforts of young children to deal with the world of inanimate objects, for example, are easily labeled as instances of nonsocial or impersonal cognition. Social situations, by contrast, are simply group situations, and any collection of people is assumed to acquire a necessary social significance as an automatic consequence of its public character. As a consequence, the process by which children are imagined to come to know and understand such social objects is easily suspected of following different principles and requiring a different theoretical account than does the cognition of nonsocial objects. In sharp contrast to this view, Piaget describes all cognitions as inherently social, and, at the same time, sets explicit criteria regarding the special circumstances under which such social interactions are presumed to have some meaningful psychological impact. Each of these separate points requires some amplification.

The question of whether Piaget's theory has any special relevance for the study of intrapersonal events has been the subject of a certain amount of debate. Because his research has emphasized the child's cognitive structuring of the environment in terms of "impersonal" categories such as space, time, and number, many readers have mistakenly assumed that his theory was intended only as an account of children alienated from their usual socio-emotional context (Feffer and Gourevitch, 1960). This confusion between the theory's potential scope and special instances of its application has prompted a variety of ill-conceived attempts to "repair" Piaget's account by shoring it up with constructs borrowed from more psychodynamically oriented views (i.e., Cobliner, 1967; Odier, 1956). The theory as such, however, was never intended as a restricted account of the private contemplations of individuals working in social isolation. As a general approach to the study of knowledge acquisition, the theory disregards conventional distinctions between social and nonsocial situations and details a formal and content-free account of the evolving structural regularities through which the contents of experience are said to be organized. At each juncture of development, the child's cognitive structures are characterized as functioning as a "structural ensemble," exercising the same formal mechanisms for organizing experience, whether such experience is gained in a private or interpersonal context. Even the general coordinations of actions, which are assumed to be the origin of these cognitive structures, are presumed by Piaget to be "interpersonal or social as well as individual, since the coordination of actions of individuals obeys the same laws as intra-individual coordination" (Piaget, 1970).

Social cognition is not, then, seen by Piaget as some separate or special brand of thought reserved for the contemplation of personal as opposed to impersonal situations. Rather, the nature, context, and content of all thought is held, in his view, to be inherently social and immune to attempts to strip it entirely of its interpersonal character. All thought, according to Piaget, presupposes as well as shapes social life, and both individual and interindividual actions interpenetrate one another and reflect the influence of common structures. As a consequence, the social and logical groupings which emerge during the course of development are not regarded as merely coincidental but are viewed as different faces of the same developmental process.

Because of this presumed isomorphism between impersonal and social interaction structures, specially contrived research settings, which artificially strip cognition of its usual social character, are understood to be methodological artifacts, and questions concerning possible relationships between personal and impersonal cognitions are regarded as misplaced. Efforts to uproot Piaget's theory and to transplant it in the analytic, associationistic, antecedent–consequent soil of American psychology, however, have typically done violence to its holistic character, driving a conceptual wedge between persons and the world of social objects with which they interact. Within the behavioral and empirical traditions of psychology, stimuli are regularly differentiated from responses, causes distinguished from their effects, and independent variables isolated from dependent variables. The imposition of this vision on any problem area tends to fragment it into isolated elements which are then seen to stand in some simple contingent relation, and which admit to easy, efficient, causal explanations.

The assimilation of Piaget's theory to this analytic tradition has operated subtly to transmute it into something it was never intended to be—an assemblage of separate parts laced together by a network of associative connections. The principal victim of this divide-and-conquer strategy has been the unity inherent in Piaget's notion of the child as a structural ensemble. Cognition, conation, and affection are separately carved out from their common structural base; knowledge is regarded as something entirely separate from the people who know it, and individuals are viewed as isolated from their social context. In the wake of this atomization a raft of uniquely American questions has arisen. Are peer group interactions responsible for cognitive development? Do advances in cognitive development alter the nature of the child's social interaction? How is impersonal cognition different from the cognition of interpersonal or social events? Much of the research characterized as social-cognitive in its focus is addressed to one or more of these questions and reflects efforts to identify contingent relations and to establish efficient causal chains in an attempt to mend together what were, in Piaget's theory, only phenotypically different expressions of the same underlying genotypic structure.

Simply to insist, as Piaget insists, that all cognition is inherently social and to say nothing more would, however, be less than helpful. Those psychologists who set about dividing subjective from objective or social from nonsocial situations presumably did so to have two things to strike together for experimental purposes. Piaget's theory similarly demands some articulation of working parts and, for this purpose, one may distinguish between those situations the social character of which makes a difference and those where it does not. Although some perspective undoubtedly always exists from which the views of any two individuals would appear importantly different, those differences need not always or even frequently be taken into account. Because, in this view, people are assumed to construct the events to which they respond, their conceptual environments are not necessarily altered by the mere introduction of additional people. Persons who actually share, or are imagined to share, viewpoints identical to one's own are conceptually redundant and pose no special accommodatory problems. Even when real differences divide people these distinctions may be filtered out by the assimilatory process through which they are understood. As a consequence, the potential impact on other people cannot be assessed in terms of their presence or absence: what does and does not constitute a social situation in a functional sense cannot be determined by a simple head count. It is only when some other person actively insists on a construction of events that is different from our own that we begin to register that situation as socially relevant. The special significance of social situations, as conventionally defined, appears then to lie only in their potential for promoting alternative constructions of the same events.

Whether a person is able to recognize or cope with the alternative views represented in some social situations is an important, but importantly different, question from whether such alternatives are present. From the perspective of the child it makes a great deal of difference whether the other persons around him organize their experience in ways which are similar to or different from his own, whether they insist on advocating their views at the expense of his own, and whether they assume any responsibility for facilitating his efforts to navigate social situations which they define differently than he. In this view the potential impact of other persons would, then, vary as a function of: (1) the number of alternative constructions of the same reality on which they insist, (2) the extent to which these divergent views differ in complexity from those advocated by the child, and (3) the costs extracted for failures to recognize, understand, or accommodate to these divergent perspectives.

Viewed from the perspective of Piaget's theory, the cognition of social objects, like the cognition of objects in general, involves a progression of assimilatory and accommodatory processes through which the child shapes and is shaped by the social situations in which he is involved. During the course of development the child engages in a range of activities which run the gamut from almost purely assimilatory to almost purely accommodatory acts, and in the process his psychological center of gravity shifts radically from an egocentric to a more objective pole of the subject–object interaction in which he is involved. When engaged in a predominately accommodatory activity, the child is largely the pawn of external events and mirrors in his own actions the formative characters of the object environment with which he deals. During more purely assimilatory activities, the child radically alters environmental events and intrudes himself into situations about which he or she is attempting to be objective.

If these difficulties were characteristic only of young children, the task of formulating a coherent picture of research in the area of social cognition would be greatly simplified. Unfortunately, however, all these difficulties are as real for the prospective researcher as for the children he may be attempting to understand and characterize, and are the source of a great deal of confusion for all parties involved. As a third-party observer the research scientist runs the double risk of laying an exaggerated emphasis on either the subject or the object pole of this subject–object interaction. That is, he may, like the child, ignore or systematically underemphasize the subjective character of all subject–object interactions. The second pitfall into which he may step is one characterized by an exaggerated emphasis on the distorting influence of the subjective process of coming to know and a tendency to ignore the contributions and constraints which objects exercise on the knowing process. Phrased somewhat differently, developmental researchers, like the children they study, must achieve some balance in the emphasis which they place on assimilatory and accommodatory processes.

Unfortunately, the developmental course of research efforts in the area of social cognition shows certain parallels to the development of the children who are at its object of study and different investigators appear to have differentially emphasized either the assimilatory or accommodatory aspects of the socio-cognitive process. Those investigators concerned with the topics of person perception, social sensitivity, social awareness, etc., have directed most of their efforts to the object pole of the subject–object interaction and have been almost exclusively concerned with detailing the particulars of the various social cues to which the child must accommodate. A second group of investigators, primarily concerned with the topics of childhood egocentrism, social decentering, and role taking, have been occupied with describing the manner in which children assimilate and overly subjectivize their experience. A third group of investigators concerned with the topic of empathy appear to vacillate between these two extreme positions. In the pages which follow, each of these three general topics of social-cognitive research will be taken up in turn and representative research studies in these areas selectively reviewed.

2. Person Perception

One easily identifiable constellation in the scattered literature on developmental social cognition is a cluster of studies commonly grouped together under the heading of "social- " or "person- perception." As is often the case with the names assigned to constellations, however, these labels are rather misleading and badly suited to characterize a group of studies which only sometimes deal with social phenomena and almost never deal with perception. By whatever name, however, this group of studies, more than any other to be considered, focuses attention on the object pole of subject–object interactions, and emphasizes the accommodatory as opposed to the assimilatory side of social cognition.

The rather heady claim that the person-perception literature rarely if ever deals with matters of perception is intended as more than a quarrel over a choice of words. The issue at stake is, rather, the extent to which the problems of social cognition can be subdivided and attacked on a piecemeal basis. According to common sense, and a substantial number of psychologists as well, people are said first to accumulate factual details about their environments and then to process these pieces of perceptual information through some set of second-stage operations which are more inferential in nature. According to this sequential view of knowledge acquisition, research attention can and should be directed toward achieving some independent understanding of the separate processes by which information is registered, encoded, and processed. The majority of investigators who have worked in the area of developmental person perception seem to subscribe to some variant of such a sequential information-processing model. As a consequence, they have raised and attempted to answer separate questions concerning the ages at which children begin to register important social cues, learn to properly label these impressions, and later fashion them into complex social judgments.

The assumption that people simply collect undigested bits of experience and squirrel them away for processing at some later date violates the basic constructivistic premise of theories such as Piaget's, and either ignores or defers the assimilatory process which these theories regard as the first step in any subject–object interaction. From such a theoretical perspective, statements about the direct impress of the object world, or the passive registration of social cues, overlook the important role which available cognitive structures play in shaping the kinds of information to which one can respond, and misrepresent the child as passively accommodating to an exclusively object-centered environment. Considered from a more constructivistic view, terms such as social sensitivity or social perception tend to create the false impression that social cognition has something to do with the child's sensory acuity. While it is true that certain social cues tend to be quite subtle, and in that sense might be easily overlooked, the majority of common social gestures, facial expressions, and voice inflections seem to occur on a sufficiently macroscopic scale as to pose little or no challenge to the resolving powers of our sensory systems. According to Piaget, the task which faces the child is not seen, therefore, as one of coming to perceive social cues in the literal sense, but of coming to know and understand the cultural meanings commonly attached to them. Because it is hinged on a set of underlying premises different from those advocated by Piaget, however, most of the person-perception literature has continued to distinguish between the registration, encoding, and inferential processing of social cues, and reports its findings in terms of these separate categories. The following summary of research follows, but does not adopt, this fractured view of social cognition.

Few studies have been designed specifically to document the common assumption that awareness of the existence of socially relevant inflectional, postural, and physiognomic changes typically increases with age. While a number of studies have shown that children become increasingly better able to identify emotions from photographs (i.e., Cooke, 1971; Gates, 1923) or recorded vocalizations (Dimitrovsky, 1964; Rothenberg, 1970), the majority of such studies have relied exclusively on verbal report as a response dimension and, consequently, confound the ability to recognize such cues with the linguistic skills required to discuss them. However, a small number of developmental studies have employed physiological and other nonverbal response dimensions in an effort to determine whether sensitivity to social or affective cues does increase with age. Although physiological correlates of social awareness provide an obvious alternative to an exclusive reliance on verbal reports, few such developmental studies employing physiological measures of social sensitivity have been carried out (Osborn and Endsley, 1971). Of the two such studies reported by Osborn and Endsley which did attempt to identify physiological correlates of childrens' responses to social, affect-laden situations, one did (Dysinger and Ruckmick, 1933) and the other did not (Sternback, 1962) find evidence of age-related changes in social sensitivity.

On those few occasions where other nonverbal, behavioral measures of social awareness have been employed, age-related changes in social sensitivity have been regularly reported. Gilbert (1969), for example, found significant differences in the frequency with which nursery school and first-grade children employed facial expressions as a basis for sorting pictures of people. Utilizing a nonverbal multiple-choice response format with stylized drawings of different affect expressions, both Borke (1971, 1973) and Deutsch (1974) have demonstrated similar age-related changes in the accuracy with which children are able to specify facial expressions appropriate to various social situations. With these scattered exceptions, however, most of the person-perception literature has relied exclusively on verbal report measures and has indexed changes in the ability of subjects to understand social situations by determining the number and complexity of the words used in describing them.

From among that group of studies relying exclusively upon verbal measures several investigators have presented evidence which suggests that with increasing age children's characterizations of others cease to focus exclusively on concrete references to physical actions and appearances, and come to include a greater proportion of statements about covert thoughts and feelings. The studies of Brierly (1966), Livesley and Bromley (1973), Peevers and Secord (1973), and Supnik (1967) concerned with children's descriptions of others all present evidence of age-related increases in number of references to internal psychological states. Only one study (Olshan, 1970), utilizing a multidimensional scaling approach, has reported no such age-related increase in the number of descriptive dimensions employed. Other investigators, utilizing a variety of psychological assessment procedures, also report regular increases in the number of references to covert thought and feeling states. In a study of 4- and 6-year-old children, Gilbert (1969), for example, found a significant increase in the frequency with which subjects referred to subjective states as opposed to physical characteristics while describing both TAT cards and the Sarbin (1954) Stick Figures. Contrasting second and sixth graders, Dymond et al. (1952) found similar age-related changes in the frequency of statements about covert thoughts and feelings in response to stimulus material similar to the TAT. These findings concerning third-party descriptions have received additional support from the research on self-characterization by Guardo and Bohan (1971), who describe similar shifts from physical to covert state descriptors in the self-referential statements of 6- through 9-year-old children.

As might have been anticipated from a more constructivistic, Piage-tian perspective, however, the distinction which the person-perception literature maintains between the registration and the inferential process-ing of social cues has been difficult to maintain, and studies of social perception and studies of social inference have tended to shade imper-ceptibly into one another. This difficulty flows from the fact that many, perhaps even the majority, of the attributions which people typically make about one another involve characterizations having no direct be-havioral referents, but referring instead to hypothetical traits or disposi-tions which must be inferred from changes in the surface structure of behavior. The giving of a gift, for example, may be witnessed in a per-ceptual sense, but to conclude that one has observed an àct of generosity is almost certainly an inference. Falling between the extremes of this continuum, however, are a whole raft of instances that cannot be unam-biguously classified as either perceptual or inferential. It is not necessar-ily obvious, for example, whether one witnesses or infers joy or aggres-sion.

Investigators working in the area of developmental person percep-tion have employed a variety of conceptual strategies in an effort to establish boundary conditions between the so-called perceptual and in-ferential phases of the social attribution process. In their studies of kind-ness, for example, Baldwin *et al.* (1969) borrow from Egon Brunswik's (1956) earlier distinction between proximal and distal perceptual cues and designate as pre-inferential only those actual behavioral changes capable of measurably influencing our perceptual apparatus. In her study of 6- through 12-year-old children, Flapan (1968) simply classified some affective cues as "obvious" and others as "non-obvious." In a recent review of the literature on interpersonal inference, Flavell (1973) has proposed a somewhat more elaborate partitioning of this information-processing sequence in which he distinguishes among the processes by which potential cues are identified (Existence), their applicability in a particular situation is recognized (Need), and their separate meanings are coordinated and collocated into social judgments (Inference). More commonly, however, the majority of investigators working in this area have simply referred to a dimension of increasing abstractness, running from the most literal of behavioral cues to the most inferential of trait attributions.

The almost universal finding of investigators who have explored this dimension is that with advancing age children come to rely increas-ingly on more abstract dispositional constructs. Utilizing an adaptation of G. A. Kelley's Role Construct Repertory Test, both Brierly (1966) and Little (1968), for example, each report significant age-related increases in the absolute number of psychological constructs employed by groups of subjects who, combined across the two studies, cover the age period of 7 through 18. Similar findings regarding general age-related increases in the number of such dispositional constructs employed and their degree of abstraction have been reported by a large number of investigators utilizing a broad range of assessment procedures and age groups (Crockett, 1965; Gilbert, 1969; Gollin, 1958; Kagan and Moss, 1960; Livesley and Bromley, 1973; Rosenbach, 1968; Supnik, 1967; Yarrow and Campbell, 1963). The general impression gained from these findings is that children younger than kindergarten age are seldom observed to use inferential psychological constructs (Whiteman, 1967), nor have such constructs been found to be a regular part of children's working vocabularies until well into middle childhood (Gollin, 1958). Corroborative findings about particular kinds of psychological constructs are also common. The early work of Heider (1958), for example, indicates that the frequency with which children make statements about intentionality is related to age. The use of motivational statements seem similarly age-related. In a study of the accuracy with which third and fifth graders were able to judge affects portrayed on audio tape recordings, Rothenberg (1970) observed that older subjects more frequently employed motivational concepts in characterizing the interactions which they overheard. Taken as a group, these studies clearly document what was probably never seriously doubted—that as children grow older they become more frequent and facile users of abstract psychological constructs.

While the main thread of the person-perception literature has unraveled from an empirically based and adult-oriented information-processing tradition, there are, within this area of research, several important splinter groups that have operated out of more established developmental theories. The most visible of these is a group of investigators who take their direction from the developmental theories of Heinz Werner (1961). In contrast to other investigators in this field, who seem content simply to document the fact that with increasing age children make increasing numbers of increasingly abstract attributions, representatives of this Wernerian tradition operate under a dual obligation to demonstrate that children's views of others become increasingly ordered and hierarchicalized, as well as increasingly differentiated. For these investigators evidence that children come to employ increasingly abstract dispositional terms carries more meaning than would a simple proliferation of parallel terms. Abstract constructs, because they subsume the concrete particulars of the specific behaviors to which they refer, are seen to imply increasingly complex patterns of relations among lower-order constructs. Evidence of age-related increases in the use of such abstract constructs is, therefore, viewed as providing an adequate demonstration of the progressive ordering and hierarchical   interesting of concepts predicted by Werner's theory.

With the goal of validating this aspect of Werner's theory, several investigators have recently set out to chart developmental changes in the levels of abstraction in children's characterizations of others. Scarlett *et al.* (1971), in a Wernerian-inspired content analysis of the interpersonal constructs which first-, third-, and fifth-grade boys used in describing their peers, found that both the number and the degree of abstraction of the constructs employed increased monitonically with age. Consistent with Wernerian theory, these findings were interpreted as demonstrating, not only an increase in the degree of differentiation of the construct systems employed, but also were taken as evidence for increased hierarchical integration. A closely related study by Peevers and Secord (1973), concerned with the process of impression formation in kindergarten through college-age subjects, similarly found a significant relationship between age and the number, variety, and degree of differentiation of the constructs employed. Evidence was also reported suggesting that the older subjects of this study more frequently employed dispositional terms which reflect a growing awareness that personal characteristics are conditional on certain situational, temporal, or internal states. Additionally, older subjects employed descriptions which were more internally consistent and attempted to explain rather than simply announce the attributions which they made. A more recent study by Bigner (1974) pursued a similar Wernerian developmental analysis of the manner in which children in kindergarten through eighth grade describe their siblings. Again these data support the view that children's characterizations of others become increasingly abstract and hierarchically integrated and not simply more detailed. Similar findings and similar interpretations regarding changes in the organizational complexity of free-response descriptions of others are offered by Livesley and Bromley (1973), Watts (1944), and Yarrow and Campbell (1963).

A somewhat different approach to the study of developmental changes in the organizational complexity of the social inference process is provided by the research of Gollin (1951, 1958), in which subjects were asked to describe their impressions of stimulus characters about whom conflicting information was presented. The results of these studies, concerned with 10-, 13-, and 16-year-old children, indicate that age was an important factor in determining the mode of organization employed by these children in their attempts to resolve apparent contradictions. Relative to their younger counterparts, the older of Gollin's subjects more frequently went beyond the concrete behavioral information provided, and introduced conceptual materials to account for the contradictions observed. Whereas the younger of these children tended to adopt uni-dimensional approaches which centered attention exclusively on one or the other of the pieces of contradictory information, or simply jux-taposed inconsistencies without attempting to resolve them, older chil-dren actively considered and attempted conceptual integrations of the conflicting information. On the basis of these findings, and the related work of Dinnerstein (1951), Gollin concluded that children of different ages utilize qualitatively different inference models in forming impres-sions of others. A similar point has been made by several investigators whose research is focused more directly on problems of empathy and role taking. Both Burns and Cavey (1957) and Greenspan et al. (1975), for example, have presented evidence suggesting that as children grow older they become better able to recognize and reconcile apparent in-congruities between situational and affective cues.

One further line of evidence concerning qualitative, age-related changes in the process by which social inferences are made is provided by the work of the Baldwins and their colleagues (Baldwin and Baldwin, 1970; Baldwin et al., 1969), who have attempted to explore the manner in which acts of kindness are understood by persons of various ages. The results of these studies indicate that adults hold expectations about the choice behavior of others which reflect a weighing and balancing of available alternatives, not evident in the social expectations of younger children. In contrast to their adult counterparts, who generally made complex, multiply determined judgments regarding the prerequisites of kindness, younger subjects typically reached their conclusions on the basis of much more limited inference strategies which depended solely upon the characteristics of the particular actions performed and not at all upon alternative courses of available actions. These findings, like those cited in the preceding paragraphs, are interpreted as supporting the hypothesis that the social judgments of young children are based on inference models which are qualitatively different from those employed by college-age adults.

As can be seen from this brief overview of person-perception re-search, the initial emphasis given to the more object-focused, accom-modatory pole of subject–object interactions has gradually given way to more explicit concerns with the changing structural characteristics of the person that exercise influence over the assimilation of potential social stimuli. If, as the above-mentioned research suggests, the manner in which children form and organize impressions of others undergoes im-portant qualitative changes during the course of development, then any adequate description of social cognition must also include an equal emphasis on the more subjective, assimilatory pole of the process of subject–object interaction. Current research in person perception appears to be moving toward some such better equilibrated perspective.

3. Role Taking, Social Decentering, and Egocentricity

In contrast to the person-perception literature which, as described in the preceding section, has tended to focus attention on the object-related, accommodatory side of subject–object interactions, research in the area of social role taking has selectively emphasized the more subject-centered, assimilatory side of the social-cognitive process. Generally intended as a corrective to a more traditional, frank situationalism (Bowers, 1973), which regards variations of performance as directly traceable to variations in the stimulus environment, much of the theorizing and research in the area of social role taking has had the effect of forcing a pendulum swing in the opposite direction, overemphasizing the extent to which the object world is transformed or perverted by assimilatory activities. By not according equal attention to reciprocal increases in the contributions made by the object pole of subject–object interactions, much of the symmetry of Piaget's original theory has been lost.

Part of this lopsided preoccupation with assimilatory processes has been the result of a self-conscious effort to dramatize the subjective bias assumed to be inherent in all cognitive processes, by selecting study problems that particularly emphasize the potentially distorting influence of assimilatory processes. This optimizing strategy is responsible, for example, for the decision on the part of persons investigating perceptual role-taking skills to choose stimulus materials which present a radically different face to observers who occupy different perspectives. It is unlikely, for instance, that a ball, which, like a variety of other potentially available stimulus materials, does not appear importantly different to persons who view it from different vantage points, would be regarded by such investigators as a proper stimulus object.

A second and more substantive reason for the failure of much of the research in the area of social role taking to adopt an evenhanded approach toward both assimilatory and accommodatory processes follows from certain of the structural assumptions upon which most of these studies rest. The cognitive structures postulated by Piaget are not generally presumed to be immediately and universally reflected under all possible circumstances where they might conceivably be expressed

(Bearison, 1974). Situational factors which mask underlying competence are, consequently, often regarded as a source of experimental noise (Flavell and Wohlwill, 1969) and, as such, are minimized whenever possible. For this reason, cognitive developmental psychologists, such as Piaget, have generally exercised a preference for research involving impersonal rather than social objects and have treated the unavoidable consequences of social interaction as a form of error variance. While the outlines of cognitive structures may be seen with most precision when they are silhouetted against a uniform backdrop involving a minimum of situational variation, this research strategy has the effect of artificially exaggerating the role of the assimilatory side of the assimilation–accommodation process.

As part of a research tradition that focuses on internal structural as opposed to situational determinants of performance, research in the area of social role taking is presented with the somewhat paradoxical task of extending into a new content area a theoretical model explicitly intended to be content free. Under the idealized expectations of Piaget's theory, the process of simultaneously considering and coordinating multiple variables or dimensions should be identical across situations regardless of their social flavor, and any exception to this somewhat unlikely set of circumstances poses serious problems with which the theory seems poorly equipped to deal. Psychological assessment procedures of all sorts are, however, typically choked with error variance and, whatever the underlying truth of the matter, different procedures almost inevitably produce different results, even when they are intended as alternative means of assessing the same thing. The entirely predictable consequence of this state of affairs is that different attempts to assess the structural characteristics of children across different content areas, or even within the same content area, have invariably produced results which are in less than perfect agreement. This has produced another instance of the "the glass is half-full—the glass is half-empty" paradox, the resolution of which often has more to do with the theoretical orientation of the person who interprets these facts, rather than the facts themselves. While the results of these various research efforts do not form a particularly coherent picture they can, nevertheless, be arrayed in a huge correlational matrix, different parts of which have become the basis for a long series of often contradictory claims about social cognition.

These various correlational studies can be roughly sorted into three broad categories. First, there is a series of studies which correlate the results of various measures of social role-taking ability with other indices of maturity. These are basically procedural studies which either accept the general theoretical premise that children become less egocentric with increasing mental or chronological age, and interpret age-related changes in the various assessment procedures of a form of test validation, or, conversely, assume that the assessment procedures are face valid tests of role-taking skill, and interpret the resulting correlation between test score change and age as providing evidence for or against the theoretical assumption that role-taking abilities do in fact improve during the course of development.

The second category of studies have more of an in-house flavor and focus on the relation between various measures of social role taking and other less explicitly interpersonal measures of cognitive development. Some of these studies involve attempts to compare decentering skills on both conservation and role-taking tasks, and are undertaken in an attempt to explicate the process of "generalizing assimilation" by which cognitive structures are understood to expand in their scope of applicability and become operative across specific content areas. Other studies in this category of research are intended to explore the network of interrelationships between various alternative measures all of which are intended as parallel procedures for indexing social role-taking skills. These studies often have a construct validational thrust or are intended to demonstrate the validity of newly developed assessment procedures.

Finally, the literature on social role taking also includes attempts to relate the results of various role-taking measures to other indices of social competence. These studies typically have more of a pragmatic character and consider potential relations between social role taking and interpersonal skills as having potential diagnostic as well as theoretical significance. Some of these studies have explored only the normal range of social competence, focusing on issues of cooperation, popularity, etc. Others have contrasted the social role-taking skills of both normal and seriously disordered children whose social incompetence is of clinical proportions.

In the following research summary, studies from each of these three categories are taken up separately and their implications for the general study of social role taking considered.

3.1. General Methodological Issues and the Relation between Social Role Taking and Mental and Chronological Age

However confident people may be about their ability to apprehend directly the character of the physical or social world, it has been generally recognized that persons of all ages respond to one another in ways which reflect idiosyncracies in the observer as well as the observed.

Dishonest men are expected to respond to others with special suspicion, lovers are assumed to be blind, and beauty is thought to lie in the eye of the beholder. Both in and out of psychology such personal biases are assumed to afflict children even more than they afflict adults, and objectivity is thought to increase with age. Much of the study of social role taking consists of efforts to detail and better understand the basis for the initial and gradually declining subjective character of children's social perceptions.

The question of when, in the course of their development, persons typically develop the capacity to adopt the roles and perspectives of others depends, of course, on how such role-taking skills are defined and on what one is willing to accept as evidence of their occurrence. Children, for example, typically learn from and pattern their activities after those around them and such imitative behaviors might, if one chose, be characterized as a form of role taking. To play at being one's self, that is, simply to behave, is not, however, what is usually intended or understood by the term role taking. Rather there is implicit in the concept of role taking a usual assumption that the child must first come to recognize the existence of a plurality of potentially different ways of being. Viewed in these terms, the question of whether or not a child may be said to play or occupy different roles is typically viewed as dependent upon the degree to which he can differentiate himself from others. The child whose total behavioral repertoire represents a kind of undifferentiated monolith and who is so fused with the persons and things around him that he has no meaningful sense of self or other, cannot, in this sense, be properly described as engaged in role-taking behavior. Role taking, in this view, requires as a prerequisite that children both recognize the existence of roles or points of view different from their own and, through a kind of conceptual boot strapping operation, clear the boundaries of their own egocentric perspective and successfully transport themselves into the role or vantage of someone else.

Both Werner and Piaget (Langer, 1969) have characterized the development of this kind of role-taking skill as occurring along an egocentrism–perspectivism dimension. In this developmental context the ability to take the role of the other is seen as a special case of a more fundamental capacity to decenter or departicularize the focus of one's conceptual activities and simultaneously to consider and coordinate two or more points of view. The term "egocentrism" is applied to that state of recurrent subject–object confusion which operates to confine an individual to a singular and highly personalized point of view while denying to others the uniqueness of their own vantage. Perspectivism, on the other hand, refers to the progressive capacity to differentiate between one's own and others' points of view. As such, perspectivism does not imply the absence of thorough-going subjectivity but the recognition of its universality (Piaget and Inhelder, 1956).

A number of different assessment procedures have been developed for the purpose of assessing role-taking skills. Although differing in many details, all these measurement strategies require subjects to describe the same objects or events from multiple points of view, and interpret as failures those responses in which information exclusively available to the subject is egocentrically attributed to those whose role he is required to assume. The general communalities which cut across these various measures tend, however, to obscure the important dimensions of difference that divide them and that raise questions about their comparability. Piaget's own assessment efforts (Piaget and Inhelder, 1956) have centered on the measurement of egocentrism in a primarily visual context and describe errors in physical rather than social perception. In this procedure, commonly referred to as the "Test of Three Mountains," subjects are asked to consider how a cluster of papier-mâché mountains might appear to someone occupying a perceptual vantage other than their own, and to communicate this understanding by selecting a picture descriptive of that vantage from a set of available photographs or line drawings. Egocentrism is expressed in this procedure by choosing, as descriptive of someone else's perspective, a picture more representative of one's own point of view.

While the physical displays employed in this and related procedures guarantee that the target stimuli present a different face to different observers, they accomplish this by inquiring into perspective-taking skills of a highly concrete and impersonal sort. Of potentially greater social significance, however, are the more figurative or metaphoric meanings of the concept of perspectivism, such as are implied when one inquires whether two persons share the same point of view about, for example, the war in Vietnam. Here the question is not one concerning lines of sight, but rather an inquiry into attitudes, feelings, and beliefs. A small number of programmatic research efforts have been directed toward the study of egocentrism in this second and more metaphoric sense.

In contrast to Piaget's more perceptually oriented procedures Feffer and his co-workers (Feffer, 1959; Feffer and Gourevitch, 1960; Feffer and Suchotliff, 1966) have focused on the measurement of egocentrism in a more interpersonal context and considered perspective-taking skills in a somewhat more social and metaphoric sense. The Role Taking Test (RTT) devised by Feffer and Gourevitch (1960) requires that subjects tell and retell stories to the same Make a Picture Story and Thematic Apperception Test (MAPS and TAT) pictures, alternately taking up the various roles of the stimulus persons portrayed. Decentered or nonegocentric thought is indexed in this procedure by descriptions which assign to the different characters alternate interpretations of the same events.

The increased social relevance of Feffer's procedures appear, however, to have been purchased at the expense of a certain degree of conceptual confusion. The projective materials employed, while explicitly interpersonal, leave largely unsettled the degree of legitimate communality existing between the various roles the subjects are asked to portray. The measurement problem introduced by this procedure arises from the fact that the child's projective assumptions about the similarities between himself and others may often be exaggerated, but, at the same time, are not necessarily entirely false. People are generally more alike than different and persons, including those depicted in the TAT and MAPS test, may often be legitimately understood to occupy identical perspectives or frames of reference. Because of this frequently occurring communality or likemindedness of thought, there is nothing inherently egocentric about assuming that two persons might share many thoughts and feelings in common. Prima facie evidence of egocentric thinking exists only when there are objective grounds for assuming that the persons whose points of view are being inquired into could not possibly share identical perspectives. The RTT makes no provisions for guaranteeing that the subject and the characters whose roles (s)he is asked to take must, of necessity, see things differently. Subjects who are unable to frame a story from two points of view and subjects who are capable but do not feel the situation requires their doing so may, therefore, perform in ways that cannot be distinguished. What is required, if one is to know with any certainty whether or not individuals are capable of adopting a role different from their own, is a procedure which engineers information in such a way that the subject and the person whose role (s)he is required to assume could not be reasonably imagined to know the same facts or share a common point of view. Unless this is accomplished, egocentric and nonegocentric reasoning may legitimately result in the same behavioral outcome, and stereotypic accuracy may easily pass for effective role taking. Nonegocentric thought, in the sense intended by Piaget (1970), is not simply a synonym for accurate social judgment but implies the ability to anticipate what someone else might think or feel, precisely when those thoughts and feelings are different from one's own. Without this important qualification egocentric and nonegocentric thought may result in the same outcome and their measurement be hopelessly confounded.

A partial solution to this information-engineering problem was recently introduced in a programmatic study of role-taking behavior reported by Flavell and his co-workers (Flavell *et al.*, 1968). One procedure described in this series of studies involved the presentation of a single cartoon sequence which, after having been previewed by the subjects, was sharply abbreviated and shown in this attenuated form to an experimental cohort in the presence of the subject. The subjects' task was to anticipate the account that would be offered by this second individual who had access to less information than themselves. This manipulation insured that the subjects and the individual whose vantage point they were asked to assume occupied demonstrably different perspectives and permitted egocentrism to be measured as a function of the degree to which privileged information exclusively available only to the subject was incorrectly attributed to an only partially informed witness or bystander.

Chandler and his co-workers (Chandler, 1971, 1973a, 1973b, 1974a, 1974b; Chandler and Greenspan, 1972; Chandler *et al.*, 1974) have expanded upon this information-engineering strategy and have developed a series of measurement procedures all of which require that subjects attempt to occupy perspectives which have been systematically arranged so that they differ from their own in precise and easily identifiable ways. One of these measures, for example, consists of a series of cartoon sequences which subjects are asked to describe, first from their own perspective, and then from the point of view of a late-arriving story character who has access to less information than themselves. By engineering available information in such a way that the respondent is in a privileged position relative to the story character whose role (s)he was asked to assume, this procedure makes it possible to determine the degree to which subjects are able effectively to set aside story details known only to themselves and adopt perspectives measureably different from their own. Although formally similar to the measurement strategy introduced by Flavell, this procedure, by incorporating the person whose point of view the subject is required to assume as a story character, solves the sometimes awkward choreographic problems that result when a real individual must be kept on hand to fulfill the role of the only partially informed bystander.

Another group of role-taking measures frequently employed in the literature consists of procedures which are less psychometric than those already described and which rely instead on efforts to infer role-taking skills from the attempts of subjects to predict the behavior of persons with whom they are required to interact. One of the most commonly employed of these procedures is a variation on the two-person guessing game, sometimes referred to by children as "school." In this procedure, utilized in the research by DeVries (1970), Flavell *et al.* (1968), Gratch (1964), and others, the child subjects and the persons with whom they interact take turns either hiding or guessing the location of an object hidden in one or another outstretched hand. The hiding and guessing strategies employed by the child are then examined for evidence that deceptions are executed or suspected in ways which take into consideration the different perspectives and different agendas of both players. Flavell *et al.* (1968), have developed and others have adopted a closely related social guessing game requiring children to anticipate the strategies that might be employed by an opponent who must guess under which of two containers a coin has been hidden. Both of these procedures share some similarity to a third measurement technique developed by Selman (1971). This procedure employs as stimulus materials groups of three objects from which at least two different pairs may be composed, depending on the classificatory dimension chosen. Subjects are first asked to select from these groups the two objects which they think go together and, on a later occasion, are required to anticipate which of the objects some second child would see as belonging with one another. The unqualified presumption that others would consistently pair the objects in ways similar to one's self is taken as an index of egocentric attribution and a failure in role-taking ability.

One additional set of assessment procedures intended to provide information about developmental changes in role taking has involved the measurement of referential communication skills. In brief, studies employing this assessment strategy (Botkin, 1966; Chandler *et al.*, 1974; Cowan, 1966; Flavell *et al.*, 1968; Greenspan and Chandler, 1973; Glucksberg *et al.*, 1966; Shantz and Wilson, 1972) have required subjects to make reference to the details of some complex stimulus array in such a way as to permit another person to follow their communications and to recognize the details of which they speak. The particular topics of communication involved in these procedures vary considerably and include such things as the giving of directions and descriptions. All these procedures are similar, however, in that they attempt to compare subjects' performances with some objective standard of adequately taking into account the special role or informational needs of one's audience.

What should be obvious from this partial survey of various measurement strategies for assessing developmental changes in role-taking skill is that large-scale differences exist in the operational definitions of, and in what various investigators are willing to accept as evidence for, role-taking ability. Although there continues to be room for debate as to whether these procedures tap the same or different underlying ability dimensions (Rubin, 1973), there are no longer any grounds for assuming that all these tasks are of the same difficulty or that success on one of these procedures guarantees success in the others. This fact has undermined confidence in the presumption that common structural prerequisites underlie these various performance measures, and has inspired several attempts to identify various qualitatively different substages in the developmental organization of role-taking abilities (DeVries, 1970; Flavell et al., 1968; Selman, 1971). Beyond these controversies, which will be considered later in this chapter, the one incontestable consequence of these obvious method variances is that no exact specification of the ages at which various role-taking competencies are acquired is possible.

While no precise statements can be made about the particular ages at which various role-taking skills emerge in the course of development, the available data are consistent with most theoretical expectations and demonstrate a steady decline in egocentrism and a steady increase in role-taking skills with advancing age (Bowers and London, 1965; Feffer and Gourevitch, 1960; Looft, 1972). Preschool children tested with the majority of these procedures have been found consistently to confuse their own views with what is known and understood by others. Primary and elementary schoolchildren also typically have difficulty distinguishing private from public information, regularly presume that others understand more than they have any right to understand, and information privileged to themselves often infiltrates and contaminates their view of what is known or understood by others. Adolescents and adults are also sometimes found to lapse into egocentric errors and are less skillful in taking other people's roles and perspectives than certain idealized theoretical statements might lead one to believe (Flavell, 1973).

The lower bound of role-taking skill—that is, the point at which such abilities are first in competence, although only occasionally and under optimal circumstances in performance—probably cannot be established with great precision (Flavell and Wohlwill, 1969). Recent work cited or carried out by Flavell (1973) and his co-workers (Masangkay et al., 1974) and the research of Borke (1971, 1973) and Deutsch (1974) all suggest that certain rudimentary forms of role taking can be observed in children as young as 2 or 3 years. Particularly those studies reported by Flavell (1973) make it obvious that, if subjects are properly prepared, encouraged, and permitted to respond in ways consistent with their performance capabilities, even toddlers are able to demonstrate some awareness of the idiosyncracies of their own or other visual experience. Although sometimes imagined as debunking Piaget's earlier findings regarding changes in role-taking ability during the concrete operations period, it is not at all obvious what these findings are supposed to contradict. Even young infants, for example, evidently appreciate that their mothers do not have eyes in the back of their heads and bother to attract or escape the attention of others, depending on their purpose. Similarly, anyone who reads to young children is aware that they quickly know what to expect on subsequent pages or understand that they can thumb back through earlier pages for another look at favorite pictures. It almost certainly would be a mistake, however, to interpret these facts as signifying that the child appreciates the existence of other latent perspectives from which such well-remembered but perceptually unavailable stimuli are potentially visible (Flavell, 1973). Without attempting to minimize the importance of such data in their own right, findings of this sort are probably best understood as precursors to, rather than contradictions of, the fact that the actual recognition and coordination of multiple cues are principally an achievement of middle childhood. The problem, of course, is to understand when and how various antecedent phenomena shade into the subsequent abilities for which they are necessary dispositions. The current research of Flavell and his students promises to help bridge the gap in understanding.

Research findings concerning the relation between role-taking skills and mental age or IQ are similar in both coarse and fine detail to the data on chronological age. With mental as with chronological age, the available evidence suggests that, if one samples from a broad enough range, clear relationships with role-taking skills emerge (Cooper and Flavell, 1975; Flavell et al., 1968). Studies which focus only on some truncated segments of this range, however, typically fail to produce significant results. The apparent motivations for the collection of such data appear to differ considerably from investigator to investigator, as do the interpretations placed on their findings. Some investigators (i.e., Deutsch, 1974) whose research focuses on children of approximately the same chronological age have turned to the use of mental age in an effort to expose differences in the developmental levels of their subjects which would otherwise be lost. Studies of this sort have generally reported significant difference in social-cognitive skills between the most and least intellectually mature of their subjects. Other investigators, concerned that calendar events only establish a time frame within which developmental processes may proceed at variable rates, have introduced data concerning the mental age of their subjects as an intended refinement. Studies of this sort (Cooper and Flavell, 1975), which typically index the developmental progress of subjects in terms of both mental and chronological ages, have consistently found mental age to be the more powerful predictor of role-taking and other socio-cognitive skills.

In contrast to studies which have reported the results of intelligence testing in terms of mental ages, investigators who have characterized their subjects in terms of intelligence quotients have most commonly done so in an attempt to consider or counter the possibility that the role-taking measures in which they were interested represented nothing more than redundant and roundabout indices of general intelligence. These studies (Chandler, 1971; Cooper and Flavell, 1975) have generally reported low positive correlations between role-taking and IQ measures, which were typically interpreted as demonstrating that most of the variance in the experimental role-taking measures could not be accounted for by difference in general intelligence. Finally, a few studies (i.e., DeVries, 1970) have attempted to sample systematically from across a broad range of general intelligence and intentionally have chosen to include low-intelligence groups that would not, under normal circumstances, be included in the public school samples most typical of research in this area. These studies seem to suggest a discontinuity in the relation between intelligence and role-taking skills, with no appreciable relation between the two measures within the broad range of normal intelligence, while, at the same time, children with sharply limited intellectual abilities are found to perform extremely poorly on tests of role-taking skill. DeVries concludes from these data that intelligence seems to be a more crucial factor than age in the development of role taking at the lower end of the psychometric range, whereas chronological age appears more important within the average or above-average range.

3.2. Decentering in and out of Social Situations

To the extent that the ability to take the roles of others is, as Piaget has proposed (Piaget, 1970), a special case of the more general capacity to decenter or departicularize the focus of one's conceptual efforts, then any problems which require the recognition and coordination of multiple dimensions of experience should, in theory, be solvable by any person possessing the prerequisite structural competencies. At this level of analysis various impersonal cognitive problems, such as the conservation of liquids, and more interpersonal problems, such as the coordination of multiple points of view, are regarded as formally similar. Whether the relevant dimensions are those of the height and width of a container or the perceptual vantages of both parties in a dyadic interpersonal interaction, the tasks of simultaneously considering and coordinating the multiple dimensions involved are held to be in some way equivalent. On the basis of this reasoning several investigators (Cooper and Flavell, 1975; Feffer, 1959; Feffer and Gourevitch, 1960; Flavell *et al.,*

1968; Goldschmid, 1968; Looft, 1972; Piaget, 1970; Rubin, 1973) have been prompted to hypothesize or search for equivalencies in the de-centering abilities of children across both impersonal and interpersonal situations. Most recently, Rubin (1973), for example, has conducted a factor analytic study relating the conservation skills of second-, fourth-, and sixth-grade children to a variety of role-taking measures. The results of this study locate measures of conservation and role-taking skills on a common decentration factor and are interpreted as supporting the view that impersonal cognition (person to object) and interpersonal cognition (person to person) are based on the same underlying decentration pro-cess. Related studies by Anthony (1959), Feffer and Gourevitch (1960), Feffer and Suchotliff (1966), and Wolfe (1963) also report an increase in both impersonal and interpersonal decentering with increasing chronological age (Feffer and Suchotliff, 1966).

In addition to these various efforts to relate decentering skills in impersonal and interpersonal situations, several investigators have also carried out studies intended to determine the nature of the interrelations between different testing instruments, all of which are understood to be alternative measures of social or interpersonal role taking. A number of different studies (Chandler, 1974b; Cowan, 1967; Flavell et al., 1968; Flavell, 1973; Masangkay et al., 1974; Rubin, 1973; Selman, 1971; Sullivan and Hunt, 1967) have, for example, provided correlational evidence re-garding the interrelations between children's abilities to coordinate spac-ial perspectives and role taking measured in a more social interactional context. In general, the results of these studies suggest low, but typically significant, relations between these two kinds of measures. Much of this apparent co-variation appears, however, to be controlled by the fact that both of the skill dimensions tapped by these procedures are indepen-dently related to age. When the effects of age are partialed out (Rubin, 1973; Sullivan and Hunt, 1967), the magnitude of the apparent interrela-tions between these measures drops substantially, leaving considerable room for doubt about the unitary character of the ability dimension which they are thought to reflect. Many of the same studies (Chandler, 1974b; Flavell et al., 1968; Rubin, 1973; Selman, 1971) have also explored the interrelations between various measures of conceptual rather than perceptual role-taking skills. The social guessing games devised or em-ployed by DeVries (1970), Deutsch (1974), and Selman (1971) have, at one time or another, been correlated with the referential communication measures of Greenspan and Chandler (1973), Krauss and Glucksberg (1969); the information suppression measures by Flavell et al. (1968), and Chandler (1973a), and the Role Taking Test of Feffer and Gourevitch (1960). The resulting network of these intercorrelations has been interpreted by Rubin (1973) as evidence for a common decentration factor. These and other primarily correlational findings do not, however, entirely settle the question as to whether competencies in these various decentering situations can be traced to a common structural base. In Rubin's study, for example, the various measures of conservation and role taking shared only 5% to 40% of their variance in common and even those relatively low-order relations were reduced or found to disappear entirely when the effects of mental or chronological age were partialed out. The results of Chandler (1974b) and Chandler *et al.* (1974) also indicate that the interrelations between these measures in normal populations are not necessarily present in certain psychiatrically disordered individuals, nor are experimentally induced changes in certain of these measures always accompanied by parallel changes in the others. The finding of these studies suggests that role-taking skills may be a necessary but not sufficient condition for competency in referential communication tasks.

The presumption of a common structural base underlying competencies in the solution of both social and nonsocial decentering problems is called into further question by the fact that acquiring competence in social role taking—in contrast to physical perspective tasks—appears to be an extremely protracted affair. As the data of Flavell (1973) indicate, certain measures of social role taking continue to present serious problems to persons well into their teen-age years. While Piaget has introduced the concept of horizontal decalage to describe those situations in which problems presumed to require formally identical modes of solution are commonly found to be solved at different junctures of development, the discovery of such horizontal decalages, sometimes extending over a decade or more, constitute something of a theoretical embarrassment and raise questions about the structural communality assumed to underlie these diverse performances.

Two general sorts of in-house explanations are available to account for the fact that solutions to social and nonsocial decentering problems are sometimes found at markedly different points in development. One of these, advocated by Flavell (1973) and Bearison (1974), is the suggestion that the various impersonal and interpersonal dimensions on which attention may be either centered or decentered become salient at different ages. The long delays between the point at which certain abilities appear first as an occasional competence and subsequently as stable performances are assumed to be traceable to such differences in cue saliency. Consistent with this situational account, Bearison (1974) has argued that the marked incompetencies in the social role-taking skills of seriously emotionally disturbed adults cannot be adequately accounted for in terms of hypothesized structural deficits. He maintains that Piaget's theory is an instance of what Van Den Daele (1969) has labeled a "simple, unitary progression model," which describes development as following a single unwavering course toward maturity and, as such, tends to minimize or ignore variations either within or between subjects of the same developmental level. For this reason Bearison feels that data from clinical populations of developmentally immature thinking in once competent but now disordered adults, or on impersonal but not social decentering, cannot be accounted for in structural terms. Such apparent instances of regression, according to this view, must be seen as performance rather than competence deficits, the explanation for which must be sought in various topic-specific situational factors. Flavell (1973) makes a similar argument to account for the long time periods that often separate initial competence from stable performance. The difficulty with such situational accounts of inter- and intra-individual differences in decentering skills is that they disregard the fact that theories such as that of Piaget have attracted interest principally because of the possibilities which they offer for accounting for such differences in formal structural terms. Although there is no longer any room for doubt that some decentering tasks are more difficult than others, this fact does not entirely foreclose on the possibility that a structural explanation of these differences is still possible.

An alternative explanation for the extended time period that separates the point at which role-taking or social decentering skills are first evidenced from the point at which they are routinely in performance is that the problem posed by the various assessment procedures currently in use are not formally equivalent, as has been usually supposed, but instead require qualitatively different cognitive structures for their solution. Every multivariate problem can, at some level, be understood to necessitate the simultaneous consideration and coordination of several different factors and, in that sense, may be viewed as a problem requiring decentering skills. It is not obvious, however, that our understanding is greatly increased by this somewhat syncretistic and overinclusive use of the term. The several dimensions which make up any multivariate problem may differ in form as well as content and the presence of these formal, content-free features may importantly influence how and when solutions to these problems fit into a developmental sequence. As discussed in the earlier sections of this chapter dealing with person perception, the various constructs and dimensions entering into the formulation of social judgments vary considerably in their degree of abstraction and should probably not be regarded as equivalent grist for an inferential mill. Some details of interpersonal interaction, such as smiles or frowns or clammy handshakes, involve directly observable changes along some single classificatory dimension and contribute to what Sigel (1964) has described as "first-order" cue concepts. The single dimensions of height and width employed in the classic conservation of quantity measures are inferential elements of this character. Similarly, as Flavell's (1973) research seems to indicate, knowledge about the visual experiences of others may, under certain circumstances, be more "object"- than "subject"-oriented, and, consequently, may involve only the most modest of inferences about others. As the questions posed become more hypothetical, however, and the inferential elements involved become more abstract, the constructs which the child must consider and coordinate begin to more closely approximate what Sigel describes as "second-order" concepts. Under these circumstances, the decentering operation ceases to involve only the ability to split one's attention among competing physicalistic dimensions and begins to require some sort of balanced decentering on elements which are, themselves, inferences or operations. To perform such operations on operations, and to take the products of one's own earlier conceptual efforts as elements in a higher-order inference process, has been proposed by Piaget (1970) as the defining feature of formal operatory thought.

In light of these considerations, the decade or more during which children gradually achieve competence in coping with situations that require social decentering skills need not be regarded as a structural anomaly or the world's most protracted horizontal decalage. Instead, the various social role-taking tasks that have been previously lumped together as all requiring structurally equivalent decentration skills may be differently understood to include a range of problems, some of which, depending on the level of abstraction of the dimensions involved, require preoperatory, concrete operatory, or even formal operatory skills.

3.3. Role Taking and Social Competence

Research of the sort considered in the two preceding sections, that is, research concerned with developmental changes in various indices of impersonal and interpersonal decentering, has something of an in-house character and is primarily intended as a means of testing the validity of Piaget's assumptions about the progressive reorganization of cognitive structures. Although sharing in some of these concerns with the internal coherence of the model, other investigators have attempted to move beyond these more parochial issues and have sought to determine the impact of evolving cognitive structures on various indicators of social competence. If, as Piaget has proposed, the character of a child's changing cognitive organization exercises controls over the kinds of social interactions in which he or she can successfully engage, then clear relations should exist between the various measures of social role taking currently in use and other expressions of social maturity. Research intended to explore these hypothesized relations has typically taken one of two forms: First, there are a series of studies which have sought to establish relations between social decentering skills and any one of several different indicators of normal social skill and maturity. These investigations of the usual interpersonal consequences of changing social decentering skills are related to a second cluster of studies concerned with the relation between social role taking and various forms of serious psychopathology. The authors of this later group of studies have seen in the concept of egocentricity a possible explanation for the etiology and symptomatic course of varying pathological forms of social incompetence.

Studies which fall within the first of these two categories have most frequently explored possible covariations between the role-taking competencies of children and their success in various peer group ventures. Goldschmid (1968), for example, found that children who, relative to their age mates, had particularly well developed conservation skills also tended to have more objective self-images, were more reflective, were described more favorably by their teachers, and were preferred by their peers. Similar relationships between social decentering skills and teacher and peer group ratings of popularity have been reported by Dymond *et al.* (1952), and Rothenberg (1970). Role-taking skills have been shown by Selman (1971) to relate to progress through Kohlberg's six stages of moral development: These stages have in turn been shown by Keasey (1971) to relate to the quality of children's social participation, their centrality in the power structure of their peer group, and their leadership qualities and popularity as rated by teachers and peers. Similar results were reported by Kohlberg (1958) relating moral development and peer group popularity. Related research with adult subjects has similarly indicated an association between role-taking skill and various measures of interpersonal competence. Cottrell and Dymond (1949), for example, analyzed the TAT productions of normal adults who scored high or low on an empathy test described as a measure of role-taking skills and found low scorers to be more rigid, introverted, uninsightful, socially inept, and characterized by unsuccessful social relations in childhood. Feffer (1959) similarly reports that the ability of adult subjects to assume different perspectives on his Role Taking Test were associated with their ability to give integrated Rorschach responses. In his review of the role-taking literature, Sarbin (1954) reports several other early studies indicating a relation between difficulties in social role taking and prejudice, ethnocentricism and authoritarianism. These scattered findings, along with the whole body of research in the area of person perception all suggest, in at least tentative ways, that differences in the ability to take the role of others frequently persist into adulthood and that persons so characterized lack age-appropriate social interactional skills.

Because of the central role assigned to social decentering skills in the normal socialization process, a number of investigators have been led to hypothesize a relation between delays in the acquisition of these skills and the development of various forms of social deviation. As a group, these studies have provided considerable support for the view that pro-social behavior is linked to the development of age-appropriate role- and perspective-taking skills. Neale (1966), Chandler (1971, 1973a), and Chandler et al. (1974) have, for example, all reported highly significant deficits in the ability of institutionalized emotionally disturbed children to identify objects depicted from points of view other than their own, or to adopt social roles different from their own. Anthony (1959) reports a similar study in which 15 psychotic children between the ages of 8 and 12 were compared with a group of 15 noninstitutionalized neurotic children on the same age on their ability to solve a version of Piaget's spacial perspectives test. While 65% of the responses of the psychotic children showed some degree of egocentrism and consistently mistook their own point of view for that of others, only 15% of the responses of the neurotic children showed such evidence of egocentric thought.

The apparent parallel between egocentric confusions of young children and the delusional concerns of psychotic adults have led various theorists such as Sarbin (1954), Cameron (1947), and Sullivan (1953) to interpret the cognitive and linguistic disorders of adult schizophrenic patients as due in whole or part to difficulties in taking the role of another. According to Cameron (1947), for example:

> Any shift from one socially defined role to another—whether this occurs in terms of manipulative, verbal, or imaginal operations—necessarily involves a shift in perspective. Clearly, the person who is ready and adroit in shifting to a succession of social roles in his behavior can anticipate the reactions of others and his own reactions with greater success than the person whose shifts are clumsy and reluctant. In short, to have ease and skill in shifting perspective means to be capable of adopting a wide range of shifting interpersonal relationships and implies a corresponding immunity from the kinds of progressive misinterpretations we encounter in behavior pathology—e.g., in paranoid states. (Cameron, 1947, p. 254.)

Similarly, Dunham (1944) has suggested that:

> The egocentric isolation of the schizophrenic causes him to gain a concep-
> tion of himself which he has no opportunities to test, because of his social
> isolation. . . . his opportunities, as well as the necessary mechanisms for
> "taking the role of the other" are distinctly limited and often completely
> lacking. As a result, in the numerous situations having emotional connota-
> tions which arise in social life, he does not know how to act, and this lack
> of knowledge of essential social conduct gives rise to a feeling of strange-
> ness. . . . (Dunham, 1944, p. 517.)

Most recently Feffer (1970) has attempted to work out a general theory of
schizophrenia, utilizing the concept of egocentrism as a major explanatory variable. He argues that decentering, that is shifting from one
focus to another, is a crucial ingredient in any valid attempt to structure
experience and that the inability to execute such decentering manoeuv-
ers is a central characteristic of schizophrenic thought disorder. Related
studies in the area of referential communication skills (Cohen et al., 1974;
Rosenberg and Cohen, 1966; Cohen, 1974) similarly indicate that
schizophrenic adults lack the ability to formulate communications which
reflect an accurate understanding of the information needs of their listeners.

A similar chain of reasoning has led several investigators to
hypothesize that deficits in role-taking skills are implicated in the etiology of various behavioral or character disorders including psychopathy
and juvenile delinquency. Gough (1948) and Gough and Peterson (1952)
have, for example, developed a role-taking theory of psychopathy in
which the primary difficulty of this clinical group is assumed to be an
inability to coordinate effectively the points of view of others with their
own. According to this view, the psychopath fails to profit from experience and expresses surprise and resentment when confronted with the
disapproval of others, principally because he cannot evaluate his own
actions from the standpoint of others and consequently cannot grant to
them the legitimacy of their disapproval or disapprobations. Such persons are unable to form deep attachments to others because they lack the
ability to know how to identify with or relate to them or to share their
thoughts and feelings (Gough, 1948). In support of this view, Gough
and Peterson (1952) report that delinquents endorsed a significantly
greater number of items suggestive of role-taking deficiencies, insen-
sitivity to interactional cues and the effect of their own behavior on
others, than did nondelinquents. In line with Gough's findings, Baker
(1954) found that prisoners, diagnosed as psychopaths on the basis of
MMPI criteria, were less able to empathize accurately with or put them-

selves in the role of others than their nonpsychopathic cellmates. More recently Martin (1968), Thompson (1968), and Warren (1965) have all presented evidence which indicates that young persons with serious delinquent histories are characteristically lacking in age-appropriate role-taking skills. The studies by Chandler and his co-workers have more firmly established the link between role-taking competency and social adaptation by demonstrating that experimentally induced changes in role taking and in referential communication skills are associated with reduction in antisocial behavior (Chandler, 1973a) and general improvements in social competency (Chandler *et al.*, 1974). Taken in combination, this weight of evidence would seem to indicate that persons who fail to achieve mature social role-taking skills, and whose thinking is egocentric beyond its normal tenure, lack the prerequisite abilities necessary to negotiate a variety of otherwise commonplace social transactions and are frequently characterized by serious failures in social adaptation.

4. Empathic Understanding

In contrast to the selective emphasis on either the subject or the object pole of subject–object interactions which has characterized the studies of person perception and role taking discussed in the first two sections of this chapter, the research literature concerned with developmental changes in empathic understanding reflects a much more speckled conceptual heritage. A number of the studies in this area are extensions of the research in social sensitivity already discussed and, like them, stress ways in which children process and learn to accommodate to affect-laden cues. Investigators operating within this tradition tend to discount or minimize the assimilatory distortions introduced by the changing structural characteristics of the child, and typically search for evidence of early achievements in the area of empathic understanding. Because of this stress on identifying early expressions of empathic ability, many of these studies are methodologic and focus on unearthing procedural quirks and measurement artifacts presumed responsible for the failure of previous research to expose the assumptive empathic skills of young children. Other investigators concerned with documenting developmental changes in empathic understanding have operated out of the same theoretical tradition as have investigators of social role taking more generally, and focus their attention on the manner in which structural limitations, assumed to characterize young children, prejudice their attempts to understand the feelings of others. Like other studies of social role taking, these investigations have stressed the distorting influence which the thoughts and feelings of their subjects exercise over efforts to recognize and understand the feeling states of others. As such, these studies emphasize the subject pole of interpersonal interactions and minimize the role which social objects themselves play in shaping empathic efforts. Added to these two lines of research is a third group of investigators whose emphasis has been on the study of children's own affective responses. For these investigators, empathic responses are simply another dimension of the child's emotionality, for which the environmental stimuli happen to be affective cues emitted by others. As a consequence of these diverse orientations, the literature on empathic understanding is something of a melting pot, without any generally agreed upon definitions or measurement procedures. Sometimes the only common feature of these investigations in their use of the term empathy, by which, of course, they mean very different things.

Much of the debate surrounding the detailing of proper definitions of the concepts of empathy, sympathy, contagion, identification, etc., reduce to a semantic squabble between persons for whom these terms have different networks of connotative meaning. The investigator who is convinced that the true meaning of empathy is not captured unless the putative empathizer feels *with*, as well as understands, other people cannot be easily persuaded, for example, by a second investigator for whom the term does not necessarily imply any such sharing of kindred emotions. Conventional usage of the language permits and includes instances of both of these meanings and an acceptable scientific definition of the term cannot be achieved by negotiation or by submitting these divergent views to some form of binding arbitration.

A first step toward a resolution of this conflict would seem to lie in a re-examination of the battle lines which have been drawn. The positions currently occupied include the assertions that empathy is: (1) *knowing* what another person feels, (2) *feeling* what another person feels, or (3) both (Iannotti and Meacham, 1974). The defense of each of these positions is impaired by two tactical problems—one analytic and the other procedural. The analytic problem stems from the divide-and-conquer strategy inherent in the crisp distinction between knowing about someone and feeling along with that person. "Attempts to divide anything into two should," according to C. P. Snow (1959, p. 9), "be regarded with much suspicion." Despite a considerable precedent in psychology for just such divisive tactics, Snow's rule of thumb seems particularly applicable in the present case. While it is possible to imagine raw feelings with no conceptual content, or strict understanding devoid of any feeling tone, instances of such psychological processes in pure culture are probably only analytic artifacts, rarely, if ever, represented in the world of real events. Knowing and feeling are, according to Piaget (1970), indissociable facets of the same event. From this perspective the attempts on the part of certain investigators (Hoffman, 1974; Feshbach, 1973) to decompose empathic responses into separable affective and cognitive components seem mistakenly analytic and unnecessarily piecemeal in their approach. A clear appreciation of another person's emotions is, in the present view, an understanding that involves one's whole person and need not be animated or humanized by the infusion of some second and independent dimension of affective experience.

A second difficulty with definitions of empathy which first divide knowledge and feelings about others is that they logically exclude the possibility of ever distinguishing between genuine empathy and egocentric projection. If it could be demonstrated that an individual first came to understand others and that as a result of this knowledge (s)he subsequently came to share with them similar feeling states, then empathy, in this double-barrel meaning of the term, could be operationally defined and empirically measured. The rub, as suggested in the preceding paragraph, is that there tends to be a simultaneity about what one comes to know and feel and the sequencing of events required by certain definitions of empathy cannot be substantiated. If feeling and knowing are regarded as separate events, and their order of occurrence cannot be established, then it might just as well be the case that the two parties involved first experienced identical emotions and only later came to "know" about the similarities between their shared feelings. Under such circumstances there would, in fact, be no requirement that the parties attend to one another at all, since they could both create the appearance of empathic understanding by simply reading off their own feelings of the moment. In more conventional usage such conclusions, whether coincidentally accurate or not, would be classified as instances of projection rather than empathy. This indeterminance is not a procedural quirk which can be made to disappear through some clever methodological gymnastic, but is an inherent part of any definition which makes a sharp distinction between knowing and feeling and insists that they occur in a specifiable order. More often than not, people in the same situations share many feelings in common and under such circumstances one may egocentrically take himself as a measure of others. Being right about another person's feelings for the wrong reasons, however, has never been seriously proposed as a criterion for empathic understanding.

Consequently, any definition that cannot distinguish empathy from those instances of stereotypic accuracy which often characterize project- ive attributions cannot be defended.

For the two reasons just outlined, much of the research concerned with developmental changes in empathic responses seems conceptually and procedurally flawed and less is understood about this complicated process than the number of available studies on the topic might rea- sonably lead one to anticipate. Among the various studies, the titles of which suggest that they deal with empathic response in children, one may, however, distinguish three generic types: The first of these at- tempts to document the particular point in development at which chil- dren begin to recognize the fact that other persons are experiencing particular kinds of emotions. Studies in this category tend to be gener- ally unconcerned with questions of role taking and the distinction be- tween self and others. Their focus, rather, is on documenting the ages at which the abilities to recognize, label, or anticipate particular feeling states occur. A second category of research involves studies which focus on the similarities between the feeling states of subjects and those of the stimulus persons on whose emotions they are asked to report. A final group of studies is an offshoot of research in the general area of role taking and centers attention on the degree to which subjects are able to decenter socially in affectively charged contexts and to identify accu- rately the feeling states of others precisely when they are different from their own. In the paragraphs which follow, each of these three research areas will be considered in turn and research studies representative of these areas discussed.

4.1. The Anticipation and Identification of Affective Cues

Reference has already been made to several studies which have focused on the abilities of young children to recognize or anticipate the affective responses of others. Of these various skills, relatively less at- tention has been directed to the study of how and when children come to recognize and label accurately the manifest feeling states of others. In contrast to the substantial adult literature on this topic (Woodworth and Schlosberg, 1960) only a handful of studies have, for example, explored the abilities of children to identify the affective implication of various facial expressions. An early study by Gates (1923) and the more recent work of Cooke (1971) do, however, suggest that the ability of children to label correctly affects from photographs of facial expressions improves with age. Dimitrovsky (1964) also reports a similar improvement in the ability of 5- through 12-year-old children to identify the emotional meaning of recorded vocalizations. Research of this sort, which artificially restricts the normal range of supporting behavioral and contextual cues, represents, however, a kind of limits testing that has little apparent ecological validity and consequently seems only peripherally related to the question of what young children do and do not understand about the affect life of others.

More commonly, research interest has been directed to the question of when children come to understand what other people *ought* to be feeling in particular affect-arousing interpersonal situations. In all these studies, children of various ages were presented with potentially affect-laden slices of social interaction and required to predict how the characters in these episodes might be feeling. With a few important exceptions, these studies have provided a series of redundant situational cues, all of which prescribe a single and unambiguous affect response. The task of the subject was to conclude what someone trapped in these situations might feel and indicate their decision by either labeling the required affect or by selecting from among a series of drawings or photographs depicting various strong emotions. Early studies by Dymond *et al.* (1952) and Ruderman (1961), for example, both required subjects to describe the likely affective responses of characters portrayed in stimulus drawings, and both reported age-related increases in this brand of empathic ability. Related studies by Feshbach and Feshbach (1969), Feshbach and Roe (1968), Klein (1970), and Mood *et al.* (1973) also support this conclusion. The reliance in many of these studies on verbal response dimensions has, however, caused some suspicion that many of the apparent failures of these primary and elementary school-age subjects were the consequence of failures in communication rather than failures in understanding.

In order to test the assumption that children often know more than they can say, several investigations have turned to the use of behavioral rather than verbal reporting channels. Borke (1971, 1973), for example, presented 3- through 8-year-old children with line drawings of faceless characters engaged in social interactions calculated to sponsor feelings of happiness, anger, fear, or sadness. Brief stories describing these events were read to the children, who were required to communicate their expectations about the affective reactions of these story characters by selecting from among four stylized drawings of various facial expressions. The results of this study, later replicated (Borke, 1973) in a cross-cultural investigation of Chinese as well as American children, indicates that accuracy in anticipating the feelings of others improved systematically with age and that children as young as age 3 are often able to match successfully pictures of facial expressions with situational contexts in which such expressions are common. Utilizing a similar methodology, slightly modernized by the introduction of videotaped rather than written story materials, Deutsch (1974) also reported what are described as empathic skills among nursery schoolchildren. Anthony (1974) has tested children of both normal and emotionally disturbed parents with procedures patterned after those of Borke, and again found that preschool children were frequently able to anticipate the feeling states of others at better-than-chance levels.

Although the nonverbal reporting procedures adopted in the research of Anthony, Borke, Deutsch, and others have helped to identify underlying abilities, sometimes masked by limitations in verbal competence, two important methodological problems remain which obscure the implication of these studies. First, the manifold available affective cues employed in these studies have typically been of a highly congruent and internally consistent sort, any part of which, taken by itself, might lead to the same accurate conclusion about the affect state of the target character. In such redundant stimulus situations it is possible to arrive at seemingly identical conclusions through radically different inferential routes. Investigators who monitor only the summarial judgments of their subjects, consequently, cannot distinguish between simple univariate solutions and more sophisticated, decentered inference strategies which consider and coordinate multiple cues.

What seems required, if conclusions are to be drawn regarding the process, as opposed to the outcome, of empathic judgments is some methodology which permits qualitatively different inferential strategies to be reflected in demonstrably different patterns of response. Two studies in the literature partially satisfy this requirement. The first of these is an early study by Burns and Cavey (1957) in which 3- to 6-year-old children were tested to determine whether they could detect incongruities between the facial expressions of various cartoon characters and the affective context in which these characters were depicted. When presented with only contextual cues—for example, a doctor poised over an empty chair with a hypodermic needle in his hand—the youngest as well as the oldest of the children tested all agreed that they or anyone else would very likely be frightened if they were in that situation. However, when shown a similar drawing which included an about-to-be-inoculated child with a large smile on his face, the older but not the younger of these children were able to discount the situational demands of contextual cues and accurately identify the feeling state of the target character. These results were interpreted as indicating that the older children employed a more complex inference strategy that permitted them to set aside stereotypic assumptions about their own or others' likely reactions and to attend to the actual facial expressions worn by the target characters.

More recently, Greenspan *et al.* (1974) reported a related study in which first- and third-grade children were presented one of two brief videotapes, both of which depicted a central character being badly beaten in a test of strength. In one of these tapes, this character's admission of defeat was accompanied by appropriate affect expression, whereas in the second he behaved incongruously and appeared pleased or amused by his own failure. The younger of the children tested with these materials seemed to overlook the incongruous information presented, regularly based their judgments on contextual cues, and expressed confidence in the accuracy of their judgments, despite the contradictions presented. The older children, by contrast, were sensitive to the incongruities present in the second tape, recognized the central character's affective expressions for what they were, were reluctant to hazard inferences about the emotional meaning of these events, and expressed a great deal of uncertainty about their judgments.

Both of these studies underscore the important role which stimulus complexity plays in determining the manner in which emphatic judgments are formed, and help to expose critical differences in the inferential strategies employed by children of different ages. Without the systematic uncoupling of the manifold of affect-related cues in the presentation of incongruous stimulus situations, an observer would be left with the mistaken impression that the youngest and oldest of the children of these two studies employed inference strategies which were quantitatively and qualitatively identical.

A second limitation inherent in the measurement strategy employed by Anthony, Borke, Deutsch, and others is the fact that the contextual demands inherent in the stimulus situations chosen are so compelling and the affective responses demanded so routine and inescapable that a subject could easily conclude what the target character might feel by simply determining what he, or in fact anyone might feel in the same situation and offering this self-referential statement as an estimate of the feelings of others. This appearance of empathic skill could, as the research of Burns and Cavey (1957) demonstrates, proceed just as well without the presence of a target character at all. While, as the studies to be described in the following section indicate, a number of investigators have regarded a matching of the affective states of subject and target as a defining feature of empathic response, any proposed measure of empathic skill that can get along equally well with or without a stimulus character seems a serious perversion of the usual meaning of the term empathy. Similarly, any procedure that does not permit an operational distinction to be drawn between the projection of one's own feelings and the accurate understanding of someone else's appears to hopelessly confound empathy with one of the few things from which it should be clearly distinguished. Projecting one's own feelings onto others is, by most standards, the exact opposite of legitimate empathic understanding. This is true despite the fact that the coincidental similarity often existing between persons frequently allows us to take ourselves as a proper measure of others and to be right in our judgments for the wrong reasons. What seems required, from the present point of view, is some methodology to allow the assessment of empathic skills in a context in which knowledge of how others are feeling can be clearly distinguished from projective attributions which sometimes give the appearance of accurate empathy. The research of Burns and Cavey (1957) and Greenspan *et al.* (1975) appears to be a step in this direction.

4.2. Feeling for or with Others versus Knowledge of Others' Feelings

A number, perhaps even the majority, of investigators concerned with the study of empathic skills have been unwilling to accept accurate knowledge of what other people are feeling as a sufficient condition for the attribution of empathic understanding. According to this view, empathy implies a kind of emotional sharing between subject and object (Feshbach, 1973) which cannot be accounted for entirely in cognitive terms. This view is part of a long tradition having roots in the study of esthetic experience, classical conditioning, and clinical practice. Theodore Lipps (Wispé, 1968), for example, employed the concept of empathy to describe those esthetic reactions in which the distinctions between self and object completely dissolve and the phenomenological forces within the object come to flow within the self. Similarly, empathy has been treated by Aronfreed (1969) and Hoffman (1974) as a special case of associative learning in which the distress of others comes to operate as a conditioned stimulus that evokes affective reactions earlier produced by one's own past experiences of distress. As such, empathy is understood to be a primitive emotional reaction which occurs long before the child has developed a sense of self or other. All that is required, in this view, is that an observer demonstrate an affective experience which is elicited by cues of a corresponding affect state in the expressive behavior of another person. Both Hoffman (1974) and Feshbach (1973) go beyond this limited notion of affective contagion and also include cognitive components in their definitions of sympathy or empathy, but the presence of some match between the affective responses of subject and object remains a central ingredient in these definitions. Stotland (1969) also makes a sharp distinction between feeling along with another and making accurate predictions about the affective states of others, and argues that it is possible to empathize with inaccurately perceived affect states or even with emotions which are entirely nonexistent. Although consistent with his own definition of primary empathy as an affective rather than a cognitive response, the view that empathy could be nothing but an emotional reaction to fictitious feelings misascribed to others does considerable violence to the usual meaning of the term.

Consistent with the emphasis which they place on a match between the feeling states of subject and object, Feshbach and her colleagues (Feshbach, 1973, Feshbach and Feshbach, 1969; Feshbach and Roe, 1968; Klein, 1970), and Mood et al. (1973) have attempted not only to assess the ability of their subjects to judge the feeling state of others, but also to secure a simultaneous reading of the emotional consequences of this inferential activity on their child subjects. In the original Feshbach and Roe (1968) study, for example, children were shown a series of slide sequences depicting stimulus characters engaged in a variety of emotionally charged interactions. Although a separate inquiry was made to establish the fact that these children correctly understood the emotional reactions of the story characters, primary attention was directed toward the self-reports of these first graders regarding their own emotional reaction to these materials. Empathy was scored whenever the self-defined feeling states of the children matched those which might reasonably be ascribed to the story characters. Defined in this way, the empathic skills of boys and girls were not found to be importantly different, nor did such "empathic" responses correlate with the ability to identify accurately the feeling states of the story characters. Later studies by this research group did establish, however, age-related increases in this index of empathic ability (Feshbach, 1973), significant correlates with aggression in boys (Feshbach and Feshbach, 1969), and relations with perceived similarity, as defined by responses to persons of the same or different racial groups (Klein, 1970).

The research of Mood et al. (1973) similarly included attempts to identify developmental changes in the empathic abilities of 3- through 5-year-old children utilizing a series of verbal stories in which the central characters were portrayed as undergoing a variety of different emotions. In contrast to the studies of Feshbach and her colleagues, however, Mood et al. took as evidence of empathy only those responses in which subjects both correctly identified the feelings of the story characters and also claimed to share in these emotions. Statements indicating affective reactions on the part of the subjects which were in agreement with emotional responses defined as correct by the investigators, but not perceived as such by the child, were termed "egocentric." The accurate identification of the feeling states of the target characters without any claims for similar feelings on their own part were scored as purely "cognitive" responses. Responses in this latter category occurred with some frequency and, as in the study of Feshbach and Roe (1968), no systematic relationships were observed between the ability to judge accurately the feeling states of others and claims for equivalent feelings on the part of these child subjects.

Several important procedural, as well as conceptual, difficulties seriously complicate the interpretation of these findings: First, as Greenspan (1973) has pointed out, repeated inquiries as to how a subject feels following the presentation of each of a series of stories or slides contains certain elements of the absurd and creates demand characteristics, the effects of which cannot be calculated. Second, even if one can imagine that children's emotions go through the kinds of kaleidoscopic changes which these procedures seem to demand, there is no guarantee that young persons are capable of accurately reporting on these rapid fluctuations in their subjective experience. Third, the bold strokes in which the affective experiences of the story characters are painted easily permit a kind of stereotypic accuracy that only vaguely resembles the kinds of affect monitoring which people usually have in mind when they speak of empathic skill. Finally, the requirement that empathy be scored only in those circumstances in which there is a match between the feeling states of subject and object makes no provision for distinguishing between empathy and projection. As Feshbach (1973) has pointed out, "both projection and empathy entail a sharing of emotional attributes between subject and object and appear to be affected by similar parameters..." (Feshbach, 1973, p. 2). The direction and sequencing of these reactions is, however, assumed by Feshbach to be different, with the emotional reaction of the subject preceding that of the object in the case of projection, and following that of the object in the case of empathy. Nothing in the assessment strategy employed by either Feshbach or by Mood et al., however, makes any provision for establishing the direction or sequence of these affective reactions and, consequently, no distinction between empathy and projection is possible. As indicated earlier, this difficulty involves more than a simple procedural flaw and rests on a distinction between feeling and knowing which, from the perspective of theorists such as Piaget, cannot be maintained.

Certain of these procedural limitations, particularly those having to do with the difficulties surrounding the use of self-report measures, can and have been partially avoided by adopting some more behavioral measure of children's affective responses. As previously described in the earlier section on person perception, physiological measures of children's emotional responses to potentially affect-arousing situations are both rare and inconclusive (Osborn and Endsley, 1971). A study of Sternback (1962), for example, failed to demonstrate any consistent physiological correlation of exposure to supposedly frightening scenes from the movie *Bambi*. Osborn and Endsley's (1971) own research on children's physiological responses to television violence is equally inconclusive and demonstrates the need for continued reliance on self-report measures.

A substantial body of research does exist which is concerned with various sympathetic and altruistic responses on the part of children to the perceived distress of others. Although these studies do provide a behavioral index of children's empathic reactions, much of this research focuses on the study of the social demand characteristics that influence the extent to which sympathetic reactions find their way into behavioral expression and, for this reason, fall outside the scope of this review. The research of Staub (1970, 1971) is, however, representative of much of this research and is described here for illustrative purposes. All these studies have involved the exposure of children to tape-recorded sounds of distress which are overheard from an adjoining room, and all measure the extent to which children of various ages are prompted to volunteer or attempt to seek out assistance for the supposedly injured child. Although these studies do suggest age-related changes of helping behavior and, by implication, the underlying empathic reactions on which such sympathetic behaviors are presumably based, the variables of social conformity and readiness to take initiative in the absence of explicit license to do so are seen by Staub to be the principal source of the performance differences observed. Even if it were possible, however, to establish an assessment context in which children felt no constraints about acting on whatever empathic feelings they might experience, it would still not be possible to distinguish between reflexive, prosocial, instrumental acts, and offers of assistance reflecting some clear appreciation of what another might be feeling.

Despite the various conceptual and methodological difficulties which characterize most of the studies in this research area there is, nevertheless, little or no room for doubt that very young children are frequently moved by the affective responses of others, that they recoil from angry emotions, and suffer along with the distress of others (Murphy, 1937). People are free, of course, to call things whatever they wish and no sanctity will be violated if one chooses to label such instances of emotional contagion as empathy. What is important, however, is that some distinction be made between such primitive spillovers of emotion and more mature responses which include some recognition of the feelings of others without getting lost in them or forgetting what is happening to whom.

4.3. Empathy and Role Taking

Those investigators who have stressed the so-called affective dimension of empathic understanding (i.e., Feshbach, 1973; Hoffman, 1974; Iannotti and Meacham, 1974; Mood *et al.*, 1973; Stotland, 1969) have argued that empathy, defined solely in cognitive terms, "has little theoretical utility beyond that contributed by the cognitive functions themselves" (Feshbach, 1973, p. 1), and "is no more than the sum of its cognitive components" (Iannotti and Meacham, 1974, p. 3). Hoffman (1974) has voiced a similar criticism of various measures of role taking and empathy, arguing that many of the assessment procedures currently in use measure only cognitive components, prerequisites to, but not identical with, these important ability dimensions. Mature, prosocial responses to the distress of others, which Hoffman labels as sympathy, require, in his view, some synthesis of primitive empathic responses and cognitive role-taking skills.

The obvious reluctance on the part of these investigators to consider empathic understanding as a special case of role-taking ability appears to stem from the coldblooded and affectively neutral implications which they attach to the concept of cognition. The intellectual appreciation *of* and the feelings which people have *for* one another seem to be regarded by these investigators as isolated elements of understanding that only sometimes interact to generate a synthesis of thought and feeling. Such interactions are assumed to be only one of a possible set of outcomes that includes emotionally detached brands of bloodless understanding as well as affective reactions unelaborated by accurate knowledge of the circumstances in which such emotions occur.

If, in contrast to this piecemeal approach to the understanding of personality organization, one adopts a less fractionated view of the sort proposed by Piaget (1970), then thoughts and feelings cease to represent isolated elements which sometimes do and sometimes do not interact. Instead, individuals are presumed to be moved and changed by their interactions with the environment in more holistic ways which, for certain analytic purposes, may be decomposed artificially into cognitive and affective components. Rather than regarding the natural synthesis of these isolatable elements as a byproduct of an occasional coming together of separable parts, their interaction is seen as the normal state of affairs and pure cognitive or pure affective acts are regarded as myths of conceptual convenience. From this perspective, the felt obligation on the part of researchers such as Feshbach and many others to flesh out what is imagined to be the exclusively cognitive character of role-taking efforts with some more affect-laden dimension of experience is regarded as misplaced. If, instead, people are regarded as engaged in efforts to understand one another in a more holistic sense, and, in the process, to be themselves moved by such understanding in ways conventionally thought of as affective as well as cognitive, then it is no longer necessary to suffix some supposedly independent affective dimension to the process of coming to know.

Even if one maintains, as does Piaget (1970), that every environmental interaction has affective as well as cognitive components, it is obviously the case that people are not always uniformly moved by the affective experiences of others, and role-taking efforts must be located, as Sarbin (1954) has suggested, along some dimension of "organismic involvement," ranging from dispassionate awareness to total emersion in the affective experiences of others. A genuine understanding of the pleasure or distress of others is assumed, however, to be a necessary occasion for some flow of counterpart feelings of one's own. As such, an individual who remains affectively neutral in the face of another person's distress would not be regarded, in this view, as having fully understood the situation while himself remaining untouched emotionally. Rather, apparent understanding unaccompanied by some appropriate and comprehensive affective experience would be viewed as evidence for the fact that such understanding is superficial and incomplete. There is no requirement in this view that the observer experience exactly the same feelings as does the person with whom he is empathizing—only that the emotional meaning of the other's situation have some counterpart emotional meaning for the observer as well. This characterization of empathic understanding, and, for that matter, understanding in general, is generally consistent with the usage made of the term in the psychotherapy literature. Rogers (1952), for example, defines empathy as the ability of the counselor to assume "the internal reference frame of the client, to perceive the world as the client sees it, to perceive the client as he is seen by himself, ... but without himself, as counselor, experiencing those hates and hopes and fears" as his own (Rogers, 1952, p. 29).

If one adopts the more holistic view of human understanding advocated here and inherent in Piaget's general developmental theory, then no sharp division exists between the processes traditionally characterized as instances of either role taking or empathy. Instead, those situations commonly regarded as instances of and occasions for the measurement of empathic skill represent opportunities for interpersonal understanding in which high levels of organismic involvement are required on the part of both subject and object. As such, taking the role of another person as he stands on the opposite side of Piaget's three papier-mâché mountains might not be characterized as a task of particularly high empathic relevance, whereas seriously attempting to adopt the perspective of a starving Asian child almost certainly would be. Which acts are described as empathic and which are not hinges then, in this view, not on the underlying process that is required, which is assumed to be the same in all instances, but on the particular events that are the subject of such attempts at interpersonal understanding.

Viewed in the terms just described, parts of the general role-taking literature, particularly those studies in which the social objects whose points of view are in question are engaged in affectively charged interpersonal interactions, provide important information about the empathic process. Many studies already reviewed (Borke, 1971, 1973; Chandler and Greenspan, 1972; Chandler et al., 1973, 1974; Deutsch, 1974; Feffer, 1970; Selman, 1971) fit parts of this prescription. The assessment procedures employed in these studies have typically dealt with affect-laden interpersonal content and require, among other things, that subjects report their understanding of the affective reactions of others. In the research of Chandler and Greenspan (1972) and Chandler et al. (1974), for example, children were asked to interpret emotionally charged events, both from their own perspective and from that of an only partially informed bystander who had access to less information than they about the larger emotional context in which these events took on meaning. In one of the story sequences employed, for instance, a series of cartoon drawings depicted a girl who, after having just seen her father off on an airplane, became sad when she later received a gift of a toy airplane in the mail. The children were asked to interpret these materials both from their own point of view and from the perspective of the postman who delivered the gift, but who had no means of knowing about the earlier departure of the story character's father. Empathic skill is tapped at two levels by this procedure. The first concerns the extent to which the children are themselves capable of appreciation why, in this situation, the receipt of a toy airplane might be a legitimate occasion for sadness on the part of the central story character. The second measure of empathic understanding centers around the extent to which the children can place themselves in the limited perspective of the postman and, recognizing the reduced informational context in which he is forced to operate, are able to grasp his legitimate confusion about what, to him, must seem a paradoxical reaction on the part of a child receiving a present.

Hoffman (1974) has argued that, while this and related procedures do require children to keep one set of facts separate from another, they do not necessarily involve a clash of perspectives and, as a result, do not directly measure role taking or empathic ability. In his view, the skill required is simply one of maintaining separate facts in isolated, watertight conceptual compartments, and the question of the ownership of these facts or feelings is seen as irrelevant. These measurement tasks would be the same, according to Hoffman, with or without the presence of a second person whose perspective is to be identified, and could proceed equally well if the children themselves were simply provided with both accounts and asked to keep them separate.

Even if this were true, the suggestion that the process of social role taking can be considered as a special case of the part–whole or class-inclusion problem is neither new nor potentially embarrassing to investigators who wish to maintain that social cognition in general, and role taking in particular, is simply the interpersonal expression of more general conceptual operations. A recent study by the author and his co-workers (Chandler and Helm, 1974) has, however, provided an indirect test of Hoffman's hypothesis that the presence of another person could be incidental to the problems presented by most current measures of role-taking ability. In this study the role-taking skills of 4-, 7-, and 11-year-old children were evaluated under conditions in which they had or had not themselves previously occupied the perspective of a second individual whose point of view they were subsequently asked to assume. Under these testing conditions, that half of the sample who had once literally occupied the perspective in question were explicitly in that circumstance which Hoffman regards as characteristic of most measures of role-taking skill. That is, they were themselves in direct possession of all of the necessary facts and had simply to keep these different views separate and conceptually intact. The remaining children, by contrast, were required to interpret a perceptival display from the perspective of another person without having themselves previously occupied that vantage. If Hoffman's hypothesis were true, this second group of children would prove to be in the same situation as the first and no per-

formance differences would be expected to distinguish them. In contrast
to these expectations the results of this study indicate that, for the
7-year-old children of this study, it made a great deal of difference
whether or not they had once previously occupied the perspective they
were later asked to assume. The facts were the same in either instance,
but, for these primary schoolchildren, it proved much easier to isolate
and preserve the integrity of different perspectives which had once been
their own. This was, however, less true for the 4-year-old subjects, who
were as quick to confuse their own and alternative perspectives as they
were the views of someone else, or for the 11-year-olds, who performed
well under either of these testing conditions.

A perhaps more telling criticism of these various measures of role-
taking ability, at least as they relate to the study of empathic understanding, is that they make no provision for the assessment of the extent to
which subjects are moved by or impacted on by their knowledge of the
affective experiences of others. No easy solution is available to this problem. Other than self-report measures, which are notoriously unreliable
in the age group of interest, no convincing assessment techniques are
available for determining the extent to which insight into other peoples'
feelings operates as a source of counterpart emotional meaning to the
subject. The repeated questioning of the children's own feelings following the serial presentation of numerous brief caricatures of human emotion (i.e., Mood *et al.*, 1973) seems to be a somewhat artificial and dubi-
ous procedure, which may well obligate a child to make claims for a level
of personal involvement or emotional responsivity which does not
seem to be warranted by the task.

If one is genuinely interested in the extent to which children are
moved or become organismically involved in the distress of others, it
will probably be necessary to examine their efforts to understand emotional events that are sufficiently real and sufficiently weighty to warrant
real concern and deserve a response having a measurable depth of feeling. Whether such an assessment situation can be created without ex-
posing subjects to real risks or hazards, whether such situations could be
set up in a usual laboratory context, or whether they could be presented
in the serial fashion required by conventional measurement strategies is
not clear. With or without solutions to these problems, however, research into the development of social role-taking skills appears less
compromised by measurement artifacts and conceptual confusion than
does research that artificially disassembles people's thoughts and feelings and then finds itself unable to reason how all these parts should be
put back in place.

5. Conclusion

The results of this survey of current research in the area of social cognition appears to support a number of tentative conclusions: First, while research in the areas of person perception, social role taking, and empathy has typically sprung up out of different kinds of conceptual soil, there does appear to be some growing confluence in the findings of these diverse studies. Whereas the person-perception literature initially evidenced a kind of situational bias and focused almost exclusively on the efforts of subjects to accommodate to a network of socially relevant cues, there has been a gradual shift in this research toward a greater appreciation of the degree to which social stimuli are filtered and shaped by the assimilatory influences of the child's changing cognitive organization. Conversely, the role-taking literature began with a decided structuralistic bias and almost exclusively emphasized the manner in which objectivity is lost to the distorting influences of assimilatory processes. More recently, however, investigators working in this area have come to attach increasing importance to the manner in which the object environment exercises accommodatory controls over the more subjective side of subject–object interaction. This gradual equilibration is seen as bringing both of these research areas closer to the kind of assimilation–accommodation balance which Piaget regards as the hallmark of any developmental process.

Second, research in all the areas reviewed began with a kind of fragmented piecemeal approach, the wounds of which give some evidence of beginning to heal. Research in the area of person perception, for example, initially articulated numerous discrete information-processing steps which now, in hindsight, appear to infuse and interpenetrate one another and to form more of a piece. Similarly, research regarding the development of role-taking and social decentering skills initially appeared to develop independently from the less interpersonal aspects of cognitive growth. These divisions also have begun to prove to be artificial distinctions between social and nonsocial cognition and have become increasingly difficult to maintain. The independent status of empathic understanding has also come increasingly into question, and equivalencies between empathy, person perception, and role taking are more and more frequently stressed. Although it is perhaps premature to hope, this pattern of increasing confluence of theory and results could very well lead to the reconstitution of the whole person in psychological research.

Finally, it should be clear from the preceding survey that developmental research in the area of social cognition is only now emerging from its own early sensorimotor period and is beginning to rework its own earlier achievements on a more abstract representational plane. While the conceptual hazards inherent in these early efforts are very real, social-cognitive research appears to be in a decided growth spurt and seems on its way toward achieving a mark of greater maturity.

References

Anthony, B. J., 1974, The development of empathy in high risk children, paper presented at the Eighth International Congress of the International Association for Child Psychiatry and Allied Professions, Philadelphia.

Anthony, E. J., 1959, An experimental approach to the psychopathology of childhood autism, *British Journal of Medical Psychology* 32:18–37.

Aronfreed, J., 1969, The concept of internalization, *in* "Handbook of Socialization Theory and Research" D. Goslin (ed.), Rand McNally, Chicago.

Baker, B., 1954, Accuracy of social perceptions of psychopathic and non-psychopathic prison inmates, unpublished manuscript.

Baldwin, A. L., Baldwin, C. P., Hilton, I. M., and Lambert, N. W., 1969, The measurement of social expectations and their development in children, Monographs of the Society for Research in Child Development, 34:(4, Serial No. 128).

Baldwin, C. P., and Baldwin, A. L., 1970, Children's judgments of kindness, *Child Development*, 41:29–47.

Bearison, D. J., 1974, The construct of regression: A Piagetian approach, *Merrill-Palmer Quarterly*, 20:21–30.

Bigner, J. J., 1974, A Wernerian developmental analysis of children's descriptions of siblings, *Child Development* 45:317–323.

Borke, H., 1971, Interpersonal perception of young children: Egocentrism or empathy?, *Developmental Psychology* 5:263–269.

Borke, H., 1972, Chandler and Greenspan's "Ersatz egocentrism": A rejoinder, *Developmental Psychology* 7:107–109.

Borke, H., 1973, The development of empathy in Chinese and American children between the ages of three and six years of age: A cross-culture study, *Developmental Psychology* 9:102–108.

Botkin, P. T., 1966, Improving communication skills in sixth-grade students through training in role-taking, Unpublished doctoral dissertation, University of Rochester.

Bowers, K. S., 1973, Situationism in psychology: An analysis and a critique, *Psychological Review* 80:307–336.

Bowers, P., and London, P., 1965, Developmental correlates of role-playing ability, *Child Development* 36:499–508.

Brierly, D. W., 1966, Children's use of personality constructs, *Bulletin of the British Psychological Society* 19:72.

Brunswik, E., 1956, "Perception and the Representive Design of Psychological Experiments" (2nd ed.), University of California Press, Berkeley, California.

Burns, N., and Cavey, L., 1957, Age differences in empathic ability among children, *Canadian Journal of Psychology* 11:227–230.

Cameron, N., 1947, "The Psychology of Behavior Disorders", Houghton-Mifflin, Boston.

Chandler, M. J., 1971, Egocentrism and childhood psychopathology: The development and application of measurement techniques, paper presented at the biennial meeting of the Society for Research in Child Development, Minneapolis.

Chandler, M. J., 1972, Egocentrism in normal and pathological child development, *in* "Determinants of Behavioral Development" F. Monks, W. Hartup, and J. DeWitt (eds.), Academic Press, New York.

Chandler, M. J., 1973a, Egocentrism and antisocial behavior: The assessment and training of social perspective-taking skills, *Developmental Psychology* 9:326–332.

Chandler, M. J., 1973b, Role theory and developmental research, paper presented at the 81st Annual Convention of the American Psychological Association, Montreal.

Chandler, M. J., 1974a, Accurate and accidental empathy, paper presented at the American Psychological Association Meeting, New Orleans, Louisiana.

Chandler, M. J., 1974b, The picture arrangement subtest of the WAIS as an index of social egocentrism: A comparative study of normal and emotionally disturbed children, *Journal of Abnormal Child Psychology* 1:340–349.

Chandler, M. J., and Greenspan, S., 1972, Ersatz egocentrism: A reply to H. Borke, *Developmental Psychology* 7:104–106.

Chandler, M. J., Helm, D., 1974, Developmental changes in the contribution of shared experience to social perspective-taking skills, paper presented at the Southeastern regional meeting of the Society for Research in Child Development, Chapel Hill.

Chandler, M. J., Greenspan, S., and Barenboim, C., 1973, Judgments of intentionality in response to videotaped and verbally presented moral dilemmas: The medium is the message, *Child Development* 44:311–320.

Chandler, M. J., Greenspan, S., and Barenboim, C., 1974, Assessment and training of role-taking and referential communication skills in institutionalized emotionally disturbed children, *Developmental Psychology* 10:546–553.

Cobliner, W. L., 1967, Psychoanalysis and the Geneva School of genetic psychology: Parelleles and counterparts, *International Journal of Psychiatry* 3:82–124.

Cohen, B. D., 1974, Referent communication disturbances in acute schizophrenia, *Journal of Abnormal Psychology* 83:1–13.

Cohen, B. D., Nachmani, G., and Rosenberg, S., 1974, Referential communication disturbances in acute schizophrenia, *Journal of Abnormal Psychology* 83(1):1–13.

Cooke, G. E., 1971, Conceptual learning in young children: A comparison of the effects of role, principle, and guided discovery strategies on conceptualization in first grade children, Unpublished doctoral dissertation, University of Oregon.

Cooper, R. C., and Flavell, J. H., 1975, Cognitive correlates of children's role-taking behavior, *Merrill-Palmer Quarterly,* in press.

Cottrell, L. W., and Dymond, R. F., 1949, The empathic response—a neglected field for research, *Psychiatry* 12:355–359.

Cowan, P. A., 1966, Cognitive egocentrism and social interaction in children, *American Psychologist* 21:623.

Cowan, P. A., 1967, The link between cognitive structures and social structures in two-child verbal interactions, paper presented at meetings of the Society for Research in Child Development.

Crockett, W. H., 1965, Cognitive complexity and impression formation, *in* "Progress in Experimental Personality Research" (Vol. 2), B. A. Maher (ed.), Academic Press, New York.

Deutsch, F., 1976, The effects of sex of subject and story character on preschoolers' perception of affective responses and interpersonal behavior in story sequences: A question of similarity of person, *Developmental Psychology,* in press.

DeVries, R., 1970, The development of role-taking as reflected by behavior of bright, average, and retarded children in a social guessing game, *Child Development* 41: 759–770.

Dimitrovsky, L., 1964, The ability to identify the emotional meaning of vocal expression at successive age levels, *in* "The Communication of Emotional Meaning" J. R. Davitz (ed.), McGraw-Hill, New York.

Dinnerstein, D., 1951, A study of the development of certain cognitive structures, unpublished doctoral dissertation, Graduate Faculty of Political and Social Science, New School for Social Research.

Dunham, H. W., 1944, The social personality of the catatonic–schizophrenic, *American Journal of Sociology* 49:508–518.

Dymond, R. F., Hughes, A. S., and Raabe, V. L., 1952, Measureable change in empathy with age, *Journal of Consulting Psychology* 16:202–206.

Dysinger, W. S., and Ruckmick, D., 1933, "The Emotional Responses of Children to the Motion Picture Situation," Macmillan, New York.

Feffer, M. H., 1959, The cognitive implications of role-taking behavior, *Journal of Personality* 27:152–168.

Feffer, M. H., 1970, A developmental analysis of interpersonal behavior, *Psychological Review* 77:197–214.

Feffer, M. H., and Gourevitch, V., 1960, Cognitive aspects of role-taking in children, *Journal of Personality* 28:383–396.

Feffer, M. H., and Suchotliff, L., 1966, Decentering implications of social interaction, *Journal of Personality and Social Psychology* 4:415–422.

Feshbach, N. D., 1973, Empathy: An interpersonal process, paper presented at the meeting of the American Psychological Association, Montreal.

Feshbach, N. D., and Feshbach, S., 1969, The relationship between empathy and aggression in two age groups, *Developmental Psychology* 1(2): 102–107.

Feshbach, N. D., and Roe, K., 1968, Empathy in six and seven-year-olds, *Child Development* 39:133–145.

Filer, A. A., 1972, Piagetian cognitive development in normal and emotionally disturbed children, unpublished doctoral dissertation, University of Rochester.

Flapan, D., 1968, "Children's Understanding of Social Interaction," Teacher's College Press, New York.

Flavell, J. H., 1970, Concept development, *in* "Carmichael's Manual of Child Psychology" (Vol. 1) P. H. Mussen (ed.), Wiley, New York, pp. 983–1059.

Flavell, J. H., 1973, The development of inferences about others, *in* "Understanding Other Persons" T. Mischel (ed.), Blackwell, Basil & Mott, Oxford, England, pp. 66–116.

Flavell, J., and Wohlwill, J., 1969, Formal and functional aspects of cognitive development, *in* "Studies in Cognitive Development," D. Elkind and J. Flavell: Essay in honor of Jean Piaget, New York, Oxford University Press.

Flavell, J. H., Botkin, P. T., Fry, C. L., Wright, J. W., and Jarvis, P. E., 1968, "The Development of Role-taking and Communication Skills in Children," Wiley, New York.

Furth, H. G., 1969, "Piaget and Knowledge: Theoretical Foundations," Prentice-Hall, Englewood Cliffs.

Gates, G. S., 1923, An experimental study of the growth of social perception, *Journal of Educational Psychology* 14:449–462.

Gilbert, D., 1969, The young child's awareness of affect, *Child Development* 39:619–636.

Glucksberg, S., and Krauss, R. M., 1967, What do people say after they have learned to talk?, *Merrill-Palmer Quarterly* 13:309–316.

Glucksberg, S., Krauss, R. M., and Weisberg, R., 1966, Referential communication in nursery school children: Methods and some preliminary findings, *Journal of Experimental Child Psychology* 3:333–342.

Goldschmid, M. L., 1968, The relation of conservation to emotional and environmental aspects of development, *Child Development* 39:579–589.

Gollin, E. S., 1951, Forming impressions of personality: A study of social perception, unpublished doctoral dissertation, Clark University.

Gollin, E. S., 1958, Organizational characteristics of social judgment: A developmental investigation, *Journal of Personality* 26:139–154.

Gough, H. G., 1948, A sociological theory of psychopathy, *American Journal of Sociology* 53:359–366.

Gough, H. G., and Peterson, D. R., 1952, The identification and measurement of predispositional factors in crime and delinquency, *Journal of Consulting Psychology* 16:207–212.

Gratch, G., 1964, Response alternation in children: A developmental study of orientations to uncertainty, *Vita Humana* 7:49–60.

Greenspan, S., 1973, The child's response to distress in others: A review of the experimental literature, unpublished manuscript.

Greenspan, S., and Chandler, M. J., 1973, The effects of referential communication training on cognitive egocentrism and social behavior in emotionally disturbed children, paper presented at the biennial meeting of the Society for Research in Child Development, Philadelphia.

Greenspan, S., Barenboim, C., and Chandler, M. J., 1974, Children's affective judgments in response to videotaped stories, paper presented at the Southeastern Regional meeting of the Society for Research in Child Development, Chapel Hill.

Greenspan, S., Barenboim, C., & Chandler, M., 1976, Empathy and pseudo-empathy: The affective judgments of first- and third-graders, *Journal of Genetic Psychology*, in press.

Guardo, C. J., and Bohan, J. B., 1971, Development of a sense of self-identity in children, *Child Development* 42:1909–1921.

Heider, F., 1958, "The Psychology of Interpersonal Relations," Wiley, New York.

Hoffman, M. L., 1974, Empathy, role-taking, guilt, and development of altruistic motives, *in* "Man and Morality" T. Likona (ed.), Holt, Rinehart and Winston, New York.

Iannotti, R. J., and Meacham, J. A., 1974, The nature, measurement, and development of empathy, paper presented at the meeting of the Eastern Psychology Association, Philadelphia.

Kagan, J., and Moss, H., 1960, Conceptual style and the use of affect labels, *Merrill-Palmer Quarterly* 6:40.

Keasey, C. B., 1971, Social participation as a factor in the moral development of preadolescence, *Developmental Psychology* 15:216–220.

Klein, R., 1970, Some factors influencing empathy in six and seven-year-old children varying in ethnic background, unpublished doctoral dissertation, University of California.

Kohlberg, L., 1958, The development of modes of moral thinking and choice in the years ten to sixteen, unpublished doctoral dissertation, University of Chicago.

Krauss, R. M., and Glucksberg, S., 1969, The development of communication: Competence as a function of age, *Child Development* 40:255–266.

Langer, J., 1969, "Theories of Development," Holt, Rinehart and Winston, New York.

Little, B. R., 1968, Age and sex differences in the use of psychological, role, and physicalistic constructs, *Bulletin of the British Psychological Society* 21:34.

Livesley, W. J., and Bromley, D. B., 1973, "Person Perception in Childhood and Adolescence," Wiley, New York.

Looft, W. R., 1972, Egocentrism and social interaction across the life span, *Psychological Bulletin* 78:73–92.

Martin, M., 1968, A role-taking theory of psychopathology, unpublished doctoral dissertation, University of Oregon.

Masangkay, Z. S., McCluskey, K. A., McIntyre, C. W., Sims-Knight, J., Vaughn, B. E., and Flavell, J. H., 1974, The early development of inferences about the visual percepts of others, *Child Development* 45:357–366.

Mood, D., Johnson, J., and Shantz, C. U., 1973, Young children's understanding of the affective states of others, paper presented at the Southeast Regional meeting of the Society for Research on Child Development.

Murphy, L. B., 1937, "Social Behavior and Child Personality: An Exploratory Study of Some Roots of Sympathy," Columbia University Press, New York.

Neale, J. M., 1966, Egocentrism in institutionalized and non-institutionalized children, *Child Development* 37:97–101.

Odier, C., 1956, "Anxiety and Magical Thinking," International University Press, New York.

Olshan, K., 1970, The multidimensional structure of person perception in children, unpublished doctoral dissertation, Rutgers–The State University.

Osborn, D. K., and Endsley, R. C., 1971, Emotional reactions of young children to T.V. violence, *Child Development* 42:321–331.

Peevers, B. H., and Secord, P. F., 1973, Developmental changes in attribution of descriptive concepts to persons, *Journal of Personality and Social Psychology* 27:120–128.

Piaget, J., 1970, Piaget's theory, *in* "Carmichael's Manual of Child Psychology," Wiley, New York, pp. 703–732.

Piaget, J., and Inhelder, B., 1956, "The Child's Conception of Space," Routledge & Kegan Paul, London.

Rogers, C., 1952, "Client-Centered Therapy," Houghton-Mifflin, Boston.

Rosenbach, D., 1968, Some factors affecting reconciliation of contradictory information on impression formation: An ontogenetic study of person perception, unpublished doctoral dissertation, Clark University.

Rosenberg, S., and Cohen, B. D., 1966, Referential processes of speakers and listeners, *Psychological Review* 73:208–231.

Rothenberg, B. B., 1970, Children's social sensitivity and their relationship to interpersonal competence and intellectual level, *Developmental Psychology* 2:335–350.

Rubin, K. H., 1973, Egocentrism in childhood: A unitary construct? *Child Development* 44:102–110.

Ruderman, D. L., 1961, An exploration of empathic ability in children and its relationship to several variables, unpublished doctoral dissertation, Columbia University.

Sarbin, T. R., 1954, Role theory, *in* "Handbook of Social Psychology" G. Lindzey (ed.), Addison-Wesley, Cambridge, Massachusetts.

Scarlett, H. H., Press, A. N., and Crockett, W. H., 1971, Children's descriptions of peers: A Wernerian developmental analysis, *Child Development* 42:439–453.

Selman, R. L., 1971, Taking another's perspective: Role-taking development in early childhood, *Child Development* 42:1721–1734.

Shantz, C. U., and Watson, J. S., 1971, Spatial abilities and spatial egocentrism in the young child, *Child Development* 42:171–181.

Shantz, C. U., and Wilson, K. E., 1972, Training communication skills in young children, *Child Development* 43:693–698.

Sigel, I. E., 1964, The attainment of concepts, *in* "Review of Child Development Research" (Vol. 1) M. L. Hoffman and L. W. Hoffman (eds.), Russell Sage Foundation, New York.

Snow, C. P., 1959, "The Two Cultures and the Scientific Revolution," Cambridge University Press, Cambridge.

Staub, E., 1970, A child in distress: The effect of focusing responsibility on children on their attempts to help, *Developmental Psychology* 2:152–153.

Staub, E., 1971, A child in distress: The influence of nurturance and modeling on children's attempts to help, *Developmental Psychology* 5:124–132.

Sternback, R. A., 1962, Assessing differential autonomic patterns in emotions, *Journal of Psychosomatic Research* 6:87–91.

Stotland, E., 1969, Exploratory investigations of empathy, *in* "Advances in Experimental Social Psychology" (Vol. 4) L. Berkowitz (ed.), Academic Press, New York, pp. 271–313.

Sullivan, E. V., and Hunt, D. E., 1967, Interpersonal and objective decentering as a function of age and social class, *Journal of Genetic Psychology* 110:199–210.

Sullivan, H. S., 1953, "The Interpersonal Theory of Psychiatry," Norton, New York.

Supnik, L., 1967, Source of information as a factor affecting the impression of others, unpublished doctoral dissertation, Clark University.

Thompson, L. A., 1968, Role playing ability and social adjustment in children, unpublished doctoral dissertation, University of Southern California.

Van Den Daele, L., 1969, Qualitative models in development analysis, *Developmental Psychology* 1:303–310.

Warren, M. Q., 1965, The community treatment project: An integration of theories of causation and correctional practice, paper read at the annual conference of the Illinois Academy of Criminology, Chicago.

Watts, A., 1944, "The Language and Mental Development of Children," Heath, Boston.

Werner, H., 1961, "Comparative Psychology of Mental Development," Science Editions, New York.

Whiteman, M., 1967, Children's conceptions of psychological causality, *Child Development* 38:143–155.

Wispe, L. G., 1968, Sympathy and empathy, *International Encyclopedia of the Social Sciences*, Vol. 15, Macmillan, New York.

Wolfe, R., 1963, The role of conceptual systems in cognitive functioning at varying levels of age and intelligence, *Journal of Personality* 31:108–123.

Woodworth, R. S., and Schlosberg, H., 1960, "Experimental Psychology: Revised Edition," Holt, New York.

Yarrow, M. R., and Campbell, J. D., 1963, Person perception in children, *Merrill-Palmer Quarterly* 9:57–72.

6

Memory from a Cognitive-Developmental Perspective

A Theoretical and Empirical Review*

LYNN S. LIBEN

1. Overview

Jean Piaget's early work was largely concerned with the identification and explanation of qualitative changes in the developing child's intellectual structure. Subsequent Genevan work has been concerned with clarifying the ways in which this general intellectual structure interacts with other cognitive processes such as perception (Piaget, 1969) and imagery (Piaget and Inhelder, 1971). More recently, Piaget and Inhelder (1973) have examined the relation between intelligence and memory, and it is this work that is reviewed in the present chapter.

The chapter begins with a discussion of the implications of a constructivist epistemology, in general, and of Piaget's theory, in particular, for memory. Piaget and Inhelder's (1973) empirical work on memory is

LYNN S. LIBEN ● The Pennsylvania State University, University Park, Pennsylvania.

*Support for the preparation of this chapter was provided, in part, by a grant from The University of Rochester, Rochester, New York. The author would like to express thanks to John A. Meacham, Sherri L. Oden, Carla J. Posnansky, and Arnold J. Sameroff for their many helpful comments on an earlier draft of this chapter.

then reviewed briefly. In the following section, some of the methodological and interpretive problems related to the Genevan research are discussed, and, where possible, these problems are evaluated by evidence from subsequent (non-Genevan) studies.

If it is the case that intellectual structure influences memory, it is necessary to identify the locus of the effect. Is the influence at the time of encoding, and/or during storage, and/or at the time of retrieval? The theoretical assumptions and empirical data related to these issues are discussed in section entitled "Loci of Operative Effects on Memory."

In the following section, Piaget and Inhelder's operative approach to memory is considered in relation to other mnemonic theories. These comparisons are included first, as a mechanism for clarifying the Genevan position and, second, as a way to evaluate how Piaget and Inhelder's approach adds to or modifies previous interpretations of the memory process.

2. The Operative Approach to Memory: Theory and Research

2.1. Theoretical Foundations

2.1.1. Acquisition of Knowledge

2.1.1.1. Epistemological Issues.   One characteristic of an organismic model such as Piaget's is that the organism is assumed to have a profound role in the construction of its own knowledge (Overton and Reese, 1973; Pepper, 1942; Reese and Overton, 1970).

> The main point of our theory is that knowledge results from *interactions* between the subject and the object, which are *richer* than what the objects can provide by themselves.... The problem we must solve, in order to explain cognitive development, is that of *invention* and not of mere copying ... the concepts of assimilation and accommodation and operational structures (which are created, not merely discovered, as a result of the subject's activities), are oriented toward this inventive construction which characterizes all living thought. (Piaget, 1970, pp. 713–714.)

Piaget's position contrasts sharply with the naive realism of the mechanistic model in which it is assumed that knowledge and organization are already in the environment, ready to be absorbed by an essentially passive organism.

The two models also differ in their conceptualization of developmental change. Under a copy theory of reality, the passage of years is presumed to provide an opportunity for additional exposure to the environment, thus permitting the organism to incorporate more and more information. Although these experiences alter the quantity of knowledge, they do not effect profound, qualitative changes in the way that the world is known, since the world's reality remains constant.

In contrast, the organismic approach proposes that there are qualitative changes with the passage of time. Through interactions between subject and object, schemes are restructured and coordinated, from the sensorimotor schemes of action through the operational schemes of formal thought.* As a consequence of these qualitative changes in cognitive structure, there are changes in the way that new stimulation from the environment is assimilated, understood, or known.

2.1.1.2. Operative and Figurative Functions. The constructivist nature of Piagetian theory is perhaps best understood in the context of operativity. "Operativity refers to the active aspect of the internal structure through which reality is assimilated and transformed into objects of practical or theoretical knowledge" (Furth, 1969, p. 57). As the internal structure changes, the objects of knowledge must change as well. For example, an infant might assimilate a partly filled bottle only to the sensorimotor scheme of grasping, whereas an 11-year-old child might assimilate the "identical" stimulus to a Euclidean spatial system, recognizing the invariant horizontality of the liquid. Although Piaget does not deny the reality of the tipped bottle, the child's knowledge of that bottle is the product of the child's interaction with the stimulus, in other words, of the way in which the child assimilates the environment to his or her operative schemes.

At the same time that the child's operative schemes transform the stimulus into objects of knowing, the child's figurative actions construct knowledge about the static, configural aspects of the stimulus. Operative functions "are characterized by their ability to transform objects. . . . The figurative functions, by contrast, have no tendency to transform objects, but tend to supply imitations of them in the broadest sense of the term" (Piaget and Inhelder, 1973, pp. 9–10). Although figurative functions—such as perception—have been referred to as "copying" ac-

---

*The English words *scheme* and *schema* are used in this paper to translate the French words *schème* and *schéma*, respectively, as in the definition of the two terms given by Inhelder (1969): "A *scheme* indicates the general structure of actions and operations. A *schema*, by contrast, is merely a simplified imagined representation of the result of a specific action" (p. 340). In the interests of clarity, even "direct" quotations from *Memory and Intelligence* (Piaget and Inhelder, 1973) have been modified to conform with this translation.

tivities (e.g., Ginsburg and Opper, 1969), they copy only insofar as they construct knowledge about *states* of reality rather than about transformations of reality. Even figurative knowledge is the result of the child's imitative activity rather than the passive reception of a predetermined reality.

Operative processes are thus intimately involved in the figurative processes. For example, in perceptual activity the intelligence determines where the eyes look, and hence influences what is seen and how it is interpreted. Thus, even figurative knowledge about states is a product both of the external configuration and of the subject's intelligence.

2.1 2. The Storage and Retrieval of Knowledge

2.1.2.1. Epistemological Issues. The issues discussed above in relation to the acquisition or construction of knowledge are equally applicable to the retention and retrieval of knowledge, that is, to memory.

According to classic associationism of the mechanistic model, memory is simply the storage of stimulus–response associations. The degree to which associations, or sets of associations, are engraved in memory is dependent upon the repetitiveness of the associations, the reinforcement of the associations, contiguities in space or time, and other environmental variables (e.g., see Anderson and Bower, 1973, for a historical review of associationism). These associations can decay over time through disuse or interference, or can be strengthened through repetition, new connections, and so on. Changes in memory under this model are quantitative in nature (Reese, 1973a, 1975).

In contrast, the holistic nature of the organismic model (Reese and Overton, 1970) dictates that memory be viewed as an integral part of the organism's structure. If it is true, first, that memory is integrally bound with the structures of intelligence, and second, that intellectual structure changes with development, then it must also be true that memory changes over time. These changes are not simply changes in the storage capacity or in the utilization and efficacy of memory strategies (although such changes do occur), but include changes in the memory code as well:

> It is customary to represent memory as a system of coding and decoding which naturally assumes the intervention of a *code*. But curiously enough, this code itself has been studied very little, as if it were taken for granted that the code stays the same throughout development. (Piaget, 1968, pp. 1–2.)

Piaget and Inhelder (1973) have studied changes in this code that occur in conjunction with the changing intellectual structure of the child.

2.1.2.2. Generalized versus Specific Aspects of Memory. As discussed above, the acquisition of knowledge involves both the operative functions, relating to that which is generalizable, and the figurative functions, concerning the specific nature of an external event. A similar contrast may be drawn in memory between the concepts of memory in the "broad" or "wide" sense and memory in the "strict" sense. Memory in the wide sense involves the conservation of schemes, where this conservation is the ability "to reproduce whatever can be generalized in a system of actions or operations (habitual, sensorimotor, conceptual, operational and other schemes)" (Piaget and Inhelder, 1973, p. 4). Conservation of schemes is mnemonic only in a general sense, since schemes are preserved by their very functioning. For example, one need not "remember" that if 12 plus 7 equals 19 then 7 plus 12 also equals 19. Such knowledge is necessarily contained in the structure of concrete operations. What distinguishes memory in the broad sense from intelligence in general is that the former is concerned specifically with the comprehension of the past, while the latter is concerned with the present and future:

> Seen in this light, the "memory in the wider sense" becomes an integral part of the intelligence, except that it is oriented, not towards present reality with its possible transformations, but towards the comprehension of the past, with its limited and frozen characteristics. (Piaget and Inhelder, 1973, p. 399.)

Memory in the strict sense bears on "situations, processes or objects as are singular and recognized or recalled as such" (Piaget and Inhelder, 1973, p. 5). However, just as figurative knowledge is influenced by operative knowledge, so memory in the strict sense is embedded in the general conservation of schemes. Thus, even memories for specific events at identifiable points in time interact with the schemes of intelligence.

2.1.2.3. Recognition, Reconstruction, and Reproduction. Piaget and Inhelder (1973) draw an additional distinction among three types of memory—recognition, reconstruction, and reproduction—with respect to the underlying figurative functions and, thus, with respect to their developmental levels.

The most primitive of the three, both ontogenetically and phylogentically, is recognition. According to Piaget, "recognition is an intrinsic part of every sensory-motor habit" (Furth, 1969, p. 150). Thus, the representation of the original stimulus allows identification on the basis of familiar perceptual and sensorimotor schemes. At the other end of the continuum of difficulty is reproduction: in the absence of external stimuli, recall must be based on a representation such as the mental image. Between the other two lies reconstruction, which combines recognition (materials are present) and evocation (materials must be rearranged). Reconstruction is particularly conducive to recall since the act of manipulating the materials tends to reactivate the schemes which had been used during the original assimilation of the memory stimulus. Thus, the three types of memory are dependent upon different figurative processes: recognition upon perception, reconstruction upon imitations, and reproduction upon mental imagery.

2.2. Genevan Research on Memory

Two kinds of evidence are needed to support the theoretical position that memories are dependent upon operativity. First, cross-sectional data must demonstrate that children of different developmental stages reproduce, reconstruct, and recognize stimuli differently, in accord with their operative levels. Second, longitudinal data must show that particular children's memories change in conjunction with their developing operative schemes.

2.2.1. The Research Paradigm

Piaget and Inhelder (1973) collected both cross-sectional and longitudinal data to study the hypothesized relation between memory and operativity using a research paradigm in which children of different developmental levels are shown a stimulus and are tested for recall after varying intervals, typically after one or two weeks and again after several months. The stimulus is never re-presented during the intervening period. Several aspects of the procedure have been varied across studies: children have been asked to describe or copy the stimulus while it is in view; reconstruction and recognition tasks have been added to reproduction tasks; and the number and spacing of recall intervals have been changed. In addition, memory stimuli have been varied both in form (pictures versus physical events) and content, including stimuli related to: (a) "Additive Logical Structures," in which a single dimension is relevant, as in seriation and transitivity; (b) "Multiplicative Logical Structures," in which two dimensions must be coordinated, as in multiplicative matrices; (c) "Causal Structures," in which cause and effect must be linked, as in an event which shows transmitted motion; and (d) "Spatial Structures," in which there are spatial configurations and transformations, as in rotations of geometrical forms.

Only highlights of Piaget and Inhelder's (1973) results are described here; the interested reader is referred to either of two brief reviews of this work (Inhelder, 1969; Piaget, 1968), or to *Memory and Intelligence* in which this work is reported in its entirety (Piaget and Inhelder, 1973).

2.2.2. Cross-Sectional and Longitudinal Data

The cross-sectional data from Piaget and Inhelder's (1973) studies supported an operative interpretation of memory. That is, reproductions of conceptual stimuli were like the responses typically produced by children of the same age on related anticipatory tasks. For example, one week after seeing a fully seriated array of sticks, many 3- to 4-year-old children drew the picture from memory as alternating large and small sticks, or as uncoordinated triplets. These errors are comparable to those committed when children of this age attempt to construct an ordered series *de novo*.

The longitudinal data from these studies are even more striking. Rather than revealing consistent decrements in memory over time—as would be expected if there is simply a fading memory trace—some memories *improved* over time, improvements which are assumed to reflect operative growth. In the most striking demonstration of this phenomenon of "long-term memory improvement," Piaget and Inhelder (1973) found that, of the children shown a seriated array of sticks, 74% produced more highly seriated drawings at the later recall session (after 8 months) than they had at an earlier recall session (after one week). Furthermore, even the memories of the other 26% of the subjects did not deteriorate but remained stable. While this study provided the strongest evidence of memory improvement, studies using other stimuli generally revealed improvement in at least one-third of the subjects tested.

It should be noted that memory improvement is expected only if there is a relatively clear correspondence between the stimulus and a simple operation. Memories may deteriorate, instead, when "two or more schemes are in active conflict because of nonsynchronous development" (Inhelder, 1969, p. 349). Piaget and Inhelder (1973) examined memory for a stimulus in which there was numerical and spatial conflict, specifically, a stimulus in which four matches were arranged in a horizontal line, with another four matches beneath the line in a flattened "W". Deteriorations in memory were noted because of the subjects' tendencies to equalize the end points of the two sets of matches (e.g., by adding extra lines to the zigzag configuration, or by extending the length of each segment of the "W"). It is likely, however, that if subjects had been retested after another long retention interval, there would have been memory improvements as the result of the growing coordination of the two previously conflicting schemes.

A second type of stimulus which would not be expected to elicit memory improvements is one in which arbitrary relations are presented. To test this expectation, Piaget and Inhelder (1973) showed children a series of geometric figures, each having a long or short, horizontal or vertical crossbar. Although there were some possibilities for the application of classification schemes (pairing geometric forms; contrasting horizontal versus vertical crossbars and short versus long crossbars), the specific combinations of elements were arbitrary, and hence not subject to classification. As expected, there were no long-term memory improvements for this stimulus because "our model did not readily lend itself to logical schematization (classification and ordination), and because its contingent aspects were considerable" (Piaget and Inhelder, 1973, p. 349).

2.2.2.1. *Comparisons among Memory Tasks.* The study using geometric figures described above was also designed to investigate the proposed relation between reconstructive and reproductive memory. Following the reproduction task at the 1-week and 6-month memory sessions, subjects were given the materials needed to reconstruct the original stimulus. As predicted, reconstructions were more like the original stimulus than were reproductions.

The finding that reconstructions are more advanced than reproductions was also confirmed in several other studies reported in *Memory and Intelligence,* but only when the schemes needed for recall were within the subject's level of development. When the necessary schemes surpassed the subject's level entirely, reconstruction and reproduction methods elicited similarly low levels of performance. A similar generalization may be made about the findings relating performance on reproduction and recognition tasks: If the subject does not understand the stimulus at all, performance on recognition and reproduction tasks is comparable; if the schemes are within the subject's general level, recognition performance is superior. Piaget and Inhelder (1973) summarize these findings as follows:

> In brief, the mnemonic process seems to be largely continuous and integral, with the schemes proper to recognition preparing the way for those proper to reconstruction and recall. The former nevertheless have a much greater accommodation potential, and hence a much greater figurative power, because, in the case of recognition, the model is present and perceptible, and all the memory has to do is to distinguish it from other models. It is this union between imitative (and later, figurative) accommodation and schematizing assimilation which explains all the mnemonic successes or deformations we have observed, so much so that all distinctions between the so-called "raw" memory and the logical memory, and hence the intelligence, appear to be purely arbitrary. (p. 408.)

2.3. Summary

In summary, Piaget and Inhelder (1973) have extended an organismic view of development to memory, hypothesizing that memory cannot be separated from the intellectual structure of the child. This assumption, coupled with the position that intellectual structures change qualitatively with development, yields two corollaries: The first is that children with different intellectual structures will remember "identical" stimuli differently. The second is that, as a particular child's intellectual structure changes, there will be a parallel restructuring of the memory code.

In support of these two corollaries, Piaget and Inhelder (1973) have presented research which demonstrates, first, that there are differences in the ways that children of different stages recall stimuli—differences which are comparable to those found in anticipatory tasks of similar kinds; and, second, that there are improvements in memory over long retention intervals which follow the path of general operative advancement.

Questions may be raised, however, about the Genevan methodology, findings, and interpretations. In the following section, some of these questions are discussed, and the empirical evidence bearing upon the answers to these questions is reviewed.

3. An Empirical and Methodological Review

3.1. Introduction

The Genevan work on memory has been greeted by a "reflexive skepticism" (Altemeyer et al., 1969) comparable to that generated by much of Piaget's earlier work. In defense of the skeptics, however, it should be noted that although Piaget and Inhelder (1973) did predict the dependence of memory on operational schemes, their initial observation of long-term memory *improvement* was serendipitous and apparently surprising.

> This led us to the (fairly obvious) conclusion that the memory of children is bound up ... with the way in which they interpret a model .... But while this result was what anyone taking the operational... view would only have expected, a chance encounter with one of our subjects persuaded us to look further into the matter. When this subject, who had been questioned about the memory test six months earlier, turned up for quite a

different investigation, and was asked what he remembered of the first one, his reply showed that he did, in fact, recall it, but that he had schematized it further. (p. x)

Subsequent investigations have been directed toward answering two major questions: First, does the phenomenon of long-term memory improvement exist, and, if so, is Piaget and Inhelder's (1973) interpretation of it correct? The answer to the first of these questions is almost certainly "yes." Long-term memory improvements have been found in studies using stimuli related to a variety of operational schemes (Altemeyer *et al.*, 1969; Crowley, 1975; Dahlem, 1968, 1969; Finkel and Crowley, 1973; Furth *et al.*, 1974; Liben, 1974, 1975b).

The answer to the second question is not, however, as clear. As has been true in other research examining memory change [for example, investigations of memory for simple pictures in the *Gestalt* tradition (see Riley, 1962) and research on reminiscence (see Buxton, 1943)], there are methodological problems linked with the test–retest paradigm which make it difficult to interpret findings conclusively (Carey, 1971). In the following sections, some of these problems and the evidence bearing on them are discussed.

3.2. Long-Term Memory Improvements: Operative and Nonoperative Explanations

3.2.1. Effects of Repeated Testing

One problem with the test–retest paradigm is that subjects obtain additional practice with every session. Thus, subjects may perform better at later recall sessions, not because of operative development, but because of additional practice on the recall task. If practice is responsible for improvement, subjects who participate in extra recall sessions should perform better than subjects who participate in fewer recall sessions during an identical time interval.

In three studies, different numbers of recall sessions have been given to different groups of subjects. In one of these studies, Dahlem (1969) showed kindergarten children an array of fully seriated sticks and asked them to reconstruct the array either (a) after 6 months only; (b) after 1 week and 6 months; (c) immediately after viewing, after 1 week and 6 months; or (d) immediately, twice after 1 week, and again after 6 months. Dahlem found no differences in 6-month memory performance as a function of the number of earlier recall sessions.

The findings of a second study, by Finkel and Crowley (1973), were less clear. Three groups of kindergarten subjects were shown one of three stimuli, each related to a different level of seriation. One stimulus was a fully seriated array of sticks (stimulus III), and two stimuli were "preseriated" arrays, one showing three small, four medium, and three large sticks in order (stimulus IIB), and the other alternating small and large sticks (stimulus IIA). One-third of each group of subjects was tested for recall after 5 months only; another third was tested after 1 week and 5 months, and the remaining third was tested after 1 day, 1 week, and 5 months. Performance differed as a function of the number of earlier recall sessions. For subjects who saw the fully seriated array, repeated testing had a positive effect on memory. For subjects who saw the preseriated arrays, repeated testing seemed to increase the incidence of memory change, although not consistently in a positive direction. It should be noted, however, that Finkel and Crowley (1973) included a recognition task within each recall session, and thus the significant effect of repeated testing may have resulted from repeated exposure to the recognition choices, rather than from practice in the recall task per se.

In the third study, Crowley (1975) also used both fully seriated (III) and preseriated (IIB) arrays. Memories were tested (a) after 6 months or (b) after 1 week and 4 months, using only reproduction tasks. Crowley found that subjects who were not given the 1-week task were more likely to forget the stimulus completely by 4 months, but given that the sticks were remembered at all, no differences in operative levels of memory performance were evident as a function of prior testing.

Thus, of the three studies in which the number of recall sessions was varied, only one (Finkel and Crowley, 1973) found that repeated testing affected the level of performance. Since this study was also the only one to include a recognition task in the recall sessions, practice per se probably affects performance less than does repeated exposure to the stimulus. It should be noted that a significant effect of either factor would suggest that some of the improvements found by Piaget and Inhelder (1973) resulted from artifacts, since their studies often included recognition and/or reconstruction tasks in the early recall sessions. It is important that future research study the effects of both these variables carefully by varying the number and content of recall sessions, and by using stimuli other than seriated arrays.

3.2.2. Attention to Relevant Attributes of Stimuli

Another possible nonoperative explanation of the child's better performance at the second recall session is that the initial recall session alerts the child to the relevant aspects of the stimulus. Altemeyer *et al.* (1969), for example, were concerned that, when a seriated array was the memory stimulus, mentioning "size" at the 1-week recall session would cause the child to restructure his or her memory in relation to size. To test this hypothesis, one group of kindergarten children was asked to "... draw me a picture and show me how *big* the sticks we looked at were" (p. 846), while the second group was asked to reproduce the array without reference to size. No significant differences were found between the groups, either at the 1-week session or in patterns of memory change over time.

Adams (1973) suggested that long-term memory improvements might be explained by improvements in children's abilities to understand the task. If this were true, children who were made aware of the relevant aspect of the task prior to the memory task would not show the usual long-term improvements. To test this hypothesis, Adams gave kindergarten children discrimination tasks prior to presenting a seriated memory stimulus. In the experimental group the relevant dimension of the discrimination task concerned seriation, while in the control group it concerned geometric shapes. Contrary to the hypothesis, an equivalent amount of improvement on the memory task was found in the experimental and control groups. (Since only change data were reported, it is unknown whether the two pretraining procedures affected absolute levels of performance differently.) The findings from the studies by Altemeyer *et al.* (1969) and Adams (1973), then, suggest that memory improvement is not highly susceptible to the extent to which the experimenter draws the child's attention to the operative component of the stimulus.

3.2.3. Evaluating Long-Term Regressions

3.2.3.1. What Is the Null Hypothesis? When Piaget and Inhelder (1973) noted the impressiveness of memory improvement, they compared the number of observed improvements to the number they presume is predicted by trace theories of memory, that is, to zero. Altemeyer *et al.* (1969) translated this comparison into Kolmogorov-Smirnov tests, in which the observed number of memory improvements is compared to the expected number under the alternative hypothesis that all memories remain stable or deteriorate over time. Using this procedure, Altemeyer *et al.* (1969) and Liben (1974, 1975b) found highly significant long-term memory improvement.

It should be apparent, however, that if temporary changes occur in variables such as attention and motivation, the child's performance could vary even without underlying changes in memory. This reason for change in performance, however, should lead to approximately equal numbers of memory progressions as regressions, since sometimes the child's motivation, attention, etc., would be better in the second session and sometimes better in the first. In contrast, if memory change reflects operative development, changes should be predominately positive, reflecting advancing operative schemes.

  3.2.3.2. *Memory Progression versus Memory Regression.* The number of memory regressions versus the number of memory progressions found by Genevan researchers differs markedly from that found by subsequent investigators. Although Piaget (1968) has not denied that under some circumstances memory regressions occur, his reports suggest that they are relatively uncommon. With a fully seriated array of sticks, Piaget (1968) found memory improvements in 74% of the subjects, and "not one instance of deterioration" (p. 4). Similarly, using an M-shaped series of sticks, 38% of the subjects improved, while none showed memory deterioration. With a stimulus of a tipped, half-filled bottle, some regressions were reported (11%), but the incidence was small in comparison to the memory progressions (31%).

  Dahlem (1968) replicated the low incidence of memory regressions with an array of seriated sticks as the memory stimulus. She found that all subjects who reconstructed the stimulus perfectly at one week also reconstructed it perfectly at six months. In addition, of subjects whose memories were imperfect at 1 week, very few showed poorer performance by 6 months. In a later study, Altemeyer *et al.* (1969) did find some regressions. These investigators did not, however, consider these regressions troublesome since there were almost two times as many progressions as regressions, and since the progressions typically represented large gains and the regressions small losses.

  Other studies, however, have found a strikingly high incidence of memory regressions. In a second study using a seriated stimulus, Dahlem (1969) again found stability in perfect performance. This time, however, she found that subjects with imperfect 1-week performance were equally likely to deteriorate as to advance by the 6-month recall session. Murray and Bausell (1971) found many more regressions than improvements among first- and second-grade children who were asked to reproduce stimuli related to conservation and seriation. It should be noted, however, that the criteria used to determine the accuracy of recall included several relatively figurative components of the stimuli which may have led to an artifically high incidence of deterioration (see Liben, 1976).

  Finkel and Crowley (1973) also found a high incidence of regressions. Of subjects who were shown a fully seriated array (a replication of Piaget and Inhelder's stimulus), about 20% improved from 1 week to 5 months, while 37% deteriorated. Of subjects who were shown the preseriation stimulus IIB, approximately equal percentages improved (40%) as deteriorated (38%). Of subjects who were shown the preseriation stimulus IIA, almost twice as many subjects improved (32%) as regressed (18%). This last finding provides only tentative support for the predicted higher incidence of progressions, however, since stimulus IIA was at a low developmental level, thereby providing much room for improvement but little for deterioration. The recognition data from the Finkel and Crowley study showed greater memory stability than did the reproduction data, but, again, the changes which did occur were approximately evenly divided between progressions and regressions.

Crowley (1975) also found an equivalent amount of memory regression and progression among subjects who had been shown a fully seriated stimulus. Of subjects who had been shown preseriation stimulus IIB, however, progressions were far more common than regressions. One reason for the discrepancy between the Finkel and Crowley (1973) and Crowley (1975) studies may be that a recognition task was included in the former but not in the latter study.

Furth et al. (1974), using four stimuli related to spatial transformations and numerical sequence, also found "massive regressions" (p. 70). Similarly, Liben (1974) found about as many deteriorations as improvements in memories for the horizontal water line in a tipped bottle and again in a later study (Liben, 1975b) for stimuli related to seriation, horizontality, and verticality concepts.

The high incidence of memory regressions relative to the number of memory improvements is a troublesome finding for Piaget and Inhelder's operative explanation of long-term memory improvement. While it would be relatively simple to excuse memory regressions as a function of "performance" variables, it is not clear why one would not, then, explain memory improvements in the same manner.

3.2.3.3. The Role of Figurative Memory. An alternative explanation of regressions which has been suggested (Furth et al., 1974; Liben, 1974; Crowley, 1975) is that regressions are produced by subjects whose developmental levels are low throughout the period of the investigation but whose 1-week reproductions are figuratively based. Thus, at 1 week, these subjects reproduce the operative element correctly on the basis of good figurative memory, but at 6 months reproduce it inaccurately because the figurative memory has faded and operative schemes have taken control.

One way to examine the power of figurative memory is to show different stimuli (e.g., fully seriated versus unseriated arrays) to different subjects and compare their reproductions. If memory is entirely dependent upon subjects' operative levels, reproductions by the two groups should be indistinguishable; if memory is largely figurative, reproductions should differ, reflecting the differences in stimuli.

Several studies have varied stimuli in this way. Altemeyer et al. (1969) showed some children a fully seriated array, and other children a randomly arranged array of sticks; Finkel and Crowley (1973) showed one fully seriated array and two preseriated (IIA, IIB) arrays; Crowley (1975) presented one fully seriated array and one preseriated array (IIB); Liben (1974) showed one stimulus in which liquid in a tipped bottle was shown correctly (horizontal group), and another stimulus in which the liquid was shown parallel to the bottle's base (nonhorizontal group), and, finally, Samuels (1975) showed some children a videotaped event which demonstrated conservation reasoning (C event) and other children an event which demonstrated nonconservation reasoning (NC event).

In all reports which give information about absolute levels of memory performance (some provide only data on memory change), it is clear that memories were strongly influenced by the memory stimulus actually shown to the child, thus confirming the power of figurative memory. In the horizontality study (Liben, 1974), extremely different patterns of reproductions were produced by the horizontal and nonhorizontal groups. Of the scorable responses produced at the 1-week and 6-month recall sessions, subjects in the horizontal group most often produced drawings with a horizontal water level, while subjects in the nonhorizontal group most often drew liquid parallel to the base of the tilted bottle. In the study on conservation (Samuels, 1975), recall consistently matched the event (C or NC) viewed by the child, given that there was sufficient recall to permit coding of the response. Using seriation, Crowley (1975) found that subjects' reproductions differed at one week as a function of the stimulus (III or IIB) shown to the subject but, unlike the other two studies, found that this difference dissipated by the 4-month recall session.

These findings support the notion of a strong figurative memory. The results of the study by Liben (1974), and to a lesser extent those of the study by Samuels (1975), suggest that figurative control extends through the later recall session. Crowley's (1975) results, on the other hand, support the notion that figurative memory fades and operativity acquires increasing control over time. One reason for the discrepancy between the two sets of studies may be that in the Liben (1974) and

Samuels (1975) studies, the alternative stimulus was operatively *incorrect* (water levels *are* horizontal; number *is* conserved through displacement) whereas in the Crowley (1975) study, the alternative stimulus was not contrary to physical fact (there is no physical truth which requires that sticks be arranged in size order). Thus, the continued power of figurative memory in the Liben and Samuels studies may be the result of the subjects' having specifically encoded and remembered an error in the stimulus. It is also possible that the amount of time required for operativity to restructure figurative memory varies as a function of the concept involved (seriation, horizontality, conservation) and as a function of the particular figurative context in which the operative component is embedded. Additional studies which vary the kinds of alternative stimuli and extend the retention intervals are needed to evaluate the hypothesis that memory regressions represent weakening figurative control and growing operative control.

3.2.3.4. Regressions: Theoretical Implications. Even if empirical support were found for the interpretation of memory regression offered above, regressions would still be problematic in Piagetian theory, since, as noted earlier, operative schemes are presumed to influence even the subject's figurative activities. Thus, if one explains regressions on the basis that operativity affects memory only weeks or months after the stimulus was viewed, the construct of operativity is weakened. A second problem with this explanation is that it is difficult to imagine how one could determine whether a child's reproduction at a particular point in time is "figurative" or "operative." One might posit that whenever a child's reproduction exceeds his or her operative level, memory must be figurative; but, without a mechanism for determining when memory is under figurative or operative control, this proposition is circular and untestable.

3.2.4. Short-Term Changes in Memory

Another approach that may be used to evaluate the operative explanation of memory improvements is to examine memory change within short periods of time. If operativity takes control of memory immediately, there should be no major differences among drawings produced immediately after viewing the stimulus, after several hours, after a day, or after one or two weeks, since operative schemes would generally not be expected to change appreciably within this time period. On the other hand, if reproductions made immediately after viewing the stimulus are still under figurative control and only later become operatively directed, then later drawings might be inferior to earlier drawings.

In either case, improvements in drawings between two early recall sessions would not be expected to occur except as artifacts of the retesting paradigm (e.g., practice in drawing) or as a consequence of uncommonly large short-term operative improvement.

Piaget and Inhelder (1973) included recall sessions immediately or 1 hour after stimulus presentation in several of their studies. In general, they found that memories remained stable between the early recall session and a session one week later. For example, between 1 hour and 1 week, memories for a double-classification stimulus remained stable in 44 of 58 subjects, deteriorated slightly in 10, and improved in 4; similarly, memories for horizontality of liquid remained stable in 21 subjects, progressed in 4, and regressed in 4.

In a study by Furth *et al.* (1974), subjects were asked either to copy four stimuli (Copy condition) or to reproduce them immediately following presentation (Noncopy condition), followed by recall sessions after 2 hours, 2 weeks, 6 months, and 1 year. The drawings of the Copy and Noncopy conditions were very similar at the initial and subsequent sessions, with only slight decreases in accuracy from the first through the third recall sessions. Dahlem (1969) also failed to find significant differences between 1-day and 1-week reproductions of a seriated array. However, she reported these data for the group as a whole, so that while it is possible that there was indeed little change, it is also possible that there was considerable change in individual subjects, but that these changes were approximately evenly divided between progressions and regressions, thus producing no overall group effect.

Finkel and Crowley (1973) reported short-term change on an individual basis and did find considerable change between reproductions at 1 day and 1 week. Of subjects who were shown a fully seriated array, only 54% produced drawings at the same developmental level at 1 day and 1 week, 32% had improved by one week, and 14% showed a decline in performance. Unfortunately, the meaning of this short-term improvement is unclear since a recognition task was included in the 1-day recall session. Additional studies which omit recognition tasks but which analyze short-term memory changes in individual subjects are needed.

3.2.5. Memory for Arbitrary Stimuli

Another means of assessing the viability of the operative explanation of memory improvement is to examine the course of memory for relatively arbitrary stimuli. If operative development underlies memory improvement, then improvement would be expected only for the components of stimuli which fit into developing operative schemes. On the other hand, if artifacts of retesting (e.g., subjects' increasing comfort) account for improvement, then memory should improve for all aspects of the stimuli, including those which are arbitrary.

Voyat (reported in Piaget and Inhelder, 1973) showed one group of 4- to 7-year-old children an array of seriated sticks which varied in color. Although about 33% of these children showed long-term memory improvement for seriation, only about 13% showed improvement for the colors. It is also interesting to note that, while no long-term regressions were found by Voyat with respect to seriation, about two-thirds of the subjects regressed with respect to color memory.

As described earlier, Piaget and Inhelder (1973) also studied memory for a stimulus with arbitrary combinations (geometric forms with horizontal and vertical crossbars). As expected, memories after 6 months were generally worse than those at 1 week (in 16 of 19 subjects); a few remained stable (3 of 19); and none progressed. A second group of subjects that was tested a full year after seeing the stimulus did show memory improvements, but only with respect to the regularities (e.g., forms were reproduced in pairs), and not with respect to the arbitrary combinations.

Liben (1974) examined memory changes separately for the operative component (horizontal water level) and figurative components (e.g., bottle shape, color) of the memory stimulus. Although some long-term improvements were found for figurative components, they were less common than improvements in the operative sphere. Finally, Crowley (1975) showed one group of children a memory stimulus unrelated to the rest of her seriation stimuli (a face) and found no evidence for memory improvement. The results of these studies suggest that although there may be occasional improvements for arbitrary elements of a stimulus, most progress occurs in relation to elements that are closely tied to operative schemes.

3.2.6. Memory for Operatively Primitive Stimuli

A related way of examining the role of artifacts versus operativity in improvement is to use memory stimuli that are operatively primitive. If memory reflects operative development, memory changes should be in the direction of higher and higher operative levels, and hence become less and less like the original primitive memory stimulus. If, on the other hand, artifacts (such as enhanced motivation) are responsible for memory improvements, then changes should be in the direction of a better and better match to the stimulus, even though the stimulus itself is operatively primitive.

In the first study to use this paradigm (Altemeyer *et al.*, 1969), one group of kindergarten children was shown a completely unorganized array of different-sized sticks. If artifacts account for long-term memory improvements, reproductions should be more unordered at 6 months than at 1 week. If operative growth accounts for memory improvement, reproductions should become increasingly ordered. Results supported the operative explanation. In a second study of this kind, Furth *et al.* (1974) showed kindergarten, first-, second-, and fourth-grade children an operatively incorrect drawing related to the Euclidean concept of verticality (a chimney at right angles to the oblique roof of a house). Using a three-category system of "unmodified" drawings (chimney reproduced as shown), "relevant" drawings (chimney reproduced in a true vertical position), and "nonrelevant" drawings (chimney omitted entirely), Furth *et al.* found a consistent increase in the percentages of relevant drawings with age, both cross-sectionally and longitudinally. A similar trend was evident in a study by Liben (1974) in which the operatively incorrect stimulus was a picture in which liquid was shown parallel to the base of a tipped bottle. The long-term changes which occurred generally showed improvements with respect to the concept of horizontality, rather than with respect to the incorrect stimulus picture.

In the three studies discussed above, the operatively incorrect stimulus was extremely primitive. Thus, if a subject reproduced the stimulus as it actually appeared at the early recall session (i.e., random arrangement of sticks; chimney at right angles to roof; liquid parallel to base of the tipped bottle), there was actually little opportunity to show operative deterioration, and much opportunity to demonstrate operative advance. It would be preferable for such studies to use operatively incorrect stimuli which lie between extremely primitive and fully developed operative levels. With such stimuli, later reproductions could evolve toward either higher or lower operative levels.

The preseriated array IIB used in the studies by Finkel and Crowley (1973) and Crowley (1975) meets this requirement. As noted earlier, the findings from these two studies are not in agreement: the former found an equivalent incidence of change toward higher and lower operative levels, while the latter found a far greater incidence of change toward higher operative levels. Since the Crowley study did not include a recognition task, these results are probably less confounded, and thus should be weighed more heavily. On balance, then, results suggest that improvements generally occur with respect to the operative concept rather than with respect to the figural stimulus itself, although research using less primitive stimuli is needed to support this conclusion more firmly.

3.2.7. Summary

The preceding review presents evidence that artifacts do contribute to the long-term memory improvements found by Piaget and Inhelder (1973), but that such artifacts alone cannot account for the observed patterns of memory. An assessment of the relative contributions of artifacts and operativity to memory change will be possible only after data from additional research are available. In the interim, other means of evaluating the operative approach must be used.

3.3. The Relation between Operative Level and Memory Performance

Another means of evaluating the operative theory of memory is to examine evidence for the hypothesized relation between operative level and memory. The operative account of long-term memory improvement would be strengthened by evidence that: (a) cross-sectional differences in memory correspond to cross-sectional differences in operative levels; (b) there is a correspondence, within subjects, between operative levels and memories; and (c) there is a correspondence, within subjects, between long-term memory change and long-term operative change. The data bearing on these relations are discussed below.

3.3.1. Cross-Sectional Evidence

As discussed earlier, Piaget and Inhelder (1973) present data from a variety of memory tasks to show that memories correspond to developmental progressions which have been documented in earlier work. Only two subsequent Piagetian memory studies have included cross-sectional designs. Furth et al. (1974) gave kindergarten, first-, second-, and fourth-grade children memory tasks related to spatial transformations and numerical progression. Pictures related to spatial transformations (a half-filled tipped glass, a chimney on a roof, and a falling stick) were assumed to tap highly advanced operative concepts, while a picture related to numerical sequence (a series of "dominoes") was assumed to be operatively easier. With the exception of the operatively incorrect chimney stimulus (described earlier), older children produced more unmodified drawings than did younger children, a finding that is consistent with the operative theory of memory.

In the other long-term memory study in which cross-sectional data were collected, Liben (1975b) tested kindergarten and fourth-grade children with stimuli related to three concepts which represent a wide operative range—seriation, horizontality, and verticality. While preoperational kindergarten children should be advancing significantly with respect to seriation, they should be at an extremely primitive level with respect to the Euclidean concepts, advancing only minimally during a 6-month interval. In contrast, fourth-grade children should have highly developed seriation schemes, but their Euclidean concepts should be in transition. The prediction was therefore made that kindergarten children would reproduce the seriation stimuli at mixed operative levels and show long-term memory improvements for these stimuli, but would be consistently poor at reproducing the Euclidean stimuli and show little improvement over the retention interval. It was also expected that fourth-grade children would reproduce the seriation stimuli accurately at both recall sessions, but would show long-term memory improvements for the Euclidean stimuli. The findings supported these predictions. Thus, the cross-sectional data, although limited, do confirm Piaget and Inhelder's (1973) position.

3.3.2. Within-Subject Analyses: Short-Term and Longitudinal Data

To support the operative explanation of memory, it is necessary to show that there is a correspondence between particular children's operative levels and memories. As has been noted elsewhere (Liben, 1974), without separate measures of operative level and memory, evidence for their relation is circular. If, for example, a given child's reproduction of some stimulus is poor, the difficulty may be attributed to inadequately developed operative schemes. If another child's memory is good, the success may be explained by a highly developed operative level. The same is true for explanations of memory change: if one child's memory improves, the improvement may be attributed to operative development; if another child's memory remains stable, it may be assumed that the underlying schemes have not advanced during the intervening period.

Within-subject data on operative level and memory were not consistently collected by Piaget and Inhelder (1973). In some studies the relation between the two was implied by presenting the memory data as a function of subjects' ages. In other studies, operative level was assessed at the beginning or conclusion of the memory task only, thus failing to provide data on operative *change*. Furthermore, the within-subject comparisons were not always made systematically and objectively. For example, in their study on long-term memory for seriation, Piaget and Inhelder (1973) report:

> In general, there was a fairly marked correspondence between the subject's operational level and the organization of his memory after the lapse of one week. The only notable exception . . . was that a number of subjects at Stage II, though unable to construct the correct series even by trial and error, nevertheless made the correct drawings. . . . However, the importance of this exception should not be exaggerated; among sixty subjects from three to 5;11 . . . they accounted for only seven cases; one 3;9-year-old (taught at a private school where particular attention was paid to drawing); two 4-year-olds (taught at the same place), and four 5-year-olds. (pp. 36–37.)

Thus, there appears to be a tendency to evaluate confirming and disconfirming evidence differently. When the expected relation between the two indices is found, the findings are taken as support for the operative theory of memory. When the expected relation is not found, reasons for the mismatch are hypothesized, as in the "drawing instruction" reason given above.

The early replication studies that measured both operative level and memory within subjects also did so at either the beginning or end of the memory task only. Dahlem (1969) assessed subjects' operative levels at the conclusion of the memory task only and found that subjects who reconstructed the seriation stimulus correctly at six months were significantly more likely to perform perfectly on another seriation (transfer) task than subjects who had not reconstructed the series perfectly. However, the relation between performance on the memory and transfer tasks was not perfect: 12 of the 40 subjects who had reproduced the seriation stimulus perfectly performed imperfectly on the transfer task, while 8 of the 89 subjects who had performed imperfectly on the memory task performed perfectly on the transfer task.

Murray and Bausell (1970) examined the relation between operative level and immediate memory by giving first- and second-grade children conservation, seriation, and horizontality problems, and then asking them to reproduce the task stimuli. For example, children were shown a picture containing two rows of objects (balls and cups), equal in number and spatially aligned. In the next picture, one row of objects (cups) was spread out and the child was asked whether both rows still contained the same number of objects. In the memory task, children were then asked to "draw the rows of balls and cups after one was moved" (p. 335). The evidence for the relation between memory and operative level was mixed: performance on the conceptual task and the memory task was significantly related in conservation of number and in seriation, but not in conservation of amount and length or in horizontality. As noted earlier, however, the criteria used in scoring the memory drawings included arbitrary components of the stimulus (e.g., in conservation of number the absolute number of objects shown on the two rows had to be correct, with the cups, not balls, in the longer row), a factor which may have led to an attenuation of the correspondence between the two measures.

Neither the study by Dahlem (1969) nor that by Murray and Bausell (1970, 1971) provided data on operative change, since operativity was assessed only once. In addition, no data on the effect of pretesting were obtained, despite the common assumption that an operative pretest necessarily interferes with performance on subsequent memory tasks (Finkel and Crowley, 1973). More recently, investigators have collected data on both these issues by testing memory and later operative levels in subjects who were, or were not, given an earlier operative pretest.

In one such study, Liben (1974) assessed operative levels of one group of fifth-grade children both before and after a memory task related to horizontality, and assessed operative levels of a second group of children following the memory task only. No differences were found between the two groups' performance on either the later operative assessment or the memory task, thus justifying the use of within-subject data. Significant correlations between operative levels and memories were found both at the early and late recall sessions, although the correlations were low. Contrary to expectation, memory change and operative change did not systematically coincide. One possible explanation for the failure to find a closer relation between the two measures is the choice of horizontality for the memory task, since recent work (Harris *et al.*, 1975; Liben, 1975c; Thomas *et al.*, 1973) has shown that even a large number of adolescents and adults fail horizontality tasks. Another possible explanation of the findings is that the assessment procedure may have been too brief to provide a reliable measure of the horizontality concept.

In a second study using a within-subjects design (Liben, 1975b), modifications were made to overcome difficulties with the earlier study. First, an extensive operative assessment procedure was used; second, memory stimuli tapped concepts of seriation and verticality as well as horizontality; and, third, the operative components of the stimuli were embedded in pictures and stories designed to enhance the attractiveness and meaningfulness of the stimuli (e.g., a picture of a cat tipping a fish bowl was used as a horizontality stimulus). Despite these methodological improvements, results were similar to the earlier study: significant but low correlations were found between performance on the operative tasks and memory performance, and no systematic relation between memory change and operative change was found. It should be noted, however, that while participation in the assessment procedure had no apparent influence on memory performance, kindergarten boys did perform better on the spatial tasks of the final assessment procedure if they had participated in the initial assessment task. This finding suggests the need for continued caution in interpreting data from studies using within-subjects designs.

To obtain within-subject data on operative level and memory, Samuels (1975) gave all subjects a conservation assessment task prior to and following the memory task. The memory stimulus was an event presented on video tape which showed children who verbalized either conservation or nonconservation reasoning. As noted earlier, subjects' memories reflected the event actually witnessed rather than their own cognitive levels. Other differences were evident, however, as a function of the subjects' cognitive levels. For example, at the 1-day recall session, Stage 3 children were more likely than Stage 2 children to offer conservation explanations of the nonconservation event (e.g., "The girl had more cars because she took more"). In addition, subjects who saw an event dissonant with their own cognitive level (e.g., Stage 3 subjects who witnessed the nonconservation event) were more likely to remember the event only vaguely by the 5-month recall session. Thus, although recall of the event itself did not differ with cognitive stage, there was evidence of operative influence. The child's skill in reproducing the verbal event may be interpreted as assimilation "at nothing other than a verbal level" [Piaget, quoted in Duckworth, 1964, p. 3], and thus, the reasons given by subjects probably reflect their real recall of the event more meaningfully. Of the small number of subjects who did show scorable long-term memory change, parallel changes in operative level were not evident.

The relation between operative level and memory was also studied by Crowley (1975). Half of her subjects were given a construction task to assess seriation before and after the memory task, while all subjects were assessed at the conclusion of the memory task. With a fully seriated array as the memory stimulus, the relation between memories and operative level was poor at 1 week but good at 4 months, an inconsistency Crowley attributes to the initial strength of figurative memory. For the preseriated array (IIB), no significant differences were found between memory scores and seriation (assessment) scores, either at the beginning or end of the study. However, the relation between long-term changes in memory and seriation scores was poor for both groups, with the correspondence poorer in the group seeing the fully seriated stimulus. Again, Crowley explains this discrepancy as a result of the spuriously high 1-week memory scores for this group as a consequence of figurative memory.

3.3.3. Conclusions

The evidence from studies which included measures of both memory and operative level does not support an operative interpretation of long-term memory improvement as unequivocally as do the cross-sectional data. Some significant associations between memory and operativity have been found (Crowley, 1975; Dahlem, 1969; Liben, 1974, 1975b; Murray and Bausell, 1970), but their magnitudes have been low. Furthermore, change scores have not coincided, although it should be recognized that change scores are by their nature unreliable since they compound two measurement errors (e.g., see Nunnally, 1973).

It is possible that the failure to find a strong relationship between memory and operative assessment results from various "performance" variables. For example, the two tasks may engage subjects' attention and motivation differently. Furthermore, the very techniques that have been used to reduce intertask confusion may have reduced intertask comparability. Different experimenters, for example, might elicit different levels of performance. It is unlikely that this is a major factor, however, since even when the same person gave both memory and assessment procedures (Liben, 1974), a poor relation between the two obtained. Another possible explanation rests in the use of different tasks to measure operative level and memory. Although attempts have been made to use operatively equivalent but figuratively different tasks for the two measures (e.g., in the study by Liben, 1975b, a plumb line on a crane was used for the memory task while a plumb line in a car was used in the assessment procedure), it is possible that the contents were not, in fact, operatively equivalent.

There have also been differences in the amount of stimulus support provided by the memory and assessment tasks. In the study by Liben (1974), for example, the memory task was entirely without figurative support (the subject was required to reproduce the memory stimulus on a blank piece of paper), while the assessment task had extensive figurative support (the subject was required to draw liquid in outlines of tipped bottles). In some cases, even the mode of response varied between the two tasks. For example, in the Samuels (1975) study, operative levels were assessed by a standard manipulative conservation procedure, whereas memory was assessed via verbal report; in the Crowley (1975) and Liben (1975b) studies, developmental level for seriation was assessed with a construction task, while memory was assessed by a production task which required drawing of the sticks.

In addition, it is still not entirely clear that assessing a subject's operative level prior to the memory task has no effect on later performance. While Liben (1974) and Crowley (1975) found no effect of initial assessment either on memory or on later operative performance, Liben (1975b) did find one effect. Although this effect was relatively small and isolated, it suggests that conclusions based on studies using withinsubjects designs must still be considered tentative. To continue to provide information on the effects of initial assessment, future research should consistently include some subjects who are assessed at the conclusion of the memory task only.

3.4. Summary

In summary, there is evidence that performance on long-term memory tasks is not highly susceptible to small variations in procedures. Negligible effects were found as a function of instructions at the one-week recall session (Altemeyer *et al.*, 1969); pretraining on relevant stimulus characteristics (Adams, 1973); repeated testing (Crowley, 1975; Dahlem, 1969); copying the stimulus during initial presentation (Furth *et al.*, 1974); or participating in an assessment task prior to the memory task (Crowley, 1975; Liben, 1974, 1975b). These results suggest that most procedural variations across Piaget and Inhelder's (1973) studies probably did not confound results significantly. On the other hand, a significant effect of repeated testing was found when a recognition task was included in the recall session (Finkel and Crowley, 1973). This finding raises some question about the validity of the long-term memory improvements found in the many studies by Piaget and Inhelder (1973) in which recognition and/or reconstruction tasks were included in the first recall session. A more conservative approach that would still provide some information about relative performance on different types of memory tasks is to postpone recognition and reconstruction tasks until after the end of the final recall session, as in the studies by Liben (1974, 1975b).

The operative explanation of memory improvement was supported by the findings that: (a) memories for figurative or arbitrary aspects of stimuli improved little over long intervals (Crowley, 1975; Liben, 1974; Voyat, in Piaget & Inhelder, 1973); (b) memory changes for operatively incorrect stimuli were generally toward higher operative levels rather than toward greater figurative accuracy (Altemeyer *et al.*, 1969; Furth *et al.*, 1974; Liben, 1974); and (c) performance on operative assessment tasks and memory are significantly related (Crowley, 1975; Dahlem, 1969; Liben, 1974, 1975b). However, the operative explanation was weakened by: (a) the high number of memory regressions (Crowley, 1975; Finkel and Crowley, 1973; Furth *et al.*, 1974; Liben, 1974, 1975b); (b) the weakness or inconsistency of the relation between operative levels and memory, (Crowley, 1975; Dahlem, 1969; Liben, 1974, 1975b; Murray and Bausell, 1970); and (c) the poor correspondence between changes in memory and changes in operative level (Crowley, 1975; Liben, 1974, 1975b; Samuels, 1975).

As discussed earlier, "performance" variables may explain the negative findings. However, such explanations are valuable only insofar as they are testable. For example, one could obtain measures on the operative comparability of figuratively different tasks used in operative and memory tasks, but it would be difficult to prove or disprove that two tasks engage subjects' attention differently.

A second explanation, also discussed earlier, is that memories remain figurative for some unspecified period of time, and only later fall under operative control. This explanation would account for several otherwise troublesome findings, specifically, the high number of memory regressions, the weakness of the relation between operative levels and memories, and the lack of correspondence between operative change and memory change. Before this explanation can be considered useful, however, it is necessary to find a way to determine if a particular memory is figuratively or operatively controlled. Furthermore, as noted earlier, such an explanation seems to weaken the power of the operativity construct. The question concerning when operativity influences memory is an important one, and it is this issue which is discussed in the following section.

4. Loci of Operative Effects on Memory

Piaget and Inhelder (1973) have explicitly hypothesized that operative schemes are effective throughout all phases of memory:

> the schemes serve as instruments of mnemonic organization and, as such, they are active during retention and recall no less than during the fixation of memories. (p. 383.)

In the following discussion, the theory and evidence related to the loci of operative effects is examined.

4.1. Perception of the Stimulus

The first question that may be posed in discussing the loci of operative effects on memory is whether the subject even *sees* the stimulus as it is presented. For the skeptic, there is no satisfactory answer to this question. If the child does *not* perceive the stimulus correctly, it may be argued that effects of operativity are not upon memory but rather upon perception. On the other hand, if the child *does* perceive the stimulus correctly, the notion that operativity influences even figurative processes is weakened.

The resolution of this problem lies in the relation between the operative schemes available to the subject versus the operative schemes needed for a high level (coordinated) assimilation of the stimulus, and, second, in the genetic order of the figurative processes. According to Piaget, if the child's operative level is near that tapped by the stimulus, then the child should be able to perceive it veridically (as shown by an ability to copy the stimulus correctly), even though he or she cannot reproduce the stimulus correctly immediately after it has been removed. On the other hand, if the subject's own level is far beneath that required for the highest-level assimilation of the stimulus, then even perception is poor. For example, Piaget and Inhelder (1973) report that when 3-year-old children were asked to copy a seriated stimulus, their copies were no better than their reproductions; but when 4-year-old children were given the same tasks, copies were like the stimulus, although reproductions were not.*

These findings reflect the genetic progression of the figurative instruments from perception, to imitation, to imagery. Higher level functioning is possible in the presence of the stimulus than in its absence, since in the former case the subject may use primitive perceptual functions to copy the stimulus, while in the latter case, the subject must use representational support of mental imagery to reproduce the model. As discussed earlier, this genetic order also explains the differences in performance on recognition, reconstruction, and reproduction tasks.

---

*Results from the "copy" tasks also prove that memory improvement cannot be attributed to advancing drawing skills: if children are able to copy the stimulus when it is in full view, they must have the graphic skills needed to reproduce it in a memory task as well.

4.2. Memory Fixation

According to Piaget and Inhelder (1973), operativity has an immediate effect on memory, so that distortions occur "just as soon as the model is removed from sight... as soon as perception ceases to act as a restraint" (p. 95). They offer the following explanation:

> ... the memory-image is at first an imitative symbol and not an extension of perception.... It follows that, in his attempts to reconstruct what he has seen but no longer perceives, the subject is reduced to symbolizing as faithfully as he can what assimilations to his schemes he made in the presence of the model: he will accordingly produce the most faithful image possible of what he has seen, but an image that is more faithful to his thought than to his perception, simply because his thought persists while the perception has gone and cannot be replaced by the image. (p. 95.)

It is important to emphasize Piaget and Inhelder's point, i.e., that memory images are not copies or visual afterimages of the stimuli, but rather represent the way in which the subject has understood or assimilated the model. Piaget and Inhelder (1973) present evidence from several studies to support this interpretation. For example, they report that one hour after showing subjects a picture of a tipped bottle, reproductions corresponded to the "Child's notions in... deductive anticipations rather than to that of his perceptions" (p. 302).

Several subsequent investigators have included tests for immediate memory in their studies. Dahlem (1968) had kindergarten children reconstruct a seriated array immediately after viewing, and found that these reconstructions were better than those made one week later. However, in a later study using the same tasks and similar children, Dahlem (1969) found that immediate and one-week reproductions were equally poor. No explanation of this discrepancy is apparent. Furthermore, although Dahlem (1968, 1969) discussed relative performance at the two sessions, little information about the absolute levels of performance was given, so that the influence of operativity on immediate memory is unclear.

As described earlier, Murray and Bausell (1970) included a test of immediate memory in their study of first- and second-grade children's memory for stimuli related to conservation, seriation, and horizontality. The stimuli related to conservation of amount and length were reproduced correctly by approximately 60% of the children; the stimulus on conservation of number was reproduced correctly by only about 30%; seriation was recalled correctly by almost 80%; and horizontality by less than 10%. These figures do suggest that children have difficulty recalling stimuli related to conceptually difficult concepts. As noted earlier, however, the relation between performance on the operative pretest and success on the memory task was substantial in only two of the five sets of stimuli (see pp. 170–171).

King and Blackstock (1971, cited in Blackstock and King, 1973) found that children (no ages reported) "could not copy a seriated configuration any better with the model present than with the model removed" (p. 256). In a later study (Blackstock and King, 1973), 4- and 5-year-old children were asked either to "recognize" or to "reconstruct" seriated arrays. In the recognition task, the subject watched the experimenter place an M&M candy under the only one of four arrays that was fully seriated. The four arrays were then spun rapidly so that they "disappeared" in a blur for 7 seconds, and then the child was asked to find the M&M. In the reconstruction task, the experimenter and subject each had a set of unseriated rods. While the sticks were partially obscured, the experimenter rearranged his sticks into a seriated row, and then asked the subject to "Make yours just like I made mine" (p. 257). Although this task is referred to as a "reconstruction" task, the experimenter's model was apparently present during the subject's construction, and thus actually posed a copying task. Unfortunately for the present issue, the two tasks were distinguished, not only by the absence or presence of the stimulus, but also by the mode of response (recognition versus reconstruction) and by the degree of feedback. Thus, the data comparing performance on copy versus reproduction tasks are uninterpretable. However, the absolute levels of performance were reported and show that, even with the model present, the percentage of subjects who constructed the seriated array correctly ranged from 47% to 73%, depending upon the particular array used. (Although significant age effects were found, absolute levels of performance were not reported as a function of age.)

Only the study by Furth et al. (1974) was specifically designed to permit evaluation of the differences between copy and reproduction drawings. Kindergarten, first-, second-, and fourth-grade children in one group were asked to copy each of four stimuli, while children of the same ages in a second group were asked to reproduce the stimuli immediately after viewing. The levels of drawings did seem to reflect subjects' operative levels (inferred from age), although, at least for some stimuli, this was equally true for copies and reproductions. For example, with a drawing of a half-filled tipped glass as the stimulus, the horizontal water level was copied correctly by 8%, 29%, 37%, and 60% of the children in each age level, respectively, and was reproduced correctly by 6%, 25%, 44%, and 77% of the children in the second group.

The findings reviewed above do provide some support for Piaget and Inhelder's contention that the child's image is "faithful to his thought," since, in many cases, immediate reproductions were distorted. On the other hand, the high incidence of memory regressions discussed earlier suggests that at least some subjects are able to extend their figurative perceptions, even for long periods of time, without apparent operative support.

Two approaches might be used to investigate the importance of this inconsistency. One approach is to study individual differences in memory skills among children. For example, if it could be shown that the children who regress over time have particularly good memories even for relatively arbitrary stimuli, then the regressions in the operative realm would be less disturbing. An extreme case, for example, would be to study "eidetic imagers" (Leask et al., 1969), whose memories would presumably reflect figural rather than operative encoding.

A second approach would be to examine the relation between immediate memory and operative level more finely, perhaps using within-subject measures. To be consistent with Piaget and Inhelder's theory, findings from such studies should show that the subjects with good immediate memories and later deteriorations are transitional with respect to the concept tapped by the stimulus.

4.3. Memory Retrieval

Piaget and Inhelder (1973) also assert that operative schemes affect processes used at the time of recall.

> Now, reconstruction most certainly involves the utilization of what schemes are at the subject's disposal during recall ... the (more or less fragmentary) conservation of a memory, must be based on that of the schemes (of habit and intelligence) and must normally be completed by a reconstruction involving the schemes currently employed. (p. 21.)

Evidence that the schemes "currently employed" differ with developmental level is available from the innumerable Piagetian studies which have demonstrated developmental changes in performance on logical and infralogical tasks. Insofar as applying schemes to a fragmentary memory is similar to responding to an anticipatory task (i.e., a task that assesses the subject's intellectual level, such as a conservation task), developmental differences in memory performance should be found. These differences would occur even if children at different developmental levels retained identical memories of the original stimulus prior to the application of reconstructive processes.

One way in which researchers have tried to dissect the role of reconstruction from memory fixation and retention is by using tasks which tap the child's decoding processes but which do not provide an opportunity for encoding, a situation that occurs when memory stimuli are omitted entirely. If different reconstructive processes are in part responsible for the developmental differences in memory drawings, there should be age differences in the drawings produced in these "no stimulus" tasks.

Altemeyer et al. (1969) suggested, for example, that if a child's spontaneous tendency to apply seriation schemes increases with age, then drawings elicited at later recall sessions would be more patterned than earlier drawings. To test this interpretation, they devised a "Spontaneous Drawing Task" in which kindergarten through second-grade children were told: "I have a picture of something in my mind, and I would like you to guess what it looks like and draw a picture of it ... here is the hint. *I am thinking about some sticks.* Now draw me a picture of some sticks" (p. 854). Unexpectedly, older children did not draw patterned arrays more often than younger children. In fact, very few children of any age produced patterned arrays of any kind. It was concluded, therefore, that the improvements found in memory tasks must be directly linked to the memory process in some way.

As has been suggested earlier (Liben, 1975a), the findings of Altemeyer et al. (1969) are surprising in light of the presumed operative influence on constructive processes. A possible explanation of the failure to find age differences in spontaneous seriation is that other characteristics of children's drawings vary with age, thereby obscuring differences in the application of seriation schemes. To test this hypothesis, Liben (1975a) repeated the procedure used by Altemeyer et al. (1969), but examined drawings for characteristics other than seriation.

As in the study by Altemeyer et al., seriated drawings were uncommon at all ages. Other age differences in drawings were, however, evident. Given that a drawing was unseriated, older children typically incorporated the sticks into representational drawings such as tepees, campfires, or log cabins, while younger children typically scattered the sticks randomly. Liben (1975a) also examines drawings made by children in a second group in which the following highly informative hint was given: "I am thinking of 10 sticks, all of different sizes. They are all standing up straight in a row. Now try to draw me a picture like the one

I am thinking about" (p. 122). With this hint, older children did seriate their drawings significantly more than did younger children.

The results of this study (Liben, 1975a) confirm that there are changing tendencies to apply increasingly advanced operative schemes to drawing tasks, even when subjects are not specifically asked to do so. This finding suggests that some of the memory improvements observed in Piagetian long-term memory experiments can be attributed to changes in the processes used at the time of retrieval. This finding need not, however, be construed as evidence against the operative approach to memory, but instead suggests that at least some of operativity's effect occurs at the time of recall.

4.4. Memory Retention

Although there is evidence that operativity affects the processes at the time of acquisition and recall, Piaget and Inhelder (1973) argue that these processes cannot alone account for reproductions: "We are therefore dealing with inferences . . . but inferences whose premises are derived simultaneously from schemes and authentic memories" (p. 387). As evidence of the contribution of authentic memory, Piaget and Inhelder (1973) point out that some reproductions that occur would never have been drawn if operative schemes were simply oriented toward the present reality. For example, several months after seeing a drawing of a partly filled bottle on its side, some 5-year-old children reproduced the bottle upright but drew the liquid coating the side of the bottle. The fact that the child turned the bottle back on its base is presumed to involve "recourse to habitual schemes" (p. 386), while the fact that the child drew the liquid on the side of the bottle involves "recourse to the memory-image" (pp. 386–387). The latter effect is attributed to memory because children at this age who are asked to anticipate water level in an upright container almost always respond correctly.

Subsequent research has also confirmed the dual roles of authentic memory and reconstruction. A comparison of the results from the studies by Altemeyer et al. (1969) and Liben (1975a), for example, confirms the insufficiency of either process alone. If operativity were itself responsible for drawings produced in seriation memory tasks, then merely hinting at the content of the stimulus should be sufficient to elicit drawings comparable to those usually produced in memory tasks. The vague hint used by Altemeyer et al. (1969), however, elicited few patterned drawings and showed no age differences. The informative hint used by Liben (1975a) did elicit patterned drawings and age differences, suggesting that the information specified in this hint is more similar to what is usually present in memory. It is apparent, however, that even this information does not mimic authentic memory completely, since the drawings produced with informative hint are not entirely comparable to those produced in memory tasks by children of the same age. For example, of the drawings produced by kindergarten children who were given the informative hint (Liben, 1975a), 35% were patterned and 10% were perfectly seriated. In comparison, of the drawings produced in a memory task given to the following year's kindergarten children from the same school (Liben, 1975b), 53% of the 1-week reproductions showed some patterning and 23% were perfectly seriated; 56% of the 5-month reproductions showed some patterning and 35% were perfectly seriated. It may be inferred from the differences in the drawings elicited by the two tasks that authentic memories contain more information than a simple record of the general content of the memory stimulus.

Piaget and Inhelder (1973) argue further that these authentic memories are subject to the influence of operativity *during* the course of retention. While it is possible that memory traces are continually revised with every advance in operative schemes, the only way in which this hypothesis may be tested is by finding a way to examine the memory image without involving retrieval processes. As explained in the earlier discussion of the fixation of memories, Piaget and Inhelder (1973) propose that the memory image is a symbolization of the way in which the subject assimilated the model to his or her operative schemes, rather than an extension of a perception. Since reproduction tasks—rather than recognition tasks—tap these memory images, and, since retrieval is necessarily involved in reproduction tasks, the memory image cannot be studied in isolation, and thus the proposal that operativity affects memory during retention appears to be untestable.

4.5. Are These Mnemonic Effects?

The evidence reviewed above supports the hypothesis that operativity affects at least the encoding and retrieval of memories. One question which has arisen in discussion of Piagetian memory research is whether an effect of operativity at retrieval should be interpreted as an effect on *memory*. In its extreme form, this question was posed by Altemeyer et al. (1969) as: "Is Memory Involved at All?" (p. 853). While it is readily apparent that children are truly remembering the content of the original stimuli (with few exceptions, children draw sticks if they are shown sticks, and bottles if shown bottles), it is less obvious that their renditions of the operative components of stimuli are mnemonic in origin, except in the broad sense of the conservation of schemes. Instead, there may be a constant trace throughout the retention interval, with different decoding mechanisms applied to this trace at the two recall sessions (Altemeyer *et al.*, 1969; Bresson, 1970; Carey, 1971). In some cases the contribution of authentic memory is unmistakable (e.g., reproductions of upright bottles with liquid coating the side), but in most cases, authentic memories and reconstructions cannot be distinguished.

In one sense, whether or not decoding changes are classified as mnemonic is a matter of definition. If memory is defined as only that which is stored, then the processes applied at acquisition and retrieval should not be included. If, however, memory is defined as that which enables one to reproduce or recognize what has been experienced in the past, then acquisition and retrieval are appropriately included in memory. Past developmental research on memory supports the second definition, since it has been concerned with changes in acquisition processes (e.g., Belmont and Butterfield, 1969; Flavell, 1970; Flavell *et al.*, 1970; Hagen, 1972; Hagen *et al.*, 1970), and, more recently, with retrieval processes (e.g., Kreutzer *et al.*, 1975; Ritter *et al.*, 1973; Salatas and Flavell, 1975). Furthermore, past studies of memory capacity *per se* have not found important developmental changes in the storage component of memory (see Belmont and Butterfield, 1969). On the basis of developmental research traditions, then, operative effects on any one of three processes—acquisition, storage, or retrieval—may be considered as effects on memory.

In a second sense, whether or not constructive processes are included in the domain of memory is a model issue. As discussed by Reese and Overton (1970), one of the corollaries of an organismic model is holism, described by Werner and Kaplan (1963) as an assumption which

> maintains that any local organ or activity is dependent upon the context, field or whole of which it is a constitutive part: its properties and functional significance are, in a large measure determined by this larger whole or context. (p. 3.)

In keeping with this corollary, "The Memory" cannot be separated from the rest of the intellectual system, a position expressed well by Bartlett (1932):

> It is perfectly true that nobody can set a ring around Memory, and explain it from within itself. ... Remembering is not a completely independent function, entirely distinct from perceiving, imaging, or even from constructive thinking, but it has intimate relations with them all. (pp. 12–13.)

The research reviewed earlier supports the notion of "intimate relations" between memory and other knowing actions. To exclude the constructive processes from what is "really memory" is, therefore, to reject
the model in which the Piagetian analysis of memory is rooted.

4.6. Summary

In summary, Piaget and Inhelder have proposed that operativity is
influential at the time of memory fixation, retrieval, and during the
retention interval itself. Support for the hypothesized operative effect at
fixation is found in studies of immediate memory: children's immediate
reproductions contain errors comparable to those made on anticipatory
tasks. As noted earlier, however, most long-term memory studies have
found a high incidence of memory regression. This finding suggests that
some children's memory images are more faithful to their perceptions
than to their thoughts even for surprisingly long periods of time.
Additional research is needed to evaluate the significance of this apparent inconsistency, e.g., determining whether children with particularly
strong figurative memories are unusually good at reproducing arbitrary
configurations, and/or are transitional with respect to the concept tapped by the memory stimulus.

There is also evidence which suggests that there are developmental
changes in the spontaneous application of operative schemes, changes
which may partly account for the cross-sectional and longitudinal differences in performance on memory tasks. Reproductions produced in
memory tasks are not, however, perfectly congruent with drawings
produced in anticipation tasks or in "no stimulus" tasks. These differences imply that the child's performance on memory tasks cannot be
accounted for by constructive strategies alone, but must include authentic memory as well.

While it is clear from the data that authentic memory plays an important role in determining children's reproductions, it is not clear that
Piaget and Inhelder are correct that operativity affects these authentic
memories *during* storage. To validate this hypothesis it would be necessary to examine the memory image without the involvement of the
subject's retrieval processes, an apparent impossibility within the operative framework.

Some researchers have questioned the legitimacy of calling operative effects on fixation and retrieval "memory" effects. Inclusion of such
effects within memory may be justified on the basis that past develop-

mental research has included acquisition and retrieval processes in the study of memory, and on the basis that the organismic model precludes the dissection of memory from constructive and reconstructive strategies.

5. The Operative Approach in the Context of Other Mnemonic Theories

5.1. Introduction

In the following sections, Piaget and Inhelder's operative approach to memory is considered in the context of alternative theories of memory.

Piaget and Inhelder (1973) most often contrast their own approach to the "classical view":

> In the classical view, according to which the memory is nothing but conservation, memory transformations must necessarily result in mnemonic distortions or memory losses. (p. 383.)

> As against this view, our observations have shown that besides these distortions or omissions, there can also be qualitative mnemonic improvements with time. (p. 384.)

The "classical view" to which Piaget and Inhelder (1973) refer is, of course, associationism. There is little question that Piaget and Inhelder's approach differs fundamentally from classic associationism. Some of these differences are highlighted below. It should be noted, however, that three of the characteristics of Piaget and Inhelder's approach which make it so unlike associationism—an active organism, memory in context, and changing (not simply fading) memory traces—do not consistently divide their theory from other approaches to memory.

With regard to the activity of the organism, Kausler (1970) has noted that contemporary theories have rejected the notion of a passive organism posited by their associationistic ancestry:

> The most striking change involves the model's conception of the subject as a passive, rote participant in the learning of a list of verbal units. Current views accept as commonplace frequent transformations of any one of the primary elements of the learning process—S units, R units, and first-order S-R habits—by an active, cognitive subject. (p. 308.)

Similarly, Piaget and Inhelder are not alone in analyzing memory in context. Bartlett, Neisser, Jenkins, and the dialecticians have all incorporated contexts of various kinds in their approaches to memory.

Finally, Piaget and Inhelder are not unique in positing changing memories. While in the "classic" view memory is conceptualized as a deteriorating trace, other theories have included notions of changing memories. In some cases, the traces themselves are assumed to undergo modification (e.g., Gestalt), while in other cases, it is performance that changes (e.g., as a result of differences in retrieval cues, as suggested by Tulving).

In the following sections, some alternative approaches to memory are discussed with particular emphasis on their view of organismic activity, contextual analysis, and memory change. Three warnings must precede this discussion. First, it should be noted that no attempt has been made to provide exhaustive coverage, either in the selection of approaches or in the treatment of those approaches which have been included. Second, although some attempt has been made to discuss similar theories together (e.g., highly contextual approaches), the sequence in which theories are discussed is not meant to imply order along a continuum (e.g., a "passive-to-active" continuum). A unilinear order of this kind is precluded by the fact that theories differ on several dimensions simultaneously. Third, neither the delineation of approaches nor the placement of theorists within these approaches is mutually exclusive. That is, elements of one approach may be contained in another (e.g., studies of the organization of memory may be considered as a subset of information processing), while a particular theorist's research may be applicable to more than one approach simultaneously. Thus, the divisions used should be interpreted as a heuristic device meant to facilitate comparisons to Piaget and Inhelder's position, rather than as a scheme for organizing and evaluating all important approaches to memory.

5.2. Alternative Approaches to Memory

5.2.1. Associationism

As noted above, one of the most extreme comparisons which may be drawn is between associationism and the operative approach to memory. Anderson and Bower (1973) identify four basic assumptions common to associationistic theories—connectionism, reductionism, sensationalism, and mechanism—all of which are linked to a mechanistic model (Reese and Overton, 1970). The definitions given by Anderson and Bower (1973) for each of the metafeatures demonstrate the ubiquity of world views. About sensationalism, for example, they say: "Certainly no one would quarrel with the claim that representations of sensory data constitute part of the contents of the mind" (p. 11). What, in Piagetian theory, would "representations of sensory data" look like? The most similar concept would probably be representations (images) derived from the organism's accommodative activity (imitation) which occurred in the presence of the stimulus. While the associationist's "representations" are linked to an epistemology of naive realism, the organismic theorist's "representations" are linked with constructivism, and thus operative and associationistic theories begin with strikingly different assumptions regarding the content of memory.

Is this difference also found in their views on the course of memory over time? In associationism:

> The process of dissolution was assumed to be passive, in the case of disuse or decay theory, or to be active, in the case of interference theory. Disuse or decay refers to the dissipation of associations with the passage of time; use or repetition maintains the bonds, which otherwise dissipate. (Reese, 1973a, p. 405.)

Even in the "active" process of interference, new associations are impinging on a still passive organism from the environment.

Thus, both the content of memory and its course over time differ radically in associationism and in Piaget's operative approach. Do the retrieval processes differ as well? In associationistic theories, retrieval is based upon chains of past associations which are reactivated. A quotation from Hobbes illustrates this position emphatically, if archaically:

> The *cause* of the *coherence* or consequence of one conception to another is their first *coherence* or consequence at that *time* when they are produced by sense: as for example, from St. Andrew the mind runneth to St. Peter, because their names are read together; from St. Peter to *stone*, for the same cause; from *stone* to *foundation* because we see them together; and for the same cause, from foundation to *church*, and from church to *people*, and from people to *tumult*; and according to this example, the mind may run almost from anything to anything. (Cited in Deese, 1965, p. 3; original source: Hobbes, 1839, p. 15.)

As we have seen earlier, the retrieval of a "trace" in Piagetian theory is assumed to be a much more active process, with the subject's operative schemes restructuring both the trace and the reconstruction at time of recall.

It is clear, then, that all aspects of memory are assumed to be fundamentally different in the two approaches, a situation which derives from the fundamental difference between the root metaphors of the two theories—machine versus organism. As noted above, however, there have been other theories which have posited more active roles for the organism. Some of these are discussed below.

5.2.2. Gestalt Psychology

One of the earliest theories in which the organism was thought to have an impact on the way stimuli were encoded was Gestalt psychology. Instead of assuming that the determinant of perception was the pattern of retinal stimulation, the Gestalt psychologists invoked innate organizational principles such as proximity and similarity to account for the way that events were perceived (Köhler, 1929). Autochthonous forces—forces in the cortex which act to simplify perception—were assumed to act during retention as well.

The Gestalt psychologists have provided empirical demonstrations of the influence of organizational forces on perception and memory. However, their work has had a "discouragingly complex and inconclusive history" (Postman, 1972, p. 4) because of methodological problems, some of which apply to the Piagetian paradigm as well. For a thorough discussion of this history, the reader is referred to an extensive review by Riley (1962).

In some ways the Gestalt position sounds Piagetian—there is an organismic effect on perception and memory, and traces become "better" with the passage of time—but, in important respects, the two positions differ. First, the Gestaltists assumed that the organizational principles were inherent in the neural structure of the brain: in Piagetian theory, the "schemes" of organization are the products of the organism's constructive interaction with the environment. Second, the Gestaltists assumed that memories became "better" in terms of increasing regularity, symmetry, and simplicity. Such changes do not parallel the memory improvements found by Piaget and Inhelder (1973), which instead show progress with respect to logical operations. Third, in Gestalt theory, successful retrieval is essentially a function of trace accessibility:

> ... the long-term availability of prior experiences for recall depends on the temporal stability of the memory traces laid down by these experiences. For example, the availability of an association is governed by the continuing cohesiveness of the underlying unitary trace.... The accessibility of available traces for recall is a function of the similarity between these traces and current stimuli. (Postman, 1972, p. 5.)

Thus, Gestalt theory is not comparable to the Piagetian approach in several fundamental ways.

Contemporary psychologists have also been interested in the role of organization in memory; a brief discussion of their work in relation to Piagetian theory follows.

5.2.3. Contemporary Approaches to Organization in Memory

Contemporary organization theorists have been concerned with the ways in which subjects organize verbal material into memory. Various paradigms (see Postman, 1972) have been used to show that subjects restructure input in accord with semantic, conceptual, or idosyncratic categories, or use organizational strategies based on list order (Tulving, 1968).

Insofar as the organism is active in affecting the way that stimuli are encoded into memory, this approach is compatible with Piaget's. However, at least some of the theorists working in this area emphasize the empiricistic origin of organizational structures. Postman (1972), for example, has said: "The bases of organization for verbal units are obviously attributable to prior linguistic experience" (p. 5). Postman further suggests that at least in some areas, "the difference between exponents of association and of organization appears to reduce largely to matters of language" (pp. 40–41).

It is misleading to classify all theorists who study organization of memory in the same way, since some have a far more constructivistic approach:

> We do not remember events in the world, but rather our encoding or interpretation of those events. Our interpretation of stimulus events depends not only upon stimulus variables but also upon subjective factors such as our attitude, and our expectation or mental set established by the prior psychological context. (Bower, 1972, pp. 93–94.)

Regardless of the epistemological orientation of the particular theorist who studies organization in memory, little interest has been shown in the memory trace once it has been established. Instead, memory is presumed to maintain the organization used by the subject during acquistion.

> The view that the level of recall reflects the stability of higher-order units is, almost by definition, a basic tenet of any organizational account of memory. Consequently, long-term retention is seen as dependent on the integrity of the structure developed during acquisition. (Postman, 1972, p. 5.)

Recall, then, is dependent upon "the reinstatement of the specific retrieval cues established during original learning" (Postman, 1972, p. 6). Tulving (1974) has taken a particularly strong position on the role of these cues, suggesting that although forgetting may in part reflect a loss of information from the trace, forgetting is largely a cue-dependent phenomenon. Furthermore, Tulving considers that it is unlikely that traces are changed or strengthened directly through the use of retrieval cues, believing instead that such cues simply facilitate access to the original trace. Variation in the adequacy of retrieval environments can also explain

> the fact that sometimes recall *increases* over a retention interval, in the absence of interpolated learning, and under conditions where the two tests are nominally identical. . . . It is entirely conceivable that changes in the retrieval environment, which we know is at least partly determined by the person's informational intake and mental activity, can become more appropriate for retrieval as well as less appropriate. (Tulving, 1974, p. 80.)

Tulving's conception of memory, like Piaget's, can explain memory improvement. However, it should be readily apparent that the improvements are fundamentally different in the two theories. In Tulving's conception, the trace is identical throughout retention, and it is only *access* to that trace that is affected by "the person's information intake and mental activity." There is neither restructuring of the trace itself nor new utilization of the content of the trace. In Piaget's conception, on the contrary, there is presumed to be qualitative restructuring of memory, and changes in the way that the authentic memory is used at the time of retrieval. Thus, while Piaget's approach to memory is like that of the contemporary organization theorists' insofar as both posit an active organism, the two differ in several important ways.

5.2.4. Psychoanalytic Approach

Although it is unusual to discuss Tulving and Freud in sequence, it is interesting to note that Tulving's concept of cue-dependent forgetting has a parallel in the psychoanalytic tradition. The implicit assumption made in the clinical setting is that events from childhood remain in memory, but are inaccessible as a result of defense mechanisms such as repression.

There has been some experimental work in the area to determine whether events not consciously recalled do, indeed, emerge in fantasy ("emergence" or the Pötzl effect"), and whether, following fantasy, recall improves ("recovery"). As in the Gestalt tradition, however, the evidence from this area is inconclusive, again, largely because of methodological problems. (The reader is referred to Haber and Erdelyi, 1967; Erdelyi, 1970; and Erdelyi and Becker, 1974 for a discussion of these issues.)

Despite the shared concept of improvement in recall, the psychoanalytic and operative views of memory have little in common. In addition to the obvious differences in focus (affective versus cognitive), the two theories view the memory trace very differently. In psychoanalytic theory, the individual is assumed to retain memories as they were initially experienced, despite profound affective changes during development. In Piagetian theory, memories are assumed to change in conjunction with operative development. A change would presumably also be expected in affective memories, so that childhood memories would be continually reinterpreted in accord with increasing cognitive and affective maturity.

5.2.5. Information Processing

Although organization theorists are implicitly concerned with what happens inside the black box of the mind, their research has generally focused on characteristics of input and output. Theorists working within the information processing paradigm have tended to focus more explicitly on the intervening processes.

In a classic information processing model proposed by Atkinson and Shiffrin (1968), memory is divided into two parts. The first—the structural components—are the locations where information is stored in some form, specifically, a sensory register, and short- and long-term memory stores. The second—the control processes—are the mechanisms used by the subject to transform or recode information and thereby transfer it to long-term storage. Processes are emphasized even more strongly in the depth-of-processing model proposed by Craik and Lockhart (1972). In this model it is proposed that there are successive stages through which a stimulus passes during processing, with different kinds of information about the stimulus being extracted in each.

Researchers have often attempted to externalize the processes used. For example, one of the control processes which has been hypothesized to prevent the loss of information from short-term memory store is rehearsal. Researchers have looked for overt evidence of rehearsal by examining lip movements (Flavell *et al.*, 1966); by allowing subjects to control the delivery of stimuli and then examining hesitation patterns as an indication of rehearsal strategies (Belmont and Butterfield, 1969); by asking subjects to "think aloud" (Fagan, 1972; Ornstein and Liberty,

1973; Rundus, 1971), and by inducing rehearsal strategies to determine whether performance changes from established baseline patterns (Hagen and Kingsley, 1968; Hagen *et al.*, 1970; Palmer and Ornstein, 1971). The reader is referred to Hagen *et al.* (1975), to Reese (1973a, 1973b, 1975), and to Brown (1975) for extensive discussions of the developmental theory and research related to the information processing approach.

Researchers using an information-processing approach, then, have stressed the activities of the subject. Developmental research in this model has been concerned with documenting the child's growing repertoire of these activities, and with his or her growing sophistication about when to apply them (Flavell, 1970; Hagen, 1972; Meacham, 1972). Despite the study of developmental changes in the control processes, however, little attention has been given to changes in information once it has entered the long-term store. It is here that there is the clearest divergence with Piaget's position.

> Now, memory changes in the course of a subject's development do not simply reflect the level of his encoding and decoding powers: *the code itself is susceptible to change* during the construction of operational schemes. (Piaget and Inhelder, 1973, p. 26.)

The developmental changes in control processes that have been documented by most American researchers are changes in the level of "encoding and decoding powers." Existing information processing models could be amended to account for longitudinal long-term memory change by adding a feedback loop which updates the memory trace as cognitive structures change. Thus, although the information processing approach is fundamentally consistent with Piagetian theory, the two theories are not yet comparable in their present form (see Reese, 1973a, 1973b, 1975, for extensive discussions of the relation between the two models).

The theories discussed next are explicitly constructivistic and emphasize strongly the context in which memory processes occur.

5.2.6. Bartlett

Bartlett (1932), like Piaget, rejected a trace theory of memory. Instead, he conceived of remembering as:

> An imaginative reconstruction, or construction, built out of the relation of our attitude towards a whole active mass of organized past reactions or experience, and to a little outstanding detail which commonly appears in image or in language form. (p. 213.)

The research paradigm developed by Bartlett (1932) is similar to that later used by Piaget and Inhelder (1973). Subjects were shown pictures or told stories which they were asked to reproduce after long intervals of time. Bartlett found that subjects tended to change elements of the pictures and stories which could not be interpreted readily within their own experiences, although subsequent researchers (e.g., Gauld and Stephenson, 1967) have raised questions about Bartlett's findings.

It should be apparent that Bartlett's and Piaget's conceptions of memory are fundamentally alike. They have, however, differed in focus. Bartlett's orientation was largely affective while Piaget's has been largely cognitive; Bartlett's focus was on continuities (e.g., of the subject's interests and attitudes) while Piaget's has been on developmental change.

5.2.7. Neisser

A later constructive theory of memory which drew heavily upon Bartlett's conception is that proposed by Neisser (1967). Like Piaget and Bartlett, Neisser, too, rejected trace theories of memory, or the "Reappearance Hypothesis," as he called it. Instead, Neisser (1967) suggested that memory is a constructive process which makes use of stored information—the "Utilization Hypothesis." Neisser's constructivistic epistemology is evident in all aspects of cognitive processing, and thus sounds much like Piaget's:

> What is the information... on which reconstruction is based? The only plausible possibility is that it consists of traces of *prior processes of construction*. There are no stored copies of finished mental events, like images or sentences, but only traces of earlier constructive activity....
>
> The present proposal is, therefore, that we store traces of earlier cognitive acts, not of the products of those acts. The traces are not simply "revived" or "reactivated" in recall; instead, the stored fragments are used as information to support a new construction. (Neisser, 1967, pp. 285–286.)

Insofar as Neisser's orientation is more cognitive than Bartlett's, his theory is closer to Piaget's. As in Bartlett's work, however, Neisser's focus is not developmental, but instead concerns "The cognitive processes... of the American adult, or at least of the college student who is so frequently the subject of psychological experiments" (Neisser, 1967, p. 11). With a shift toward developmental concerns, Neisser's theory would be like Piaget's, given that the basic assumptions of both theories are so similar.

5.2.8. Dialectic Approach

The dialectic approach to memory also emphasizes the importance of context for memory, but defines context even more broadly than did Bartlett or Neisser. In addition to the individual subject's interests, attitudes, values, and personal experiences, the entire cultural and historical context is considered to be essential for a dialectic analysis of memory (Kvale, 1976; Meacham, 1972; Reese, 1975). Insofar as the dialectic approach prohibits the study of memory in isolation, it may be likened to the Piagetian position.

A second characteristic of the dialectic approach—the insistence upon change—is also compatible with Piagetian theory (Reese, 1975). However, the type of change focused upon differs in the two approaches. In the Piagetian approach, change is viewed in relation to the individual's cognitive development, whereas, in the dialectic approach, change is interpreted in relation to the social, cultural, and political change in the society.

The two positions might also be contrasted with regard to the types of materials used to study memory. One of the major criticisms of past memory research from the dialectical view (Kvale, 1976; Reese, 1975) is that tasks have been intentionally stripped of meaning. Criticized most vehemently have been nonsense syllables, but tipped bottles and seriated sticks might be criticized as well. Materials that are highly meaningful in relation to the social environment and real goals would be more compatible with a dialectical approach. In fact, Soviet "research emphasizes the importance of incorporating material to be remembered within an activity of the subject" (Meacham, 1972, p. 209), and might consider as invalid tasks in which memory *per se* is the goal (Reese, 1975). Further discussion of Soviet work on "involuntary memory" may be found in Brown (1975) and Meacham (1976).

Dissatisfaction with nonsense syllables and other rote memorization tasks has not, however, been limited to the dialecticians. More recently, many traditional American psychologists have been voicing dissatisfaction, and have thus turned to a contextual study of memory. A brief review of this work follows.

5.2.9. Contextualism, Constructive Theory, and Assimilation Theory

Dissatisfaction with rote memory tasks was expressed by Jenkins (1971) who asked:

> Why ... do we study our normals with such "abnormal" kinds of materials? ... If we are really interested in reconstruction, in integration, in

cognitive memory and the like, why do we force our subjects to use such arbitrary and impoverished materials? (p. 283.)

In replacing these tasks and the associationistic model from which they were derived, Jenkins (1974) has turned to a contextual approach.

A contextualist interpretation of experience requires that the total meaning or quality of events be considered, including both environmental and organismic context.

> The quality of the event is the resultant of the interaction of the experiencer and the world, that is, the interaction of the organism and the physical relations that provide support for the experience. (Jenkins, 1974, p. 786.)

This contextual orientation obviously shares many basic features with the Piagetian approach, a similarity which extends to the study of memory: "Contextualism calls us back to considering what the subject believes and knows when we talk of memory" (Jenkins, 1974, p. 793).

The importance of context has been demonstrated by studies in which appropriate contexts are, or are not, provided for stimuli. Dooling and Lachman (1971), for example, showed that subjects who were given an integrating theme for prose passages were better able to retain the information in those passages than were subjects not given an appropriate context. Similarly, Bransford and Johnson (1972) found that prose passages were understood and remembered better when preceded by a pictorial context which integrated the meaning of otherwise seemingly unconnected sentences. Bower *et al.* (1975) have shown a similar effect for memory of pictures: figurally impoverished pictures (nonsense "droodles") were remembered better by subjects who were given a meaningful context for the pictures than by subjects who were not. These studies indicate the importance of a context for assimilating and remembering information.

The work on semantic memory initiated by Barclay, Bransford, and Franks (Barclay, 1973; Bransford *et al.*, 1972; Bransford and Franks, 1971) has also demonstrated that subjects' memories are determined by more than the stimulus proper. Arguing against the position that what is stored in memory is information about the linguistic structure of semantic input, Bransford and Franks (1971) presented sets of semantically related sentences to subjects who were later (3–5 minutes) asked to identify sentences as old or new. Subjects confidently recognized new sentences as "old" if the sentences integrated the meanings of the original individual sentences. New sentences that could not be derived from the ideas expressed in the original sentences were, in contrast, correctly identified as new.

In other studies designed to assess semantic integration (Barclay, 1973; Bransford *et al.*, 1972), subjects falsely recognized as "old" sentences that contained logical inferences drawn from the information provided in the original sentences. A passage from Barclay (1973) summarizes assimilation theory well and illustrates its affinity with Piaget's operative approach to memory:

> The fundamental component of assimilation theory is the comprehension device, which relates sentential information to one's knowledge system, in part through logical operations. In this respect, sentence comprehension is simply one manifestation of the general process of comprehension referred to as knowledge acquisition. (p. 253.)

Similar tasks have been given to children. In a study by Paris and Carter (1973), second- and fifth-grade children falsely recognized sentences which were true inferences derived from the information given in the actual sentences. Paris and Carter (1973) specifically note the similarity of the assimilative process in semantic memory and the assimilation–accommodation process postulated by Piaget:

> In both approaches memory is regarded as a constantly changing accumulation of knowledge. Implicit within this accommodating process is the proposition that what is retrieved from memory is not just some fractional component of what is stored. Perhaps the synthetic, organizational operations applied to the stored information and the consequent changes are critical and necessary for retention. (p. 113.)

Results supporting a constructive theory of memory were also found by Paris and Mahoney (1974) with both verbal and pictorial stimuli: second- and fourth-grade children had difficulty discriminating true inferences from original sentences. Other work by Paris and his associates is reviewed by Brown (1975).

The importance of subjects' constructions in memory has also been demonstrated by Loftus (1975). Subjects were shown a relatively complex event (e.g., a movie showing a car accident) and were then asked various "eyewitness" questions. In some cases, new (erroneous) information was given incidentally in early questions. For example, a subject might be asked: "About how fast was the car going as it approached the stop sign?" when, in fact, a yield sign, not a stop sign, had been shown in the movie. Subjects' answers to subsequent questions suggest that the new information had been incorporated into previously established memories, so that in the example given above, subjects were likely to answer "yes" when asked: "Did you see a stop sign?"

The constructive approaches to memory discussed above recognize, as do Piaget and Inhelder, the importance of context for memory, a context that includes not only the stimulus environment, but also the subject's own cognitive activity. The theories differ, however, in their focus on developmental changes in these activities.

5.3. Summary

The preceding review has shown that Piaget and Inhelder's approach has much in common with other theories of memory. There are other theorists who (a) attribute active, constructive roles to the organism in the formation and retrieval of memories; (b) view memory within a broader context, incorporating various aspects of the individual's knowledge, logic, attitudes, and culture; (c) propose highly constructive memory processes; and (d) provide for changes in memory performance over time, either by postulating changes in the traces themselves or by postulating changes in the accessibility of the trace.

Despite these areas of overlap, however, the operative theory of memory remains unique because of its fundamentally developmental nature. While other theories of memory have accommodated developmental change, or have the potential for doing so, it is only the Genevan approach in which development itself serves as the point of departure for the study of memory. In fact, Piaget and Inhelder (1973) appear to consider their work on memory as important, not so much for its implication for memory, but rather for its confirmation of cognitive-developmental theory in general:

> There is one aspect of these studies that has greatly encouraged us in our work: the surprising discovery, in a sphere apparently remote from that of cognitive operations, of a precise succession of operational stages, whose existence we ourselves might have begun to doubt had we listened to all those who do not, or rather do not yet, believe in the validity of the operational approach. (p. xi.)

Developmentalists who have studied memory have generally emphasized changes in the processes used to encode and decode information, while psychologists who have been concerned with changes in memories over time (e.g., Gestalt psychologists; Bartlett) have not generally been concerned with developmental change. Only in the operative approach has memory change been linked to qualitative changes in intellectual structure, changes that are themselves the product of the subject's constructions through interaction with the environment.

6. Conclusions

It should be apparent that Piaget and Inhelder (1973) have, indeed, contributed something new to a "field that has been so extensively worked over as has memory" (Inhelder, 1969, p. 361). Although several of their basic assumptions are shared by other theorists, their interpretation of memory within the context of the cognitively developing child is unique.

It should be equally apparent, however, that the research evidence reviewed in this chapter does not provide unmitigated support for the operative approach to memory. First, the role of artifacts may not yet be dismissed on the basis of existing research. While some procedural variables have been shown to have little effect on performance, other variables apparently do influence performance significantly, and still others play an unknown role. It would be helpful if Piagetian researchers would use methodologies from other research traditions which were developed in response to criticisms of test–retest designs (for example, in research on reminiscence, see Ammons and Irion, 1954; Buxton, 1943; in research on Gestalt, see Riley, 1962).

Second, while replications have confirmed that long-term memory improvements occur, and that memory performance differs among children of different operative levels (as inferred from age), the findings from within-subject research designs have not been as positive. Specifically, the relation between individuals' performance on the two measures has been weak (although significant), with memory change and operative change rarely coinciding.

As discussed earlier, these inconsistencies may result, in part, from differences in the tasks used to assess operative level and memory, differences that may be due to the use of different materials and/or to the different amount of interest, motivation, etc., elicited by the two tasks. A second reason for inconsistencies may be the instability of performance by subjects who are in transitional states with respect to the concept tapped by the stimulus (e.g., see Flavell, 1971; Flavell and Wohlwill, 1969).

A third explanation may lie in the relation between figurative and operative processes. While Piaget and Inhelder have proposed that memories reflect thoughts, rather than perceptions, the evidence suggests that this may be true only in relatively extreme cases, that is, when the subject's operative level is far below that tapped by the stimulus. In less extreme situations, the child may be able to extend his or her perception, even for relatively long periods of time.

The relatively "pure figurative memory" implied by this description raises several difficult theoretical and empirical questions. For example, if figurative memory is not understood as part of the more general conservation of schemes, would it then be vulnerable to decay and/or interference as is the associationists' memory trace? Another important problem, raised earlier, concerns what mechanism could be used to determine whether a particular memory is "figurative" or "operative." Without such a mechanism, hypotheses about their differential functioning are untestable. It is necessary, therefore, that future work be directed not only to improving empirical methodologies, but also toward answering these and related theoretical questions.

In evaluating the success of Piaget and Inhelder's (1973) work on memory, it is important to remember its organismic roots. As Overton and Reese (1973) have noted, the kinds of questions asked are determined by world views:

> As long as a group maintains the mechanistic position and its corollaries of unidirectionality and linearity, [the question]—"How much?"—will continue to constitute a meaningful issue.... In marked contrast, for a group that accepts the organismic position and its corollary of reciprocal causation... the questions of "Which one?" and "How much?" lose all meaning.... The viable question from the organismic position is the question "How?" (p. 81.)

Not surprisingly, Piaget and Inhelder's (1973) own goals fit those of the organismic model:

> We are simply aiming at a qualitative analysis... we are merely trying to discover the mechanisms of the memory and of their relationship to those at work in imagery and intelligence. (p. 18.)

In the final analysis, then, whether or not Piaget and Inhelder's (1973) approach to memory is accepted depends, not only upon the adequacy of the empirical evidence, but also upon the fundamental acceptance or rejection of the organismic model in which their approach is rooted.

References

Adams, W., 1973, Effect of pretraining on long-term memory improvement, *Developmental Psychology* 9:433. (Also extended report, by same title.)

Altemeyer, R., Fulton, D., and Berney, K., 1969, Long-term memory improvement: confirmation of a finding by Piaget, *Child Development* 40:845–857.

Ammons, H., and Irion, A., 1954, À note on the Ballard reminiscence phenomenon, *Journal of Experimental Psychology 48*: 184–186.

Anderson, J., and Bower, G., 1973, "Human Associative Memory," Wiley, New York.

Atkinson, R., and Shiffrin, R., 1968, Human memory: A proposed system and its control processes, *in* "The Psychology of Learning and Motivation: Advances in Research and Theory" (Vol. II) K. Spence and J. Spence (eds.), Academic Press, New York, pp. 89–195.

Barclay, J., 1973, The role of comprehension in remembering sentences, *Cognitive Psychology 4*:229–254.

Bartlett, F., 1932, "Remembering: A Study in Experimental and Social Psychology," Cambridge University Press, Cambridge.

Belmont, J., and Butterfield, E., 1969, The relations of short-term memory to development and intelligence, *in* "Advances in Child Development and Behavior" (Vol. 4) L. Lipsett and H. Reese (eds.), Academic Press, New York, pp. 29–82.

Blackstock, E., and King, W., 1973, Recognition and reconstruction memory for seriation in four- and five-year-olds, *Developmental Psychology 9*:255–259.

Bower, G., 1972, A selective review of organizational factors in memory, *in* "Organization of Memory" E. Tulving and W. Donaldson (eds.), Academic Press, New York, pp. 93–137.

Bower, G., Karlin, M., and Dueck, A., 1975, Comprehension and memory for pictures, *Memory and Cognition 3*:216–220.

Bransford, J., and Franks, J. 1971, The abstraction of linguistic ideas, *Cognitive Psychology 2*:331–350.

Bransford, J., and Johnson, M., 1972, Contextual prerequisites for understanding: some investigations of comprehension and recall. *Journal of Verbal Learning and Verbal Behavior 11*:717–726.

Bransford, J., Barclay, J., and Franks, J., 1972, Sentence memory: A constructive versus interpretive approach, *Cognitive Psychology 3*:193–209.

Bresson, F., 1970, Excerpt from Discussion of Piaget Memory Presentation, *in* "Symposium de l'Association de Psychologie Scientifique de Langue Française," Presses Universitaires de France, translated by Peter Carey.

Brown, A., 1975, The development of memory: knowing, knowing about knowing, and knowing how to know, *in* "Advances in Child Development and Behavior" (Vol. 10) H. Reese (ed.), Academic Press, New York, pp. 103–152.

Buxton, C., 1943, The status of research in reminiscence, *Psychological Bulletin 40*:313–340.

Carey, P., 1971, An information-processing interpretation of Piaget's memory experiments, paper presented at the Biennial Meeting of the Society for Research in Child Development, Minneapolis.

Craik, F., and Lockhart, R., 1972, Levels of processing: a framework for memory research, *Journal of Verbal Learning and Verbal Behavior 11*:671–684.

Crowley, C., 1975, The development of the concept of seriation and its role in short- and long-term memory of fully seriated and preseriation arrays, unpublished Doctoral Dissertation, University of Washington.

Dahlem, N., 1968, Reconstructive memory in children, *Psychonomic Science 13*:331–332.

Dahlem, N., 1969, Reconstructive memory in children revisited, *Psychonomic Science 101*–102.

Deese, J., 1965, "The Structure of Associations in Language and Thought," Johns Hopkins Press, Baltimore.

Dooling, D., and Lachman, R., 1971, Effects of comprehension on retention of prose. *Journal of Experimental Psychology 88*:216–222.

Duckworth, E., 1964, Piaget rediscovered, *in* "Piaget Rediscovered" R. Ripple and V. Rockcastle (eds.), Cornell University, Ithaca, New York, pp. 1–5.

Erdelyi, M., 1970, Recovery of unavailable perceptual input, *Cognitive Psychology* 1:99–113.

Erdelyi, M., and Becker, J., 1974, Hypermnesia for pictures, *Cognitive Psychology* 6:159–161.

Fagan, J., 1972, Rehearsal and free recall in children of superior and average intelligence, *Psychonomic Science* 28:352–354.

Finkel, D., and Crowley, C., 1973, Improvement in children's long-term memory for seriated sticks: change in memory storage or coding rules? paper presented at the Biennial Meeting of the Society for Research in Child Development, Philadelphia.

Flavell, J., 1970, Developmental studies of mediated memory, *in* "Advances in Child Development and Behavior" (Vol. 5) L. Lipsitt and H. Reese (eds.), Academic Press, New York, pp. 181–211.

Flavell, J., 1971, Stage-related properties of cognitive development, *Cognitive Psychology* 2:421–453.

Flavell, J., and Wohlwill, J., 1969, Formal and functional aspects of cognitive development, *in* "Studies in Cognitive Development" D. Elkind and J. Flavell (eds.), Oxford University Press, New York, pp. 67–120.

Flavell, J., Beach, D., and Chinsky, J., 1966, Spontaneous verbal rehearsal in a memory task as a function of age, *Child Development* 37:283–299.

Flavell, J., Friedrichs, A., and Hoyt, J., 1970, Developmental changes in memorization processes, *Cognitive Psychology* 1:324–340.

Furth, H., 1969, "Piaget and Knowledge," Prentice-Hall, Englewood Cliffs, New Jersey.

Furth, H., Ross, B., and Youniss, J., 1974, Operative understanding in children's immediate and long-term reproductions of drawings, *Child Development* 45:63–70.

Gauld, A., and Stephenson, G., 1967, Some experiments relating to Bartlett's theory of remembering, *British Journal of Psychology* 58:39–49.

Ginsburg, H., and Opper, S., 1969, "Piaget's Theory of Intellectual Development," Prentice-Hall, Englewood Cliffs, New Jersey.

Haber, R., and Erdelyi, M., 1967, Emergence and recovery of initially unavailable perceptual material, *Journal of Verbal Learning and Verbal Behavior* 26:618–628.

Hagen, J., 1972, Strategies for remembering, *in* "Information Processing in Children," S. Farnham-Diggory (ed.), Academic Press, New York, pp. 65–79.

Hagen, J., and Kingsley, P., 1968, Labeling effects in short-term memory, *Child Development* 39:113–121.

Hagen, J., Jongeward, R., and Kail, R., 1975, Cognitive perspectives on the development of memory, *in* "Advances in Child Development and Behavior" (Vol. 10) H. Reese (ed.), Academic Press, New York, pp. 57–101.

Hagen, J., Meacham, J., and Mesibov, G., 1970, Verbal labeling, rehearsal, and short-term memory, *Cognitive Psychology* 1:47–58.

Harris, L. J., Hanley, C., and Best, C. T., 1975, Conservation of horizontality: sex differences in sixth-graders and college students, paper presented at Biennial Meetings of the Society for Research in Child Development, Denver.

Hobbes, T., 1839, "Human Nature," John Bohn, London.

Inhelder, B., 1969, Memory and intelligence in the child, *in* "Studies in Cognitive Development" D. Elkind and J. Flavell (eds.), Oxford U., New York, pp. 337–364.

Jenkins, J., 1971, Second discussant's comments: What's left to say?, *Human Development* 14:279–286.

Jenkins, J., 1974, Remember that old theory of memory? Well, forget it!, *American Psychologist* 29:785–795.

Kausler, D., 1970, Retention—Forgetting as a nomological network for developmental research, *in* "Life-span Developmental Psychology" L. Goulet and P. Baltes (eds.), Academic Press, New York, pp. 305–353.

King, W., and Blackstock, E., 1971, Reconstruction memory for seriation in young children: Effect of presence of a model on performance, unpublished manuscript, City University of New York.

Köhler, W., 1929, "Gestalt Psychology," Liveright, New York.

Kreutzer, M., Leonard, C., and Flavell, J., 1975, An interview study of children's knowledge about memory, Monographs of the Society for Research in Child Development, Vol. 159.

Kvale, S., 1976, Memory and dialectics: some reflections on Ebbinghaus and Mao Tse-Tung, *in* "The Development of Dialectical Operations" K. Riegel (ed.), Karger, Basel.

Leask, J., Haber, R. N., and Haber, R. B., 1969, Eidetic imagery in children: II. Longitudinal and experimental results, *Psychonomic Monograph Supplements* 3(35):25–48.

Liben, L., 1974, Operative understanding of horizontality and its relation to long-term memory, *Child Development* 45:416–424.

Liben, L., 1975a, Evidence for developmental differences in spontaneous seriation and its implications for past research on long-term memory improvement, *Developmental Psychology* 11:121–125.

Liben, L., 1975b, Long-term memory for pictures related to seriation, horizontality, and verticality concepts, *Developmental Psychology* 11:795–806.

Liben, L., 1975c, Adolescents' Euclidean concepts: Effects of sex, cognitive style and intellectual abilities, paper presented at the 83rd Annual Convention of the American Psychological Association, Chicago.

Liben, L., 1976, Memory in the context of cognitive development: The Piagetian approach, *in* "Perspectives on the Development of Memory and Cognition" R. V. Kail, Jr. and J. Hagen (eds.), Lawrence Erlbaum, Hillsdale, New Jersey.

Loftus, E., 1975, Reconstructive processes in eyewitness testimony, paper presented in a symposium, Constructive Processes in Memory at the 83rd Annual Convention of the American Psychological Association, Chicago.

Meacham, J., 1972, The development of memory abilities in the individual and society, *Human Development* 15:205–228.

Meacham, J., 1976, Soviet investigations of memory development, *in* "Perspectives on the Development of Memory and Cognition" R. V. Kail, Jr. and J. Hagen (eds.), Lawrence Earlbaum, Hillsdale, New Jersey.

Murray, F., and Bausell, R., 1970, Memory and conservation, *Psychonomic Science* 21(6):334–335.

Murray, F., and Bausell, R., 1971, Memory and conservation, paper presented at the Biennial Meetings of the Society for Research in Child Development, Minneapolis.

Neisser, U., 1967, "Cognitive Psychology," Appleton-Century-Crofts, New York.

Nunnally, J., 1973, Research strategies and measurement methods for investigating human development, *in* "Life-Span Developmental Psychology" J. Nesselroade and H. Reese (eds.), Academic Press, New York, pp. 87–109.

Ornstein, P., and Liberty, C., 1973, Rehearsal processes in children's memory, paper presented at Biennial Meetings of the Society for Research in Child Development, Philadelphia.

Overton, W., and Reese, H., 1973, Models of development: Methodological implications, *in* "Life-Span Developmental Psychology" J. Nesselroade and H. Reese (eds.), Academic Press, New York, pp. 65–86.

Palmer, S., and Ornstein, P., 1971, Role of rehearsal strategy in serial probed recall, *Journal of Experimental Psychology* 88:60–66.

Paris, S., and Carter, A., 1973, Semantic and constructive aspects of sentence memory in children, *Developmental Psychology* 9:109–113.

Paris, S., and Mahoney, G., 1974, Cognitive integration in children's memory for sentences and pictures, *Child Development* 45:633–642.

Pepper, S., C., 1942, "World Hypotheses," University of California Press, Berkeley.

Piaget, J., 1968, "On the Development of Memory and Identity," Clark University Press, Barre, Massachusetts.

Piaget, J., 1969, "The Mechanisms of Perception," Basic Books, New York.

Piaget, J., 1970, Piaget's theory, *in* "Carmichael's Manual of Child Psychology" P. Mussen (ed.), Wiley, New York, pp. 703–732.

Piaget, J., and Inhelder, B., 1971, "Mental Imagery in the Child," Basic Books, New York.

Piaget, J., and Inhelder, B., 1973, "Memory and Intelligence," Basic Books, New York.

Postman, L., 1972, A pragmatic view of organization theory, *in* "Organization of Memory" E. Tulving and W. Donaldson (eds.), Academic Press, New York, pp. 3–48.

Reese, H., 1973a, Models of memory and models of development, *Human Development* 16:397–416.

Reese, H. W., 1973b, Life-span models of memory, *The Gerontologist* 13:472–478.

Reese, H. 1975, Information processing and the development of memory, unpublished manuscript, West Virginia University.

Reese, H., and Overton, W., 1970, Models of development and theories of development, *in* "Life-span Developmental Psychology" L. Goulet and P. Baltes (eds.), Academic Press, New York, pp. 115–145.

Riley, D., 1962, Memory for form, *in* "Psychology in the Making" L. Postman (ed.), Knopf, New York, pp. 402–465.

Ritter, K., Kaprove, B., Fitch, J., and Flavell, J., 1973, The development of retrieval strategies in young children, *Cognitive Psychology* 5:310–321.

Rundus, D., 1971, Analysis of rehearsal processes in free recall, *Journal of Experimental Psychology* 89:63–77.

Salatas, H., and Flavell, J., 1975, Retrieval of recently learned information: development of strategies and control skills, unpublished manuscript, University of Minnesota.

Samuels, M., 1975, Scheme influences on long term event recall in children, unpublished manuscript, Hospital for Sick Children, Toronto.

Thomas, H. Jamison, W., and Hummel, D., 1973, Observation is insufficient for discovering that the surface of still water is invariantly horizontal, *Science* 181:173–174.

Tulving, E., 1968, Theoretical issues in free recall, *in* "Verbal Behavior and General Behavior Theory" T. Dixon and D. Horton (eds.), Prentice-Hall, Englewood Cliffs, New Jersey, pp. 2–36.

Tulving, E., 1974, Cue-dependent forgetting, *American Scientist* 62:74–82.

Werner, H., and Kaplan, B., 1963, "Symbol Formation," Wiley, New York.

7

Logical Concept Attainment during the Aging Years

Issues in the Neo-Piagetian Research Literature*

FRANK H. HOOPER and NANCY W. SHEEHAN

1. Introduction

While there is little question that Piaget's theory and associated research represent the preeminent conception of logical concept development currently extant, it is also clear that the Genevan orientation to developmental issues offers very little information concerning significant behavioral change beyond the years of adolescence. In brief, the orthodox Piagetian perspective is rather exclusively restricted to the initial years of the human life-span, i.e., birth to maturity. Once the formal operations apex is attained, stability is predicted and no provision for significant cognitive changes, especially of a qualitative nature, is made (cf. Flavell, 1970a; Piaget, 1972b). This conceptual viewpoint is clearly at variance with a considerable number of normative research investigations of Piagetian concept attainment in mature and elderly adults (see recent reviews by Denny, 1974a; Hooper, 1973b; Papalia and Bielby, 1974). The purposes of the present chapter are threefold: (1) to review the norma-

FRANK H. HOOPER and NANCY W. SHEEHAN • Child and Family Studies Program, University of Wisconsin, Madison, Wisconsin.

*This chapter is dedicated to the memory of our colleague, teacher, and friend, William R. Looft.

tive and experimental assessments of aged individuals' performances on Piagetian logical-concept tasks; (2) to evaluate this empirical evidence with regard to putative qualitative or structural changes such as those commonly associated with the childhood and adolescent age intervals; and (3) to speculate as to the role certain corollary factors may play in determining the performance of aged individuals on logical-concept tasks.

The present chapter assumes a fundamental life-span developmental orientation to the elucidation of age-related cognitive changes following maturity (Bayley, 1963; Goulet and Baltes, 1970). Thus, we seek to elaborate and extend the general organismic perspective to encompass all portions of the human life-span. The incorporation of empirical data and associated conceptual speculation concerning the cognitive functioning of mature adults and aged individuals on logical-reasoning tasks highlights the contributions of Werner (e.g., Langer, 1970; Werner, 1948, 1957; Werner and Kaplan, 1963) rather than those of Piaget and his associates (e.g., Piaget, 1972b; Piaget and Inhelder, 1969). The presence of bidirectional developmental changes across the life-span are generally not acknowledged as viable possibilities in orthodox Piagetian theory (see, however, the second footnote on page 209 below).

A review of the present literature on aging reveals the pervasive influence of the investigator's underlying model of development. It is clear that the general world view (Hooper, 1973a; Looft, 1973; Overton and Reese, 1973; Reese and Overton, 1970) and the specific model of the aging process (Birren, 1959; Schaie, 1973) employed place major constraints upon the methodology, research designs, and general expectations of the developmental investigator. For example, it is possible to view the normal aging process as representing a stability, an irreversible decrement, or a decrement with compensation state of affairs (Schaie, 1973). Orthodox Piagetian theory would seem to suggest a stability viewpoint. Thus Piaget and Inhelder (1969) state:

> ... Finally, after the age of 11 or 12, nascent formal thought restructures the concrete operations by subordinating them to new structures *whose development will continue throughout adolescence and all of later life*. (pp. 152–153, emphasis added.)

Generally speaking, the inevitable decrement viewpoint is held by theorists who emphasize the biological basis of aging phenomena, e.g., impaired neurophysiological functioning (Bondareff, 1959; Magladery, 1959). In contrast, the stability and decrement with compensation models usually locate the causal aging factors in social learning settings and emphasize the role of past and current experiential determinants or environmentally based response contingency relationships (e.g., Baltes, 1973; Baltes and Labouvie, 1973; Cumming and Henry, 1961). Ignoring the criterion of parsimony, it may well be that the "ideal" model of the normative aging process would be a transactional–dialectical model which would subsume both biological and sociocultural determinants (cf. Looft, 1973; Riegel, 1973a).

The adoption of a dialectical or relational model of aging phenomena leads to a consideration of *multiple* causative factors. A number of these may be seen to be at issue in the studies reviewed below. These include general health status and the degree of organic brain impairment, present and past levels of social interaction/isolation, occupational status and related degrees of specialization, socioeconomic status, levels of formal education, the effects of institutionalization, long-term sociocultural influences, and the relationship of logical-concept task performances to other intelligence and personality measures. This latter category would include indices of cognitive style (e.g., measures of behavioral rigidity, field independence/dependence, etc.), tests of linguistic competence, information processing, and memory ability, and conventional psychometrically based measures of intellectual functioning such as those associated with the distinction between fluid and crystallized general intelligence factors (cf. Horn, 1967, 1970). All these possible contributing or corollary factors are, or course, in addition to the ubiquitous chronological age variable.

It will be seen that the operational role of many of these potentially confounding (or at least confusing) factors may be related to the conceptual distinction between competence and performance features of intellectual functioning (Bearison, 1974; Botwinick, 1967; Flavell and Wohlwill, 1969; Hooper *et al.*, 1971). To overly simplify, this differentiation seeks to identify and distinguish structural components from transitory performance variables in optimal cognitive functioning. From the present developmental perspective this implies a separation of stage-dependent structural attributes, e.g., the special properties associated with the eight logical *groupements* which are said to underly the concrete operations period of middle childhood (Piaget, 1972a), from task-specific factors such as motivational salience, instructional set, amount and level of language sophistication required, type and complexity of stimulus materials employed, time limits, and so forth. Very often it appears that the Genevans cite cases of intra- and interindividual uniformity as support for structural (competence) determination and relegate cases of demonstrated variability to more trivial (from their orientation) performance factors. The post hoc nature of the horizontal decalage construct is one example of this orientation.

What we are searching for, of course, are the "stagelike" structural properties of aged individuals' conceptual functioning. Thus, from the Genevan structuralist perspective, the degree of intertask performance correspondence should be notable (Flavell, 1970b, 1971; Hooper, 1973a, 1973b; Wohlwill, 1963, 1973). Judging by the elusiveness of this stage characteristic in most empirical assessments of young children and adolescents (cf. Bingham-Newman and Hooper, 1975; Brainerd, 1974) it is quite likely that our search will be complicated and error-prone. The fundamental issues may be summarized as follows: (1) Whether the performances of normal adults from a representative sampling of sociocultural and occupational populations on logical-reasoning tasks merit the stage designation to the same degree (i.e., in terms of structural synchrony and cultural universalism) as that accorded to the earlier-appearing developmental stages, and (2) whether the performance difficulties of elderly subjects on formal, concrete, and sensorimotor concept tasks denote competence deficits and hence merit an appellation of qualitative regression?

A preliminary word of caution is in order insofar as the subject sampling procedures and assessment designs of the present research literature are concerned. All the studies have employed the relatively simple and admittedly economical cross-sectional assessment design. Cross-sectional designs yield information concerning age differences rather than age changes (Baltes, 1968; Schaie, 1965, 1973). Yet the majority of the authors' intentions appear to be the explication of ontogenetic change over the life-span. Since the cross-sectional approach (as a preexperimental design, Campbell and Stanley, 1963) confounds age differences with cohort or generational distinctions, it cannot provide any direct information concerning ontogenetic age changes. Moreover, representative sampling becomes increasingly difficult as the adult and aging portions of the life-span are assessed. This follows from the well-documented influences of selective participation and selective survival (Baltes, 1968; Riegel and Riegel, 1972). Estimates of age differences are biased (usually in a positive direction) to the extent that survival rate is associated with the measurements in question. Finally, although cross-sectional investigations can provide information regarding relative item difficulties across the age groups and concept task arrays at issue, they fail to offer any data concerning developmental acquisition (or regression) *sequences* or the salient question of inter-item relationships over time (Wohlwill, 1973). These questions can be attacked only by longitudinal or time-lag assessment designs.

2. Investigations of Piagetian Concept Performances during the Aging Years*

2.1. Infralogical Abilities in the Elderly

A number of studies (see Table I)† have investigated conservation abilities in adults and the elderly. Several studies have indicated that for those conservation abilities for which there exists, in studies of young children, a horizontal decalage in the order of item difficulty (e.g., conservation of mass, weight, and volume), this same relative difficulty pattern appears to be shown in the performance of aged subjects (Ajuriaguerra et al., 1964; Papalia, 1972a; Papalia et al., 1973b; Rubin et al., 1973).

Papalia (1972a) in a life-span cross-sectional investigation of conservation ability tested 96 middle-class subjects ranging in age from 6 to 65 years and over on a battery of conservation tasks (number, mass, weight, and volume). Papalia found that earlier-appearing logical abilities were maintained by elderly subjects far more frequently than were abilities presumed to appear later. The ability to conserve number, the earliest-appearing concrete operational ability, was maintained by all subjects 11 years and older. For other quantity concepts, the percentages of subjects in the oldest age group (65 and over) who conserved substance, weight, and volume were 62%, 50%, and 6%, respectively. Papalia interpreted the poor performance of elderly subjects on tasks of intermediate and higher-level difficulty as representing "a regression with age to less complex modes of responding (Papalia, 1972a, p. 240)." Lower-level performance on the part of elderly subjects was interpreted as related to decreased neurological intactness with advanced age. This interpretation reflects a previously hypothesized relationship between

---

*The reader should note that there is a considerable degree of task overlap in the studies reported in Tables I and II.
†The present review will not include investigations of Piagetian moral concepts in adults or the elderly (cf. Kohlberg, 1973), nor will specific studies of institutionalized subjects demonstrating advanced senile dementia, for example, be covered. A number of studies in the French experimental literature, e.g., Ajuriaguerra et al. (1967) (time concepts and representative concrete operational tasks [linear and inverse order, horizontal coordinates, topological representation, conservation of quantity, weight, and volume]); Ajuriaguerra et al. (1965) (object permanence tasks and sensorimotor tasks assessing operational schemata); Ajuriaguerra et al. (1966) (spatial orientation and representation tasks[ideomotor apraxia]), have been conducted by Ajuriaguerra and his associates in Geneva.

Table I. Studies of Infralogical Abilities in Elderly Adults

Study	Subjects[a]	Abilities	Results
Chap and Sinnott, 1975	Institutionalized [68–73 years of age (n = 10); 78–83 years of age (n = 8)]; community-active [68–73 years of age (n = 12), 78–83 years of age (n = 4)].	Discrete substance, weight, length (classification, simple and temporal seriation, combinatorial reasoning).	Performance patterns noted to support structural relationships among abilities. Main effects of age and institutionalization significant (maximal difference in younger comparison groups).
Eisner, 1973	65–83 years ($\bar{X}$ = 71.7) community-living free of organic impairment (n = 10); 64–91 years ($\bar{X}$ = 74.4) institutionalized, moderate organic impairment (n = 10); 78–90 years ($\bar{X}$ = 84) institutionalized, severe organic impairment (n = 10).	Surface area, number, substance, continuous quantity, weight, discontinuous quantity, volume conservation.	Community-living Ss free of brain damage passed *all* concrete tasks, 80% passed formal tasks. Severity of brain damage significantly affected performance.
Garber, Simmons, and Robinson, 1974	61–79 years ($\bar{X}$ = 67.6) (institutionalized males); 6.10–8.7 years (n = 13).	Conservation of surface area with altered motivational and instructional sets.	23% of children and 82% of elderly males successfully solved task.
Kominski and Coppinger, 1968	Ages: 50–59; 60–69; 70 and over. All institutionalized veterans (n = 102).	Conservation of surface area with altered instructional set.	All 3 age groups performed at low levels of conservation ability. No difference due to instructional set.

Papalia, 1972	16 Ss from each of the following age groups: 6–7; 11–13; 18–19; 30–54; 55–64; 65 and over (n = 96).	Number, mass, weight, and volume.	Age difference in performance noted for more difficult tasks. The percentages of elderly Ss passing number, mass, weight, and volume were 100%, 62%, 50%, and 6%, respectively.
Papalia, Kennedy, and Sheehan, 1973	63–92 years ($\bar{X}$ = 74.4) (N = 48). Formal education—5–19 years ($\bar{X}$ = 10.7).	Conservation of surface area.	Only 13% (n = 13) passed task.
Papalia, Salverson, and True, 1973	64–85 years ($\bar{X}$ = 73.3) Formal education—$\bar{X}$ = 10.7 (N = 48).	Mass, weight, and volume.	A possible reverse horizontal decalage noted for these abilities w/66.9%, 43.7%, and 20.9% passing mass, weight, and volume.
Rubin, 1973a	70–85 years—Institutionalized 71–85 (n = 28) and noninstitutionalized 70–85 (n = 27).	Space, number, mass, weight, continuous quantity, and spatial egocentrism.	Conservation performance significantly lower for institutionalized Ss.
Rubin, Attewell, Tierney, and Tumulo, 1973	$\bar{X}$ ages: 7.63 (n = 30); 11.55 (n = 31); 21.07 (n = 26; 44.1 (n = 18); 76.33 (n = 27).	Space, number, mass, weight, continuous quantity, and spatial egocentrism.	For conservation and egocentrism, a curvilinear relationship with age was noted. Elderly Ss showed similar performance levels to two youngest groups.
Sanders, Laurendeau, and Bergeron, 1966	Ages: 20–39; 40–59; 60 and over. Oldest Ss institutionalized and noninstitutionalized (N = 155).	Conservation of surface area.	Percentage of Ss passing declined from 84% (20–39), 72% (40–59), to 24.2% (60+) over the age range.

aAll Ss are community-living residents unless indicated.

Piagetian task performance and fluid intelligence (cf. Hooper et al., 1971).

If, however, the hypothesized relationship between fluid intelligence and Piagetian logical abilities is correct, one would not expect that cognitive functioning would be most efficient for the 55- to 64-year-old age group, since neurological decline and the associated loss of fluid abilities begins during young adulthood. According to Papalia (1972a), the apex of cognitive functioning appeared during the years from 55 to 64 years of age. Analyses for the effect of education and sex revealed no significant effects.

In a similar cross-sectional life-span study, Rubin et al. (1973) investigated the status of logical abilities across the life-span. Administering measures of space, number, substance, weight, and continuous quantity conservation in addition to a measure of spatial egocentrism to 132 subjects ranging from young to elderly, Rubin et al. (1973) noted similar age trends to those noted by Papalia (1972a). The authors suggested that the observed lowered cognitive performance among elderly subjects was due to the possible interaction between increased neurological decrement and increased social isolation which affects elderly adults. For all age groups tested, sex did not significantly affect performance.

Papalia et al. (1973b) assessed mass, weight, and volume conservation in 48 noninstitutionalized elderly subjects. The findings generally replicated those of Papalia (1972a) whereby lower relative performances were noted for increasingly difficult or later-appearing logical abilities. Analysis for sex differences indicated that males demonstrated higher levels of conservation ability than did females. This relationship, however, was only significant for weight conservation.

The performance of institutionalized and community-living elderly subjects ranging in age from 70 to 85 on measures of conservation ability (two-dimensional space, number, substance, weight, and continuous quantity) and a measure of spatial egocentrism was compared by Rubin (1973a). Of the total 55 subjects (27 noninstitutionalized and 28 institutionalized), significant differences in performance were noted between the institutionalized and noninstitutionalized group on the conservation measures. Rubin interpreted the poor performance of institutionalized elderly as due to the decreased social interaction caused by their institutionalization. This interpretation, however, misses a vital distinction between institutionalized and noninstitutionalized elderly adults. Without information concerning differences between the community and institutionalized elderly subjects regarding the amount of pathology in each group, the conclusion regarding the cause of differences in performance as due solely to place of residence is conjectural.

Differences in performance between community-living and institutionalized elderly were also noted by Chap and Sinnott (1975). Employing Piagetian measures of conservation of discrete substance, weight and length, classification, simple and temporal seriation, and combinatorial reasoning, the study compared the performance of 18 institutionalized and 16 community-active subjects. Community-active subjects performed significantly better than did institutionalized subjects. While studies such as Chap and Sinnott (1975) and Rubin (1973a) discuss the lack of meaningful social interaction for institutionalized elderly as responsible for the lowered performance of these groups, they do not provide any in-depth field analyses of social interaction levels (of a quantitative or qualitative nature) in their respective subsamples as justification for this interpretation.

Eisner (1973) investigated the effect of chronic brain syndrome on conservation performance. Using the Goldschmid and Bentler Concept Assessment Test plus a measure of volume conservation, Eisner compared 10 community subjects free from signs of chronic brain syndrome (ages 64 to 91), 10 institutionalized subjects (ages 64 to 91) with moderate chronic brain syndrome, and 10 institutionalized subjects (ages 78 to 90) with severe chronic brain syndrome. All community subjects free of chronic brain syndrome passed all tasks at the concrete level and 80% of these subjects passed the volume conservation task. Institutionalized subjects with moderate chronic brain syndrome performed far less well than subjects free of signs of organic brain impairment. Subjects with severe organic brain syndrome passed far fewer tasks (at the concrete level and at the task representing formal level functioning) than the moderate chronic brain syndrome group. In contrast to previous investigations which noted the putative disappearance of logical abilities in the reverse order of their acquisition, Eisner did not confirm this finding. Community subjects free of signs of chronic brain syndrome in the present study showed no signs of intellectual decline which previous studies had noted. Generally, however, low levels of concrete reasoning abilities were noted for both groups of institutionalized elderly suffering from moderate to severe chronic brain syndrome. Eisner's data, however, may be confounded since it is not possible to conclude that the differences in performance noted for the chronic brain syndrome individuals' were due to their disease, to institutionalization per se, or to a combination of these factors. Moreover, chronological age and chronic brain syndrome severity were also confounded in this study.

As Table I indicates, studies which assessed surface area conservation in elderly subjects have not unequivocally revealed an inevitable decrement of this ability. Sanders et al. (1966) investigated the ability to conserve surface area in subjects ranging in age from 20 to 60 years and over. Subjects in the oldest age group (60 years and over) performed at significantly lower levels on the area conservation task than did subjects in either the 20- to 30-year-old group or the 40- to 59-year-old group. The percentages of subjects successfully solving the area task were 84% (20- to 30-year-olds), 72% (40- to 59-year-olds), and 24.2% (60 years and over). Despite the fact that subjects in the oldest age group were drawn from institutional and noninstitutional settings, no analysis was conducted to determine the possible effect of institutionalization on performance. Analyses for the influence of sex and level of education revealed no significant sex differences, and a significant relationship between education and performance for only the 20- to 39-year old group.

Kominski and Coppinger (1968) also assessed area conservation in 102 institutionalized veterans. Subjects were drawn from each of three age groups: 50–59, 60–69, and 70 and over. Investigators altered the task instructions to ascertain whether instructional set may significantly affect performance. Half of the subjects in each age group received abstract instructions while the other half received experience-oriented instructions. Results indicated that all three age groups performed at low levels of conservation ability. There were no differences in performance due to different instructional sets.

Papalia *et al.* (1973a) examined the viability of surface area conservation in community-living elderly adults ranging in age from 63 to 92 years. The results indicated that only 13 of the entire 48 subjects conserved area. While no significant sex differences were noted, the level of formal schooling did significantly affect task performance.

In contrast to the findings of Kominski and Coppinger (1968), Sanders *et al.* (1966), and Papalia *et al.* (1973a) that the ability to conserve surface area disintegrates in old age, Garber *et al.* (1974) found that 82% of institutionalized elderly men (63 to 79 years of age) could successfully solve the area conservation task. Garber *et al.* (1974) attempted to alter the motivational set of elderly subjects by expressing a strong belief in elderly adults' ability to think logically and enlisting each subject's cooperation in confirming their belief. In addition to altering the motivational set, the authors did not use the "childish" task format of cows and barns employed by previous studies. Rather, they used simple geometric cubes to assess area conservation. The results of this investigation highlight the importance of considering noncognitive factors (e.g., motivation and task format) which may affect the cognitive performance of elderly adults. The results of the Garber *et al.* (1974) study, however, are confounded to an unknown degree due to an unacknowledged training component (i.e., the mixed presentation of equal and nonequal stimulus arrays) in their investigation which was not present in previous studies.

2.2. Logical Abilities in the Elderly

2.2.1. Concrete Operations Abilities

Fewer studies have assessed the status of logical abilities (classes, relations, probability, formal reasoning) than the previously reviewed investigations of various conservation abilities (see Table II). Studies of classification abilities have investigated the performance of adults and elderly subjects on measures of free classification, class inclusion, and multiple classification. Annett (1959) examined the classification performance of children (5 to 11 years of age) and adults (18 to 73 years of age) on a classification sorting task. The author noted that adults above and below 40 years of age classified according to different criteria. With increased age there was an increase in the use of complementary criteria and a decrease in the number of similarity responses.

Denney (1974a) in a review of empirical investigations of classificatory behavior of children and adults concluded that studies of free classification in elderly adults have generally found that the elderly's performance relies on the use of complementary criteria similar to that used by children. Elderly adults and children tend to categorize stimuli according to complementary criteria rather than on the basis of similarity. Similarity categorizations are based upon common attributes which items share either perceptually or categorically (e.g., a nail and a screw). Complementary categorizations, on the other hand, are based upon some functional interrelationship among the items based either upon the individual's past experience or some aspect of the testing situation (e.g., a nail and a hammer). Denney suggested, however, that the reason for the similarity in response preferences between children and the elderly in their use of complementary criteria for classifying objects may be that to classify according to complementary criteria "constitutes a more natural way of organizing one's experience" (Denney, 1974a, p. 49), rather than representing structural regression.

Denney and Lennon (1972) compared free classification responses in middle-aged and elderly subjects. Subjects were asked to put the stimuli that were "alike or *went together*" (emphasis added) into groups. Differences in arranging the stimulus array indicated that middle-aged subjects arranged the stimuli into piles of similar items, while elderly adults tended to group according to complementary criteria. The elderly thus tended to make either representations of real objects or elaborate designs with the stimulus materials. The authors noted the similarity between the performance of elderly adults and performance previously noted with children.

Table II. Logical Abilities in Elderly Subjects

Study	Subjects[a]	Abilities	Results
Annett, 1959	5–11 years; 19–73 years.	Sorting task.	Adults above 40 used different criteria than those below 40. Older Ss increased their use of complementary criteria.
Denney, 1974b	35–95 years ($N = 214$) $\overline{X}$ ages: 46.27 ($n = 64$), 66.84 ($n = 25$); and nursing-home residents 78.38 ($n = 125$).	Sorting.	Ss over 60 used complementary criteria significantly more than other age Ss. No significant difference between nursing-home residents and community-living elderly Ss based upon type of response or completeness of response.
Denney and Cornelius, 1975	Middle age ($\overline{X} = 34.53$); 67–92 ($\overline{X} = 73.19$); 67–92 ($\overline{X} = 76.22$) (institutionalized) ($n = 32$; $N = 96$).	Class inclusion; multiple classification.	Age and living situation significantly affected performance on both tasks. Middle-age Ss performed significantly better than the combined other Ss. Community-living elderly Ss performed significantly better than the institutionalized Ss.
Denney and Lennon, 1972	25–55 years ($\overline{X} = 37.73$) ($n = 32$); 67–95 years ($\overline{X} = 80.06$) ($n = 32$.	Sorting task.	Elderly Ss sorted on the basis of complementary criteria. Middle-age Ss sorted on similarity basis.

Hawley and Kelly, 1973	Four age groups (25–34; 45–54; 55–64; 65–74) drawn from high and low educational levels (N = 84).	Formal operations (chemical combinations, Nassefat's Probabilities Test and Conservation of Volume Tests (WAIS subtests—Digit Backward and Digit Symbol, Voc.).	Age and Piagetian task performance generally unrelated. Only one item on Probabilities Test showed a negative correlation with age (due primarily to the low-education group). Crystallized intelligence measure more strongly correlated with formal reasoning performance.
Muhs, Papalia, and Hooper, 1976	Ages: 5–7; 8–10; 11–13; 14–20; 21–30; 31–50; 51–65; 65 and over (n = 20; N = 160).	Some–all; class inclusion; combinatorial reasoning; transitivity of length and weight; conservation of length, weight, area; auditory sequencing; auditory memory; visual presentation memory; S–B Voc.; RPMT.	Significant age effects for all measures except weight transitivity. Decrements with advancing age noted for combinatorial reasoning, class inclusion, surface area conservation, visual orientation memory, and RPMT.
Overton and Clayton, 1976	80 female Ss with $\bar{X}$ ages: 19.05 (n = 20); 64.90 (n = 20); 73.25 (n = 20); 76.35 (n = 20) institutionalized.	Transitivity, two formal operations tasks (pendulum & a combinatorial pendulum card sorting task) and the RPMT.	Significant age effects noted for both the pendulum and card-sorting task. No age effect noted for transitivity. No differences noted in the performance of institutionalized and non-institutionalized elderly. RPMT significantly related to performance on both formal tasks. An overall significant negative correlation was noted between the crystallized measure and transitivity. For specific age levels, these correlations were not significant.

(Continued)

Table II. (Continued)

Study	Subjects[a]	Abilities	Results
Sheehan and Papalia, 1974	18 Ss in each of the following age groups: 6–7; 11–13; 18–21; 30–64; 65 and over ($N = 90$).	Class inclusion (animism); field dependence–independence.	Significant improvement beyond adolescence and no significant decline past age 65 on class-inclusion performance.
Storck, 1975	Ages: 6–9; 10–13; 14–17; 18–25; 26–35; 36–45; 46–55; 56–65; 66–over ($n = 20$; $N = 180$).	Some–all; multiple classification; class inclusion; transitivity of length and weight; multiple seriation; conservation of length and weight (identity and equivalence); combinatorial reasoning, and conservation of volume.	Statistically significant curvilinear age patterns noted for multiple classification; multiple seriation; volume and combinatorial reasoning. Age X sex interactions noted for multiple classification (favoring aged females) and conservation of equivalence (favoring youngest males).
Storck, Looft, and Hooper, 1972	Ages: 55–79 ($N = 24$).	Multiple classification (multiple seriation, weight, volume, TBR, RPMT, S–B Voc., and egocentrism).	Multiple classification more difficult than multiple seriation. All Ss passed conservation of weight while far fewer Ss passed volume ($n = 13$). RPMT performance significantly related to seriation, classification, TBR composite, and two subtests of TBR (Motor-Cognitive and Psychomotor Speed). Vocabulary was unrelated to Piagetian task performance.

[a]All Ss are community-living residents unless indicated.

A second study by Denney (1974b) investigated free classification in 214 subjects ranging in age from 35 to 95 years. Subjects were asked to put the stimuli that were "alike or *the same*" (emphasis added) together. Subjects' responses in the free classification task were scored as either (a) design (complementary criteria) or (b) similarity. Results indicated that subjects over 60 years of age employed design or complementary criteria significantly more often than other age groups. Age trends revealed a decrease in the use of shape and use of size and shape as criteria for categorization, and an increase in design and color responses. In contrast to the high percentage of elderly subjects who used design in the Denney and Lennon study (1972), the majority of elderly subjects in the Denney (1974b) investigation used similarity as the basis of their grouping. Differences between these two studies of free classification highlight the possible effect of performance differences related to task format (see specific instructions above). No differences were noted between elderly subjects drawn from a nursing home or the community. For the entire sample, sex was not significantly related to task performance. In a secondary investigation, Denney (1974b) attempted to determine whether elderly adults were unable to classify according to similarity because of regression to earlier more primitive thought structures or whether elderly adults simply chose to respond to a more natural way as is seen in nature (e.g., complementary criteria). The results of this study will be discussed in the last section of this review dealing with training studies of logical abilities.

Denney and Cornelius (1975) tested 96 white middle-class adults from each of three groups: middle age, community elderly (67–92 years of age) and institutionalized elderly (67–92 years of age) on a measure of class inclusion and one of multiple classification. A comparison of class-inclusion performance between middle-aged subjects and combined institutionalized and community elderly revealed significant performance differences between the two groups. Significant differences were noted between institutionalized and noninstitutionalized elderly. Performance on the multiple-classification task indicated significant differences between the three groups. Middle-aged subjects outperformed both community and institutionalized elderly adults. A comparison between the two groups of elderly indicated significant differences based upon place of residence. Community-living situations favored better performance.

Storck *et al.* (1972) investigated the interrelationships among Piagetian measures of logical-reasoning abilities and traditional measures of intelligence in 24 healthy community-living adults ranging in age from 55 to 79 years. Measures of Piagetian abilities administered were weight and volume conservation, multiple classification, multiple seriation, and an egocentrism measure. All subjects successfully passed weight conservation, six subjects failed multiple classification, one subject failed multiple seriation, and 11 failed volume conservation. Seven subjects were unable to pass any item on the egocentrism task. Traditional measures included the vocabulary subtest from the Stanford-Binet Intelligence Scale, the RPMT, and the Test of Behavioral Rigidity (Schaie, 1960). Vocabulary was unrelated to performance on any of the Piagetian measures. Results further indicated there was a significant positive relationship between the RPMT and both multiple classification and multiple seriation. Egocentrism was generally unrelated to any of the measures employed.

Sheehan and Papalia (1974) administered a measure of class inclusion to elderly subjects in their study of animistic thinking across the life-span. Age trends for class inclusion showed a significant age effect, and performance continued to improve through the college age level. In contrast to Denney and Cornelius (1974) findings, class-inclusion performance did not significantly decline past age 65.

Storck (1975) conducted a life-span investigation of Piagetian abilities in subjects ranging in age from 6 to 91 years of age. Administering a wide array of Piagetian tasks including three classification tasks (some–all, multiple classification, and class inclusion), three relational tasks (transitivity of length and weight, and multiple seriation), four conservation tasks (length and weight identity and equivalence format), and two formal operations tasks (combinatorial reasoning and volume conservation), Storck's results indicated a statistically significant curvilinear age pattern for multiple classification, multiple seriation, volume conservation, and combinatorial reasoning. No age effect was noted for conservation of length and weight, transitivity of length, and weight and class inclusion.

In a life-span cross-sectional design, Muhs et al. (1976) assessed conservation of length, weight, and surface area, length and weight transitivity, some–all understanding, class inclusion, combinatorial reasoning, in addition to standardized measures of auditory memory (forward digit and word series), visual orientation memory, vocabulary (Stanford-Binet subtest) and the RCPMT. Subjects were 10 males and 10 females at each of the following age ranges: 5–7 years ($\bar{X} = 6.20$ years), 8–10 years ($\bar{X} = 9.05$ years), 11–13 years ($\bar{X} = 11.65$ years), 14–20 years ($\bar{X} = 15.8$ years), 21–30 years ($\bar{X} = 25.2$ years), 31–50 years ($\bar{X} = 37.90$ years), 51–65 years ($\bar{X} = 56.85$ years), and 65 years and older ($\bar{X} = 74.75$ years). Analyses indicated that order of presentation and sex-difference main effects were notably absent except for the combinatorial reasoning task, in which female subjects were superior to their male counterparts.

As anticipated, χ^2 comparisons indicated significant age-group main effects for the majority of the measures. The only exceptions were the transitivity of length and weight tasks. Significant age/sex interactions were found for the digit series memory, combinatorial reasoning, and conservation of surface area tasks. Curvilinear age trends were evident for the combinatorial reasoning, class inclusion, conservation of surface area, RCPMT, and visual-orientation memory tasks.

2.2.2 Formal Operational Abilities

According to Piagetian theory, the highest level of logical thinking occurs with the attainment of formal operational thought. Piaget (1972b) has commented on the nature and evolution of formal operational thought noting the influence of an individual's specific aptitudes and occupational specializations. He further commented that:

> all normal subjects attain the stage of formal operations or structuring if not between 11–12 and 14–15 years, in any case between 15 and 20 years. However, individuals may reach this stage in different areas according to their aptitudes and their professional specializations (advanced studies or different types of apprenticeship for various trades): the way in which these formal structures are used, however, is not necessarily the same in all cases. (Piaget, 1972b, pp. 9–10.)

Due to the somewhat variable nature of formal thought, there have been few studies of formal thinking in adults and the elderly. Smedslund (1963) noted that adult subjects in two experiments were unable to use correlational reasoning in estimating probability. In both experiments, adult subjects failed to understand the concept of probability.

A number of studies of volume conservation, often considered to be an index of formal reasoning, have noted sizable percentages of nonconserving adult subjects (e.g., Elkind, 1961, 1962; Graves, 1972; Higgens-Trenk and Gaite, 1971; Papalia, 1972a; Storck, 1975).

Investigations which have examined volume conservation performances in elderly adults typically find that these subjects pass the volume conservation task far less frequently than concrete operations conservation measures (Eisner, 1973; Papalia, 1972; Papalia et al., 1973b; Storck et al., 1972).

In similar fashion, combinatorial reasoning has been found to be significantly more difficult than various concrete tasks for elderly subjects (Chap and Sinnot, 1975; Muhs et al., 1976; Storck, 1975). For a general review of formal operational thought in mature and adult subjects, see Blasi and Hoeffel, 1975.

Another investigation of formal reasoning (Overton & Clayton, 1976) compared the performance of four groups of adult women (college coeds, 60- to 69-year-old women, 70- to 79-year-old women, and 70- to 79-year-old women residing in an old-age home) on two measures of formal reasoning, the pendulum task and a derived card sorting task. A significant age effect was noted for these two measures. With advanced age, women were less successful at solving both formal reasoning tasks. An earlier-appearing concrete logical ability, transitive inference, showed no such age effect. In addition to examining the status of formal operational thought, Overton and Clayton investigated the relationship between traditional intelligence measures (the Raven Progressive Matrices Test—RPMT and the verbal subtest of the WAIS) and logical reasoning. For the entire sample, there was a significant and overall relationship between the measure of fluid intelligence (the RPMT) and both formal operational tasks. A comparison of the oldest age groups by place of residence revealed no effect due to institutionalization.

Hawley and Kelley (1973) also investigated the relationship between formal operational thought and fluid and crystallized intelligence in males ranging in age from 25 to 74 years of age. Subjects were drawn from each of four age groups: 25–34, 45–54, 55–64, and 65–74. Within each age group subjects were characterized as either high educational level (four or more years of college) or low educational level (12 years of formal schooling or less). All subjects were administered three formal operations tasks (chemical combinations, Nassefat's Probabilities Test, and Conservation of Volume Test), two measures of fluid intelligence (WAIS subtests—Digit Backward and Digit Symbol) and one measure of crystallized intelligence (WAIS vocabulary). Results indicated that for the high-education males all correlations between age and Piagetian task performance were nonsignificant. For the entire sample, age and Piagetian task performance were nonsignificant. For the entire sample, age and Piagetian task performance were negatively correlated for only one item, the first item on the Probabilities Test due to the influence of the low-education males. In contrast to the results of Overton and Clayton (1976), crystallized intelligence was more closely related to Piagetian task performance than was either measure of fluid intelligence. Age trends suggested that, in contrast to the age-related decline noted for Digit Symbol performance, the ability to reason at the formal level remained stable over all the age ranges studied. Differences in performance between the high and low-education males suggest the important influence of education rather than age on formal reasoning abilities. The authors speculate that fluid and crystallized intelligence may differentially contribute toward the ability to solve successfully concrete and formal reasoning tasks.

2.3. Studies of Animistic and Egocentric Thought

In addition to describing logical and infralogical abilities in adults and the elderly, researchers have attempted to describe developmental changes in other Piagetian abilities. These abilities include animistic reasoning and cognitive egocentrism.

2.3.1. Animism

Animism or the tendency of young children to attribute life to inanimate objects was described in Piaget's early work (Piaget, 1929, 1933). Adults are presumed to be free of animistic thinking. Looft and Bartz (1969) have provided an excellent review of investigations of animism in children, college students, and the elderly. Two studies which assessed animism in elderly adults obtained similar results. Each study, however, interpreted the results in markedly different ways. Dennis and Mallinger (1949) investigated animistic thinking in 36 elderly adults 70 years of age and older. Of these subjects 75% gave animistic responses typical of those given by children. The authors concluded that these findings represent a regression to childhood-level concepts. Studies which have investigated animism in college-age subjects, however, have also revealed high levels of animistic thinking among the subjects tested (e.g., Bell, 1954; Crannell, 1954; Crowell and Dole, 1957; Dennis, 1953, 1957; Mikulak, 1970; Papalia, 1972b; Voeks, 1954).

In contrast to the conclusions of Dennis and Mallinger (1949), the results of a cross-sectional life-span study of animism (Sheehan and Papalia, 1974) which found high levels of animistic thinking at all age levels suggested that the tendency to respond animistically rather than representing a primitive level of responding may represent the adult's awareness of the "dialectical nature of life" (cf. Riegel, 1974). Collateral findings based upon each subject's performance on a measure of cognitive style, Witkin's Embedded Figures Test, and a class-inclusion measure supported the authors' argument that the presence in adult and elderly subjects of animistic responses does not represent primitive thought structures. The level of adult and elderly animistic responses was unrelated to either performance on the cognitive style measure or class inclusion, while the level of animistic responses was significantly related to both measures for the 11- to 13-year-old age group.

2.3.2. Egocentrism

The ability to decenter or take the perspective of another is a central concept in Piagetian theory. The construct of egocentrism, however, while playing an important role in theoretical assumptions of Piaget's theory is a somewhat confusing concept. Previous empirical investigations of the various forms of egocentrism in children (e.g., spatial, communicative, role taking) have revealed a mixed picture regarding the unidimensionality of this construct (e.g., Rubin, 1973b, contrasted with Shantz, 1968). The principal assumption regarding egocentrism maintains that, until an individual is able to decenter, he will be unable adequately to solve logical operations tasks. Fixation on one's own perspective, thus, interferes with successful problem-solving.

Looft and Charles (1971) investigated egocentrism in young and old adults. Each subject was individually tested to assess his/her level of cognitive egocentrism. Subsequently subjects were grouped into three types of pairs within each age group. The pairs consisted of the following combinations based on each subject's score on the cognitive measure of egocentrism: lo–lo egocentrism, hi–lo egocentrism, and hi–hi egocentrism. Pairs of subjects were then required to engage in a social–interaction task which required subjects working in pairs to complete a matrix with a variety of objects similar to his/her partner without looking at the partner's matrix. Elderly adults, while significantly less able to decenter on the cognitive egocentrism task, were as effective as younger subjects in the social-interaction task. The only significant difference noted betwen old and young subjects in the social-interaction task was the amount of time necessary for elderly adults to solve the task. This finding is consistent with those previously noted in the gerontological research concerning the need of elderly subjects to progress at their own pace. The elderly were generally conservative and exhibited a cautious approach in accomplishing the task. When elderly subjects were provided social feedback concerning their performance on the social-interaction task, they were able to solve the task. In contrast, on the cognitive egocentrism where no feedback was provided, the elderly performed at a significantly lower level than the younger subjects.

Rubin (1974) in a cross-sectional life-span study compared two measures of egocentrism. Using a spatial measure and a communicative egocentrism measure, Rubin found a nonsignificant relationship between the two forms of egocentrism for the elderly subjects. The peak of cognitive functioning was noted for the college-age group. Educational level was not related to performance on the egocentrism measures.

Rubin et al. (1973) employed a measure of spatial egocentrism. Using a cross-sectional life-span design, the results of this study allow a comparison of all differences in the ability to decenter among the different age groups. Performance on the spatial egocentrism task revealed a curvilinear relationship with age. Elderly subjects' performance on the spatial task was significantly inferior to that of college-age and middle-age subjects. The putative "regression" of elderly subjects on the spatial task was not so severe as that for conservation performance. No significant performance effects were noted for the sex or education factors.

Similar age trends for spatial egocentrism were noted in a life-span study by Bielby and Papalia (1975) which investigated the relationship between spatial egocentrism and moral development by interviewing 72 subjects ranging from 10 to 65 years of age and over. Performance on the spatial egocentrism task revealed a curvilinear relationship with age. The ability to decenter continued to show improvement through young adulthood and then declined significantly with age. Males showed consistent superiority in the ability adequately to solve the decentration problem.

Rubin (1973a) compared the performance of 27 noninstitutionalized and 28 institutionalized elderly subjects on a measure of spatial egocentrism and various measures of conservation. A comparison of the egocentrism scores of institutionalized and noninstitutionalized elderly revealed substantial performance differences. While the institutionalized elderly performed at a lower level, this difference did not reach significance. Despite the lack of any statistically significant difference between institutionalized and noninstitutionalized elderly, Rubin discussed the superior ability of community elderly to decenter due to their presumed greater level of social interaction. Rubin's strongly stated conclusions concerning the effect of institutionalization upon the ability to decenter seem unwarranted due to the lack of any significant difference between noninstitutionalized and institutionalized elderly adults on the spatial egocentrism measure.

With the exception of Looft and Charles (1971) and Rubin (1974), investigations of egocentrism in elderly adults have used only one rather specific measure of egocentrism, spatial egocentrism. Clearly, additional studies which employ more than a single measure of egocentrism must be conducted before any definite understanding of this characteristic in old age is possible. The ability to assume alternate spatial orientations is only one limited aspect of the ability to take the perspective of another into account. As Looft and Charles (1971) have noted, there is considerable difference between the spatial measure in which no feedback is provided and other more social forms of taking the perspective of another individual. Looft (1972) provides a review of egocentrism and social interaction across the life-span. Despite the paucity of research with adult and elderly subjects, Looft maintains the need to explore the viability of this construct for understanding the cognitive functioning of the elderly.

2.4. Training Logical Operations in Old Age

As described previously, proponents of a stability or a decrement with compensation model of the aging process (Schaie, 1973) suggest that experimental training-instruction research may provide valuable information concerning the determinants of intellectual functioning and related learning potentials (cf. Baltes, 1973; Baltes and Schaie, 1973; Wohlwill, 1973). Effective instructional strategies which have been employed with elderly subjects have included modeling techniques (Denney, 1974b; Denney and Denney, 1974), operant conditioning (Hoyer *et al.*, 1973; Labouvie-Vief *et al.*, 1974), corrective feedback (Hornblum and Overton, 1976; Schultz and Hoyer, 1976), and self-instructional strategies (Meichenbaum, 1974; Vief and Gonda, 1976; see Table III). In general, these investigations have sought to determine whether the observed age differences in cognitive functioning between young adults and the elderly are due to structural regression or attributable to performance factors mediated by age-related environmental conditions which may suppress cognitive performance. Overall, attempts to train logical abilities in elderly adults have proved successful when near transfer is employed as the criterion of success.

Denney (1974b) trained 24 elderly nursing-home residents ranging in age from 65 to 91 years to classify geometric shapes on the basis of similarity in contrast to their previously preferred basis of categorization. After the experimental subjects were exposed to a brief modeling training condition, they showed significant improvement in classifying on the basis of similarity. Trained subjects showed some generalization to the second posttest, but this difference was not significant. Despite the short duration of the training, subjects in the experimental group showed significant improvement. Denney concluded that training was effective and that the previously noted lower level of performance among elderly adults was, therefore, not likely due to neural disintegration factors.

Schultz and Hoyer (1976) conducted a training study employing 36 community-living elderly adults, ranging in age from 61 to 88 years, on a measure of spatial egocentrism. In addition to the egocentrism task, other measures included were the space, number, and word fluency subtests of the Primary Mental Abilities Test, the Identical Pictures Test, the RPMT, and a measure of volume conservation. Subjects were assigned to one of three training conditions: (a) corrective feedback, (b) nonreinforced practice, and (c) control. Subjects in the feedback condition showed significant improvement on the spatial egocentrism task. No difference was noted between subjects in the practice and con-

Table III. Training Studies of Piagetian and Related Abilities in Elderly Subjects

Study	Subjects[a]	Ability	Type of training	Results
Denney, 1974b	65–91 years nursing-home residents ($N = 24$).	Free classification based on similarity responses.	Modeling.	Training significantly increased similarity classification. Some generalization, but not significant.
Hornblum and Overton, 1976	22 Ss ages 65.1–75.9 ($\bar{X} = 71$) (8 nonconservers and 14 partial conservers).	Surface area.	(1) Feedback (2) No feedback Control group Subjects matched age, educational level, and Quick Test score.	Feedback group made substantial gains during training and performed significantly better than the control on the near-transfer task and four of the five far-transfer tasks. A delayed posttest administered six weeks following training to six Ss indicated the effects of feedback were maintained.

(Continued)

Table III. (Continued)

Study	Subjects[a]	Ability	Type of training	Results
Rubin, 1976	Trained grade two (7.03); untrained grade two (7.03); grade five (10.41); grade seven (12.59); young adult (22.21); middle age (47.26); elderly (73.61) and institutionalized elderly (81.84). All Ss required to reach criterion on posttest conservation measures to be included in the extinction phase of the experimental manipulation.	Conservation of discrete and continuous quantity.	Extinction.	Significant differences in resistance to extinction for different age groups. Young adult group most resistant with the exception of the middle-age group. Middle-aged more resistant than both grade-two groups, grade-five children, and institutionalized elderly. Elderly Ss were more resistant than grade-two and grade-five children. No significant differences were noted between the two groups of elderly Ss.
Schultz and Hoyer, 1976	61–88 years (N = 36).	Spatial egocentrism.	(1) Feedback. (2) Practice. (3) Control.	Feedback condition produced significant improvement. No difference between practice and control groups.
Tomlinson-Keasey, 1972	$\bar{X}$ ages: 11.9 (n = 24); 19.7 (n = 24); and 54 (n = 24).	Formal tasks (pendulum, balance, and flexibility).	(1) Systematic elucidation of problem-solving steps from simple to complex.	All three age groups of experimental Ss showed significant improvement on immediate posttest.

			(2) Control.	No improvements on the delayed posttest for different tasks. Near transfer gains on delayed posttest for girls and coeds showed significant increase from pretest levels.
Vief and Gonda, 1976	63–95 years ($\bar{X} = 76$) $n = 15$ female Ss each of four groups.	Inductive reasoning problems (Letter Sets Test) Transfer task; RPMT.	(1) Cognitive Training. (2) Anxiety Training. (3) Unspecified Training. (4) No Training.	Ss in groups 1 and 2 showed significant improvement on the trained task on immediate posttest. On the delayed posttest only the Unspecified Training group showed improvement. Evidence of transfer (Raven) for group 3 and some generalization for group 1.

[a]All Ss are community-living residents unless indicated.

trol conditions. Significant correlations were noted between age and egocentrism, the RPMT and egocentrism, and the PMA-space subtest and egocentrism. These findings generally support the relationship between fluid intelligence and spatial egocentrism. In view of the efficacy of training in the present study, the authors concluded that the requisite structures and operations were present in the elderly subjects. The influence of age-related environmental factors rather than intraindividual ontogenetic changes, the authors suggest, may be responsible for the apparent decline.

A third training study which employed a somewhat younger group of mature women compared the training performance of three groups of women (11.9, 19.7, and 54 years of age) on formal operations tasks (Tomlinson-Keasey, 1972). Three formal-level tasks—the pendulum, the balance, and a flexibility problem—were employed in the pretest, training, and posttest. Training consisted of taking each subject from her present level of knowledge to a greater understanding of the variables involved in successfully solving the task (prediction, testing, and conclusions). The posttest required each subject to explain the tasks to another subject. Performance on the flexibility problem constituted a measure of near transfer while performance on two new formal tasks (chemical combinations and the toy train) constituted measures of far transfer. Comparison between the experimental and control group revealed a significant effect of training. Training, however, was most effective for the college-age women. Near transfer gains on the delayed posttest were significantly above pretest levels for the girls and college coeds.

Hornblum and Overton (1976) initially assessed area and volume conservation in 60 noninstitutionalized elderly females. The assessment tasks included three area conservation tasks and three volume conservation tasks (interior volume, occupied volume, and displacement volume). For individual tasks, the percentage of subjects passing ranged from 43.3% to 75%. Based upon a qualitative stage designation, only 33.3% of these elderly subjects were classified as conservers across all the tasks. The performance decrement noted among the elderly subjects tested was in general agreement with the findings of previous studies.

In an attempt to determine whether these findings actually represent characteristic structural disintegration which accompanies aging or mere performance difficulties which affect elderly subjects, a training study was subsequently conducted. Twenty-two subjects from the first assessment were selected to participate in the training. Based upon the earlier assessment, eight subjects were classified as nonconservers, while the remaining Ss were classified as partial conservers. Subjects were assigned to either a simple feedback or control group. Subjects in each group were matched. Training consisted of a 20-trial procedure on a task similar to the conservation-of-surfaces task.

Results of training on the immediate posttest indicated the feedback group performed significantly better than the control group on the near-transfer task and four of the five far-transfer tasks. A delayed posttest administered to six subjects indicated that improvement was maintained for at least six weeks following training. The strength and consistency of the improvement of the experimental group are offered as strong support for the employment of a performance/competence distinction among elderly individuals.

In a training study related to Piagetian logical reasoning, Vief and Gonda (1976) employed a training, immediate posttest, and delayed posttest paradigm to determine if training improved elderly subjects' performance on complex reasoning problems. Sixty elderly female subjects were randomly assigned to one of four groups (two instructional and two control). Subjects in the instructional training groups received either Cognitive Training similar to that of Meichenbaum (1974) or Cognitive Training coupled with Anxiety Training. Subjects in the two control conditions received either No Training or Unspecified Training (practice with no specific instructions). Results indicated that on the immediate posttest subjects in the two training groups outperformed control subjects. On the delayed posttest, however, the training groups no longer maintained their advantage. The Unspecified Training group performed significantly better than the No Training group. The effect of training generalized to performance on the Raven most effectively for the Unspecified Training with slight improvement for the Cognitive Training group. The effect of training and the generalizability to a dissimilar task, the authors suggest, indicates the plasticity of intellectual behavior in old age.

Additional evidence against an inevitable, irreversible decline in problem-solving strategies in the elderly was noted by Denney and Denney (1974). Subjects ranging in age from 70 to 90 years of age were assigned to one of three conditions: (a) exemplary modeling, (b) cognitive-strategy modeling, and (c) control. All subjects in a previous study had asked no constraint-seeking questions, questions that eliminate a class of items, similar to those used in 20 questions. Subjects in both training conditions after observing a model significantly increased the number of constraint-seeking questions and decreased the number of questions required for solution of the posttest problem. Subjects in both modeling conditions rapidly acquired the appropriate problem-solving strategy, suggesting that the skill was readily available in the repertoire of the elderly subjects and easily elicited by training.

Employing a cross-sectional life-span experimental design, Rubin (1976) compared the extinction rates for conservation and discontinuous and continuous quantity for subjects who had reached criterion for these concepts on a posttest. Eight groups of subjects—trained and untrained second-grade children, fifth graders, seventh graders, young adults, middle-age adults, and community-living and institutionalized elderly—were exposed to experimental manipulation to extinguish quantity conservation responses. Analyses among the various groups noted significant differences in susceptibility to the extinction. Further comparisons revealed that the young-adult group was significantly more resistant to extinction than all other groups except the middle-age subjects. Elderly subjects were more resistant to extinction than the fifth-grade children and both groups of grade-two children. Finally, middle-age subjects were more resistant than the second and fifth graders and the institutionalized elderly group. Education for the adult age ranges did not significantly affect the ability to resist extinction.

According to Rubin (1976), the differences in resistance to counter-suggestion concerning conservation quantity concepts among the adult groups is support for a neurological decrement interpretation of the data. However, it should be noted that there was no significant difference in the rate of extinction between the middle-age and elderly groups. Alternately, the results lend themselves to an interpretation of the effect of various performance factors which may affect different age groups in markedly different ways, such as a greater tendency on the part of the elderly to agree with the experimenter.

3. Discussion

In this section, we shall consider a number of factors which are potential determinants of logical concept proficiency in mature and aged individuals. These factors include neurophysiological deficits, social-interaction variables as present in institutionalized contrasted with noninstitutionalized population samples, formal educational experi-ence, and the possible relationship of logical-concept functioning to other measures of intellectual prowess. Next, we will consider some of the major methodological constraints present in the current cognitive assessment literature. Finally, the general implications of the present research findings will be evaluated in terms of competence/performance distinctions in cognitive functioning and related assessment.

3.1. Factors Which May Influence the Performance of Aged Individuals

3.1.1. Neurological Intactness and Piagetian Task Performance

A popular explanation for the apparent decline of Piagetian cognitive functioning in the later years implicates the role of inevitable neurological decline which accompanies the aging process as a factor responsible for the apparent decline (cf. Hooper et al., 1971). However, no direct relationship between neurological decline and Piagetian task performance has been empirically established.

The original speculation of Hooper et al. (1971) noted an apparent similarity between Piagetian logical concepts and fluid intellectual abilities (cf. Horn, 1967, 1970). The authors suggested that, due to the putative relationship between Piagetian abilities and fluid intelligence, Piagetian abilities should exhibit the same inevitable decline noted for fluid intelligence. Other investigators have accepted this explanation to account for the lowered Piagetian cognitive performance noted among elderly individuals. Several researchers who have empirically investigated the possible relationship between fluid intelligence and Piagetian abilities, however, have not provided conclusive evidence for this argument (Hawley and Kelly, 1973; Muhs et al., 1976; Overton and Clayton, 1972). Rather, it would appear that, while Piagetian abilities and fluid intelligence may be related to a certain extent, there is no evidence to suggest that these abilities follow an identical developmental course. A more comprehensive coverage of this relationship is dealt with in a section of the conclusion.

In contrast to the speculation of Hooper et al. (1971), which specified that the inevitable loss of neurological intactness results in an inevitable regression to earlier levels of cognitive functioning, other writers have suggested that pathological neural dysfunction (e.g., chronic brain syndrome) may account for lowered cognitive performance among elderly individuals. D. Eisner's data (1973), while suggestive of the possible effect of neurological deficiency is, however, confounded to unknown degrees. The work of Ajuriaguerra and his colleagues (Ajuriaguerra and Tissot, 1966; Ajuriaguerra et al., 1964; Ajuriaguerra et al., 1965; Ajuriaguerra et al., 1966; Ajuriaguerra et al., 1967) with elderly patients suffering from senile dementia offers additional support for the regressive effect of pathological neural dysfunction on Piagetian task performance.

Neither argument, however, clearly specifies the role of neurological intactness as a factor affecting Piagetian task performances among elderly individuals. While it is clear that neurological intactness plays an important contributary or causative role in maintaining Piagetian logical reasoning abilities, further research must be conducted to specify this relationship.

3.1.2. Social-Interaction Factors and the Role of Institutionalization

The effect of environmental variables upon the cognitive performance of the elderly has yet to be comprehensively explored. Studies which have purportedly assessed differences in environmental factors include comparisons between institutionalized and noninstitutionalized elderly subjects. These studies, however, have not consistently noted differences between institutionalized and community-living subjects. Several studies have noted the superior performance of community-living subjects (Chap and Sinnott, 1975; Denney and Cornelius, 1975; Eisner, 1973). Other studies which have included "institutionalized" subjects have found either no difference (Denney, 1974b; Overton and Clayton, 1976) or failed to analyze for specific differences due to institutionalization (Garber et al., 1974; Kominski and Coppinger, 1968; Sanders et al., 1966).

Studies which have found significant differences have generally failed to delineate clearly the type and quality of care provided by the institution, the degree of pathology or impairment among the residents, and the length of institutionalization for the subjects tested. Obvious differences may therefore exist in either environmental variables (e.g., quality of care, degree of social interaction, etc.) or the degree or amount of pathology among residents or some complex interaction among the variables. Conclusions such as those of Rubin (1973a) or Chap and Sinnot (1975), which attribute differences in performance between community-living and institutionalized to the decreased social interaction in institutionalized settings, have failed to recognize the complex nature of institutionalization. Studies attempting to assess the effect of institutionalization upon performance have generally confounded institutionalization or neurological impairment (cf. Eisner, 1973).

The failure of studies of institutionalization to detect consistent differences due to institutionalization does not, however, negate the role of environmental variables. Rather, it highlights the need for more precise environmental measures. Information regarding specific aspects of the environment which facilitate or maintain competent behavior may provide better estimates of the relationship between cognitive functioning and environmental influences (Lawton, 1972) than those provided by the global variable of institutionalization per se. In addition, the findings of Denney (1974b), Garber *et al.* (1974), and Overton and Clayton (1972) question the pervasive "decremental" influence of institutionalization upon cognitive performance of elderly subjects. Therefore, the variable of "institutionalization," as presently defined or operationalized, has failed to provide significant information concerning any direct or indirect causal relationships between "institutionalization" and performance.

3.1.3. The Role of Formal Educational Factors

It is commonly acknowledged that the Piagetian system minimizes the role of formal schooling factors as major determinants of concrete operations-concept acquisition. The empirical assessment literature (e.g., Goodnow, 1962, 1969; Goodnow and Bethon, 1966; Sigel and Mermelstein, 1965) would appear to support this contention although the potential modifiability of logical concepts in laboratory or quasi-laboratory settings remains an equivocal issue (cf. training experiment evaluations by Brainerd, 1973; Brainerd and Allen, 1971; contrasted with Beilin, 1971; Klausmeier and Hooper, 1974; Inhelder and Sinclair, 1969; Wohlwill, 1970, 1973). In relative contrast, the acquisition of formal operational thought is considered to be subject to educational and occupational specialization (Goodnow, 1969; Piaget, 1972b).

A sizable number of studies have examined the relationship of years of formal schooling to Piagetian concept task performances. Overall, the results of these investigations are decidedly ambiguous. Nine studies have failed to find significant relationships between education and logical-concept performances. Graves (1972) found that in a sample of 60 minimally educated adults (8 years or less of formal schooling) 78% passed quantity conservation, 67% passed weight conservation, while only 24% passed the volume conservation task. However, years of education was significantly related to quantity conservation only. Sanders *et al.* (1966) found a significant education/surface area conservation relationship only for the 20- to 39-year-old subsample. In the Papalia (1971) study, the correlation values ranged from -0.25 (weight conservation in the 55–64-year-old group) to $+0.33$ (weight conservation in the 30–54-year-old group) and were uniformly nonsignificant.

Educational level does not appear to influence performance on cognitive egocentrism measures. Thus Rubin (1974) found nonsignificant correlations for both spatial and communicative egocentrism indices. In the Rubin *et al.* (1973) investigation correlations ranged from -0.11 (conservation total score) and $+0.09$ (spatial egocentrism) for the elderly subject subsample to $+0.36$ (spatial egocentrism) and $+0.36$ (conservation) for the middle-aged subjects. All these coefficients failed to reach acceptable significance levels. In similar fashion, a covariance analysis (years of formal education as covariate) of perceptual role-taking egocentrism in a cross-sectional life-span assessment design was only marginally significant for a subsample of adult and elderly subjects (Bielby and Papalia, 1975).

The correlations between years of education and logical task performance ranged from -0.02 (volume conservation) to $+.24$ (multiple classification) in the Storck *et al.* (1972) study (all values were nonsignificant). In the Denney and Cornelius (1974) investigation of classificatory abilities, no significant educational-level relationships were found for the class-inclusion task performances or for the female subjects' multiple-classification abilities. Educational status did, however, discriminate for male multiple-classification performances. Finally, Rubin (1976) assessed the relationship of educational level to resistance to conservation extinction (continuous and discontinuous quantity task formats). Nonsignificant relationships were observed for both the middle-aged and elderly subject subsamples.

In contrast to these findings, six investigations have found significant education/concept performance relationships for a variety of task settings. Chap and Sinnott (1975) found a correlation of $+0.52$ ($p < 0.01$) between years of schooling and overall success on a series of concrete and formal operations tasks. Papalia *et al.* (1973b) reported correlations of $+0.24$ ($p < 0.05$) for weight and volume conservation, and $+0.34$ ($p < 0.01$) for quantity conservation and educational status in a sample of 48 elderly adults. The comparison value for the male subsample volume conservation/education case was $+0.59$ ($p < 0.01$). In the Storck (1975) life-span investigation, significant correlations between years of education and concept performances (total sample of 180) ranged from $+0.14$ for class inclusion to $+0.53$ for combinatorial reasoning. Excluding the tasks of lowest item difficulty (some–all understanding and transitive inference), the average intercorrelation value was $+0.29$.

Much stronger relationships were found in the studies by Papalia *et al.* (1973a), Hawley and Kelly (1973), and Muhs *et al.* (1976). In the Papalia *et al.* (1973a) investigation, the correlation between years of education and conservation-of-surface-area performance (sample of 48 63–92-year-old subjects) was $+.035$ ($p < 0.02$). More importantly, since age and years of education were positively related ($+0.74$, $p < 0.001$) a partial correlation coefficient (task/education) was calculated with chronological age as the covariate. The resultant correlation coefficient was a remarkable $+0.98$ ($p < .001$)! With the age range in question, it is apparent that the Papalia *et al.* (1973a) sample must have included a very highly educated group of elderly individuals. Hawley and Kelly's (1973) sample included 42 low-education and 40 high-education males across the age range 25 to 74 years. Markedly superior performance was noted for the highly educated subsample while there was an *absence* of chronological age trends for the series of formal operations period measures (four volume and four probability tasks). The average intercorrelation between education status (Hollingshead Scale—high = 1 to low = 7) and formal task performance was -0.38.

Muhs *et al.* (1976) included years of formal education as a variable in the relationship analyses conducted in a cross-sectional life-span assessment design. The intercorrelations for the adolescent to adult subsample ($N = 60$, age = 15 to 50 years) averaged $+0.27$. For the older subsample, the corresponding value was $+0.32$. Deleting the relatively easy some–all understanding task resulted in respective average correlation values of $+0.31$ and $+0.37$. Moreover, covariance analyses of the educational factor (chronological age as the covariate) for the four oldest age groups ($N = 80$; 21 $-$ 66 + years of age) were significant for the measures of combinatorial reasoning, class inclusion, conservation of weight and surface area. Only the least difficult concrete-operations measures (some–all understanding, length and weight transitivity, and conservation of length) were not significantly related to the educational index.

In retrospect, it is clear that the influence of educational status on Piagetian concept performances depends upon the subject sampling procedure and specific assessment tasks employed. As anticipated, the relationship is stronger for the late-appearing concrete and formal operations tasks (Chap and Sinnott, 1975; Hawley and Kelly, 1973; Muhs *et al.*, 1976; Papalia *et al.*, 1973a). Educational level does not appear to be influential in studies of egocentric reasoning (Bielby and Papalia, 1975; Rubin, 1974; Rubin *et al.*, 1973). In those studies in which significant intercorrelations were found, the average coefficients fell in the range of $+0.30$ to $+0.40$, thus putatively accounting for 10% to 16% of the common variance. Of course, these correlational investigations convey very little concerning the manner in which educational factors bear upon concept task performances or the specific role educational experiences may play in acquiring or maintaining logical-concept proficiency.

3.1.4. The Relationship of Logical-Concept Proficiency to Other Intelligence Measures

While a number of investigators have examined the dimensionality of Piagetian concept task arrays and/or the relationship to conventional

intelligence measures in samples of children and adolescents (e.g., Berzonsky, 1971; Hooper et al., 1974; Nassefat, 1963; O'Bryan and MacArthur, 1969; Rubin, 1973b; Stephens, 1972; Vernon, 1965), far fewer
studies have been concerned with these interrelationships during the
mature and aging years. The majority of the latter endeavors have compared logical-concept skills to performances on measures of the general
intellectual factors of fluid (G_f) and crystallized (G_c) intelligence (cf.
Horn, 1967, 1970). Hooper et al. (1971) speculated that the usual Piagetian task requirements are more closely related to the neurologically
derived fluid factor, which is relatively free of cultural, schooling, and
specific life experiences.

Overton and Clayton (1976) compared the performances of 80
female subjects from three age levels (20, 65, and 73 years) on a concrete
operations task, length transitivity, a formal-level reasoning task, the
pendulum problem, and a related card-sorting task to an index of fluid
intelligence (the RPMT) and a crystallized measure (the verbal subtest of
the Wechsler Adult Intelligence Scale). As predicted, the formal operations measures were more highly related to the fluid measure ($+0.23, p$
$< 0.05; +0.44, p < 0.01$) than to the crystallized index ($+0.01, +0.06$). The
correlation of the transitivity measure with the RPMT score was $+0.17$
(n.s.) and with the WAIS vocabulary was -0.37 ($p < 0.01$). Storck et al.
(1972) included the RPMT and the Stanford-Binet vocabulary subtest in
an assessment of 24 elderly subjects. The fluid intelligence index was
significantly related to the multiplicative classification ($+0.52, p < 0.01$)
and seriation ($+0.44, p < 0.05$) measures while the vocabulary test scores
failed to correlate with any of the Piagetian task performances. Storck
(1975) also included the RCPMT and the Stanford-Binet vocabulary subtest in her life-span analysis of logical reasoning abilities. The average
intercorrelation of the vocabulary index with the Piagetian task series
was $+0.26$ while the counterpart value for the RPMT was $+0.37$. For the
subset of more difficult concept tasks (mulitplicative classification, multiplicative seriation, class inclusion, and combinatorial reasoning) the
comparison values were $+0.31$ (crystallized index) and $+0.54$ (fluid index), respectively.

In the Schultz and Hoyer (1976) instructional study, correlations
were obtained among the major posttest scores, the RPMT, and the
Primary Mental Abilities subtests of space, number, and word fluency.
While the word-fluency subtest (a measure more closely associated with
crystallized intelligence) correlations were uniformly nonsignificant, the
RPMT correlated significantly with spatial egocentrism objective scores
($+0.47, p < 0.005$) and egocentrism wrong answers ($-0.44, p < 0.005$).
In addition, the PMA spatial reasoning measure (fluid intelligence in-

dex) correlated significantly ($+0.45$, $p < 0.005$) with egocentrism objective scores, -0.46, $p < 0.005$ with egocentric responses and -0.38, $p < 0.01$ with egocentrism wrong answers.

Less confirmatory evidence for the differential relationship between fluid and crystallized intelligence indices and Piagetian task performances is provided in the studies of Hawley and Kelly (1973) and Muhs *et al.* (1976). Hawley and Kelly (1973) compared WAIS vocabulary (crystallized measure) and WAIS digit backward and digit symbol (fluid measures) scores to formal-reasoning task performances in their sample of 84 males aged 25 to 74 years. The average intercorrelation value for the vocabulary index with the Piagetian volume and probability tasks was $+0.45$. The comparison average intercorrelation for the fluid measures with formal reasoning was only $+0.34$. The Muhs *et al.* (1976) investigation included both the RCPMT and the Stanford-Binet vocabulary subtest. The average intercorrelations for the Piagetian task array and the former measure was $+0.38$ while the counterpart value for the crystallized index was $+0.39$, hardly evidence for a distinctive interrelationship. However, if a subset of classificatory measures are examined, average values of $+0.50$ (fluid intelligence case) and $+0.41$ (crystallized intelligence case) were observed.

These investigations of the relationship between conventional psychometric measures of intellectual abilities and Piagetian logical concept assessments highlight a number of conceptual and methodological difficulties. On the methodological side, there is the major problem of distinguishing variance attributable to method factors versus trait or construct variables. In the Storck (1975) and Storck *et al.* (1972) studies, for example, the significant RPMT and multiple-class and seriation correlation values may represent shared method variance since a common matrix task format was employed. A more general issue concerns just how large the obtained correlation coefficients should be to signify genuine structural interdependencies. In the studies reviewed above, few instances were observed where more than 20% to 30% of the shared variance was indicated. It is obvious also that the choice of particular fluid versus crystallized measures is critical. The singular nonconfirmatory findings by Hawley and Kelly (1973) may be a result of employing different fluid intelligence task formates (WAIS subtests in contrast to the popular RPMT measure). On the conceptual side, it must be remembered that the hypothetical general intelligence factors originally proposed by Cattell and Horn are not, strictly speaking, orthogonal factors at all. They are, in fact, correlated over much of the life-span and this is borne out by the highly significant correlations among the fluid and crystallized indices in the studies reviewed above (in all cases, for example, the S-B vocabulary subtest was found to be significantly related to the RPMT). Thus, attempts to distinguish logical-concept attainment and stability on the basis of distinctive fluid versus crystallized test variances may be questionable. Certainly a minimum requirement would seem to be a composite battery of fluid and crystallized indices administered in conjunction with a representative array of concrete and formal logical-reasoning tasks. This would permit multivariate analyses to be conducted, e.g., comparison of factor structures for samples of individuals at various points on the life-span continuum.

These reservations notwithstanding, fluid intelligence measures do appear to be differentially related to logical-concept proficiency. This is particularly the case for the late-appearing concrete-operations tasks such as those dealing with classificatory skills and formal operations-level measures (see, however, the discrepant findings by Hawley and Kelly, 1973, reviewed above).

3.2. Methodological Issues

Despite current discussions of methodological issues involved in the study of adulthood and aging and/or life-span developmental change (Hooper, 1973a, 1973b; Nesselroade and Reese, 1973; Schaie, 1973), relatively few of the studies just reviewed have appeared to be concerned with methodological considerations in assessing logical reasoning in mature and elderly subjects. The apparent lack of concern for essential methodological issues consequently makes any attempt to review and synthesize the available findings an extremely difficult task.

Many of the issues discussed in this section are obviously not unique to Piagetian research with adult and elderly subjects. These issues include: (a) differences between age changes and age differences, (b) validity and reliability of the tasks employed, (c) problems of sampling, and (d) appropriate tools for data analysis. Other issues which specifically relate to Piagetian search have also generally been ignored. These include the determination of structural relationships among the measures, stage correspondence, and convergence.

The first general methodological concern, estimation of age changes vs. age differences in Piagetian task performance, remains unsettled. Currently available studies have employed *only* cross-sectional design strategies rather than either longitudinal or sequential designs. The lack of longitudinal data, however, has seemingly been of little concern to certain investigators who have concluded that significant age differences in performance for the oldest age groups tested constitutes evidence for structural disintegration or regression. Without essential longitudinal data, conclusions concerning a loss of logical abilities are highly tentative or at best speculative.

In addition to lacking longitudinal information, many studies have also lacked essential information on normative adult logical functioning. The use of restricted age ranges has resulted in a lack of information concerning age trends in performance across the life-span.

The second unresolved methodological issue concerns the validity and reliability of Piagetian tasks administered to adult and elderly subjects. In simply administering Piagetian tasks previously used with children to mature individuals, one cannot necessarily assume that the task is measuring the same ability. Criticisms have been directed toward the use of "childish" task formats (e.g., cows and barns) in attempting to assess logical reasoning in adults (c.f. H. Eisner, 1974; Garber et al., 1974). In addition, the simplistic, often repetitive questioning which typifies Piagetian assessment (e.g., "Does one of the balls weigh more?" "Does one of the balls weigh less?") may establish either a nonlogical set or disinterest in the testing situation. The use of such "childomorphic" tasks may logically elicit childlike responses rather than logical responses from older subjects.

Similarly, assessment tasks used to measure certain abilities (e.g., volume conservation) often exhibit wide variations in the task formats employed (Elkind, 1961; Hornblum and Overton, 1975; Lovell and Ogilvie, 1961). The generality of conservation responses across such a wide range of task formats putatively measuring the same ability has yet to be established. There is presently no information concerning the reliability of Piagetian tasks when used with adult and elderly subjects.

The few studies which have addressed methodological issues have examined alterations in task instructions or format (Garber et al., 1974; Kominski and Coppinger; 1968; Muhs et al., 1976). These studies have attempted to determine the effect of differences between performance elicited by the "childish" task formats typical of Piagetian tasks and more abstract or experience-oriented instructions. Neither Kominski and Coppinger (1968) nor Muhs et al. (1976) noted significant differences attributable to task format. In contrast, Garber et al. (1974), although lacking a comparison group, attributed subjects' high rate of success to the use of highly motivating and more straightforward task instructions.

Changes in task format have been relatively minor (e.g., grass to be eaten vs. grass to be mowed). Researchers have not yet creatively addressed themselves to devising task formats more relevant to the situation of adult or elderly subjects.

Problems in sampling, the third general methodological issue, undoubtedly affect the often confusing results regarding the stability or decline logical reasoning in the later years. Investigations generally have briefly described the composition of their sampling as "predominately middle class," "community-active," or "institutionalized." Due to the increased variability which affects the composition of the oldest segments of the populations, greater care and precision clearly should be exercised in selecting a sample.

Attempts to select or stratify subjects on a particular variable, such as education (Hawley and Kelley, 1973) or degree of neurological intactness (Eisner, 1973), may serve to describe more accurately logical-reasoning abilities in various subgroups within the population of elderly individuals. In general, sampling within Piagetian studies has appeared to lack any systematic design or consistent approach. Therefore, investigations often confound age and institutionalization and/or age and neurological intactness, or age and the presence of chronic disease. No study has successfully disentangled the possible effect of these factors, which highlights the need for more precise sampling designs.

The appropriateness of many of the statistical techniques employed by Piagetian researchers is often questionable. Researchers consistently have employed quantitative analyses to assess concepts that are qualitative in nature (cf. Wohlwill, 1973). Thus, researchers who have studied adulthood cognitive functioning have failed to employ qualitative assessment techniques (e.g., Bentler's monotonicity analysis, 1973) when clearly appropriate.

The final methodological consideration specifically related to empirical attempts to extend Piaget's theory to the adulthood and aging years concerns the provision of information regarding the structural relationships among these logical abilities. Due to the theory's assumptions regarding stage correspondence, any attempt to extend the theory ultimately rests upon establishing the viability of the stage construct in the later years. The lack of available empirical evidence for the existence of any structural relationships among Piagetian logical abilities stands in sharp contrast to several authors' conclusions concerning the apparent "structural regression" of logical abilities in old age (Papalia, 1972a; Rubin, 1974; Rubin et al., 1973).

Very few studies of adults and/or elderly subjects have provided information concerning intertask performance correspondence related to the issues of stage correspondence and convergence, partly because many studies have failed to provide multivariate task assessments. Other studies for various reasons (e.g., small subject samples, lack of appropriate analyses, etc.) have also failed to provide this essential information. Studies which have attempted to address this essential methodological issue include Storck *et al.* (1972), Storck (1975), Muhs *et al.* (1976), and Chap and Sinnott (1975).

4. Conclusions

The reader will recall the point that the "model" of development employed by a particular investigator may have a marked influence on the observations and attendant generalizations which are emphasized. Thus, conclusions stressing stability over time, qualitative disintegration and regression, inherent stability masked by superficial performance deficits, and inevitable neurological decline have all been put forth. In reality, these models of the aging process are taxonomic descriptions or "labels" for the phenomena at issue. They seldom tell us anything concerning the underlying determinants of aging.

One promising alternative to these approaches takes as a point of departure the distinction between competence and performance determinants of cognitive functioning. A number of investigators interested in developmental phenomena beyond the years of adolescence have employed this construct (e.g., Baltes and Labouvie, 1973; Bearison, 1974; Hooper *et al.*, 1971; Hornblum and Overton, 1976; Riegel, 1973b; Schultz and Hoyer, 1974; Sheehan, 1976). It is clear that, in the present context, Piagetian structural units are denoted by the competence dimensions, i.e., ". . . which is a formal, logical representation of the structure of some domain . . . " (Flavell and Wohlwill, 1969, p. 71), while performance denotes ". . . the psychological processes by which the information embodied in competence actually gets accessed and utilized in real situations" (Flavell and Wohlwill, 1969, p. 71). As stated previously, our task is to separate the transitory, situationally dependent performance factors from the theoretically more important structural units.

Some of the empirical research reviewed above bears on these issues. To the extent that general fluid (G_f) factor(s) are implicated in logical-concept proficiency, a case of competence involvement is indicated. Cases of genuine neurophysiological decrements associated with lowered concept efficiency would favor a competence explanation. In similar fashion, if the performance patterns of elderly subjects reveal a high degree of consistency across a rank-ordered array of concept tasks (ordered in terms of logical complexity), then structural bases are indicated (Chap and Sinnott, 1975; Muhs *et al.*, 1976). In the Muhs *et al.* (1976) investigation, for example, the factor patterns of the youngest subjects (aged 5 to 14 years) and oldest subjects (aged 51 to 80 years) were much more similar to each other than either was to the mature adult sample. In contrast, the small number of successful experimental training studies currently extant (see Table III) would suggest that the lowered logical-concept proficiency of the elderly subjects is due to transitionary performance factors rather than structural disintegration–regression per se (e.g., Denny, 1974b; Hornblum and Overton, 1976; Schultz and Hoyer, 1976).

Certain recent theoretical discussions suggest that the Genevan orientation to lowered logical-concept "scores" among the elderly or even in mature adult groups are based upon performance rather than competence factors (Bearison, 1974; Piaget, 1972b; Smedslund, 1963). Thus Piaget (1960) has stated " . . . I am for example at an operatory level for only a small part of the day . . . the rest of the time I am dealing with empirical trial and error" (p. 126). Smedslund (1963) has commented further:

> The present data lead to the following interpretation of the Piaget–Inhelder theory: The analyses in this theory are seen as referring to the *optimal performance* at each developmental stage. Thus, a child capable of concrete reasoning in some situations may be functioning at a prelogical level in others, but will never reason at a formal level. An adult who is able to apply correlational reasoning in a highly simplified situation may regress to a particularistic or to an absolute frequency approach in many everyday life situations. Briefly, it is assumed that the developmental stages are descriptive of different levels of cognitive functioning, and that adults may, at various times, function at any of these levels, although under optimal conditions they are capable of formal, hypothetico-deductive reasoning. The empirical problem in each case is to determine under what range of conditions a given person will function at a given level. The present data support the hypothesis that this range is very restricted, or even non-existent, in most adults as far as the concept of correlation is concerned. (Smedslund, 1963, p. 173.)

A study currently in progress at the University of Wisconsin is an attempt to examine several selected performance factors which may mask the cognitive competence of elderly individuals (Sheehan, 1975). Employing a 2 × 2 factorial design, this investigation will examine the effects of instructional set and age of experimenter (elderly vs. young) upon the performance of 80 elderly women administered a battery of Piagetian tasks. In addition, the possible effects of the level of social interaction and neurological intactness upon performance will also be examined. If there is a notable absence of treatment main effects and interactions while the elderly subjects show uniformly low levels of logical-concept functioning, performance-factor explanations would appear to be excluded. As a consequence, within the obvious limits of a cross-sectional assessment design, bidirectional qualitative change for the latter portion of the life-span could be contended (cf. Roberton, 1972; Werner, 1957). This would obviously demand an extensive modification in the orthodox Piagetian view of developmental change.

However, one should not be optimistically beguiled by the simplicity of the competence/performance model. Thus, certain recent comments such as:

> The ontological status of structures is a subtle one in that on the one hand they have no existence apart from the organism, and on the other hand, they are not behavioral entities that can be directly assessed through behavioral measures. . . . There can be no experiential correlates of the cognitive structures per se because they do not exist to be discovered in the environment; they must be created anew by each developing individual. (Bearison, 1974, p. 24.)

may well question the role of any observer of cognitive functioning (no matter what portion of the human life-span is at issue). Moreover, the same author has dealt with the thorny problem of genuine structural regression as follows:

> An individual who is unable to conserve because of the debilitating effects of situational factors is, in a formal sense, no different than the individual who is conserving; both have attained the prerequisite structures for conservation. On the other hand, an individual who is unable to conserve because he lacks structures by which the logical necessity of conservation can be understood has, in a formal sense, not achieved the stage of concrete-operational thought. The theoretical and practical implications concerning the treatment of these two individuals are strikingly disparate, yet behaviorally, in terms of their performance on a task for conservation, they appear very similar. (Bearison, 1974, p. 26.)

The question, of course, remains of how to discern the subtle distinctions between these two types of individual performances, and it is particularly germane to examinations of cognitive functioning in the elderly. We would contend that the competence/performance model is of value only insofar as it promotes understanding (i.e., explanatory or predictive power) of the underlying aging or developmental processes. In brief, the competence/performance distinction is only an heuristic device. All deep structure competencies are "real" only insofar as they can be empirically demonstrated via performances of some type at some point in time!

In accord with the preceding competence/performance discussions, before any valid estimate of true age changes in Piagetian cognitive functioning can be determined, greater concern must be directed toward understanding the effects of environmental change upon performance. These environmental influences include cohort-specific changes, e.g., the level and impact of formal schooling and more general long-term sociocultural change. The confounding effect of cohort differences in masking age-related cognitive changes has been well established within the intelligence testing literature. Within the Piagetian research, however, the effects of cohort changes have yet to be analyzed since none of the studies has employed sequential design strategies. The exclusive use of cross-sectional designs in assessing logical functioning in the adulthood years effectively mitigates against any estimate of cohort-specific changes.

In addition to cohort-specific changes which may affect the performance of elderly individuals, the reader should be aware, as Piaget's genetic view of history emphasizes, of the potential influence of long-term sociocultural changes which have relegated elderly individuals to an often roleless existence. As Looft (1973) has poignantly noted, the elderly in contemporary society are "left to spend their last years in disengagement, isolation, and reminiscence" (p. 50) no longer occupying their former roles as the educators and socializers of youth. One presently can only speculate regarding the impact of such changes upon the cognitive functioning of today's elderly.

It is clear that current models of the aging process cannot do justice to a life-span orientation or incorporate the empirical findings presented herein. The Piagetian model as it is now interpreted is unable to handle the effects of such long-term sociocultural change as discussed above. Despite the dialectical basis of Piaget's theory (Riegel, 1973b), "it fails to make the transition from the formal intellectualism of Kant to the concrete dialecticism of Hegel" (p. 363). The dialectical basis of Piaget's theory rests upon its assumptions of assimilation and accommodation which interact to produce ever higher levels of equilibrium. The theory, however, appears to impart primordial status to assimilation over accommodation. The accomplishments and actions of the individual as thus viewed have theoretically little impact *upon* the environment. The actions of the individual are thus circumscribed within a closed system.

A truly dialectical or relational model incorporates the influences of historical, sociological, and demographic factors which influence social and mental development (Looft, 1973). The need to incorporate these factors into a theory to understand cognitive functioning is most obvious during the adult and aging years. At this macrolevel, the individual and environment experience an interdependent relationship. Not only is the individual changed by the impact of his environment, but he is also simultaneously an agent of change.

The dialectic model views development as an interaction of the inner biological and outer historical conditions (Riegel, 1973b). In addition to the outer manifestations which the dialectical model employs to explain an individual's development, the internal functions allow for the existence of contradiction which enables mature and creative thought to coexist. Within the model, the mature individual, rather than being increasingly isolated from reality, has come to accept the contradictory nature of experience. Applications of this dialectic model to the particular issues concerned with adulthood and old age include moral development (Meacham, 1975), egocentrism and relativistic thinking (Chandler, 1975), memory functions (Kvale, 1975), and intellectual development (Riegel, 1973b; see also Hooper, 1973b).

The complex nature of attempts to describe, explain, and modify Piagetian cognitive functioning during the adult and later years clearly necessitates the adoption of a dialectical model of development. While the noted variability in cognitive performance on Piagetian tasks proves to be problematic to a strict interpretation of Piaget's theory, the dialectual model clearly allows for intra-individual variation at the level of maturity.

The adoption of a modified Piagetian dialectical perspective to the adult and aging years of the life-span serves to highlight the superficiality to date of our normative assessment efforts. Rather than a faddish preoccupation with the administration of Piagetian logical-concept tasks to ever and ever older subject samples as a research objective in and of itself (a penchant for which the present authors ruefully admit), what is required is a research program with a dual emphasis: First, the explicit incorporation of empirical results into a given model of development is necessary; very few of the investigators whose work is cited herein have attempted to systematically relate their normative or experimental findings to an existant model of development. Second, the assessment of elderly individuals must recognize the role these persons play in a modern technological society. Thus, there is a distinct need for the employment of cognitive measures which are ecologically valid and realistic vis-à-vis the aged in today's world. Approximate answers to the salient questions posed in this review await these developments.

References

Ajuriaguerra, J. de, et Tissot, R., 1966, Application clinique de la psychologie génétiques, *in* "Psychologie et Épistémologie Génétiques, Thèmes Piagétiens" F. Bresson (ed.), Dunod, Paris, p. 33.

Ajuriaguerra, J. de, Rey-Belley-Muller, M., et Tissot, 1964, A propos de quelques problèmes posés par le déficit opératoire des viellards atteints de démence dégénérative en début d'évolution, *Cortex* 1:103.

Ajuriaguerra, J. de, Kluser, J., Velghe, J., et Tissot, R., 1965, Praxies idéatoires et permanence de l'objet. Quelques aspects de leur désintégration conjointe dans les syndromes démentiels du grand âge, *Psychiatria et Neurologia* 150:306.

Ajuriaguerra, J. de, Richard, J., Rodriguez, R., et Tissot, R., 1966, Quelques aspects de la désintégration des praxies idéomatrices dans les démences du grand âge, *Cortex Cérébral* 2:438.

Ajuriaguerra, J. de, Boehme, M., Richard, J., Sinclair, H., et Tissot, R. 1967, Désintégration des notions de temps dans les démences dégénératives du grand âge, *Encephale* 5:385.

Annett, M., 1959, The classification of instances of four common class concepts by children and adults, *British Journal of Educational Psychology* 29:223.

Baltes, P., 1968, Longitudinal and cross-sectional sequences in the study of age and generation effects, *Human Development* 11:145.

Baltes, P., 1973, Psychological intervention in old age, *Gerontologist* 13(1):4.

Baltes, P. B., and Labouvie, G., 1973, Adult development of intellectual performance: Description, explanation, and modification, *in* "The Psychology of Adult Development and Aging" C. Eisdorfer and M. Lawton (eds.), American Psychological Association, Washington, D.C.

Baltes, P. B., and Schaie, K. W., 1973, On life-span developmental research paradigms: Retrospects and prospects, *in* "Life-Span Developmental Psychology: Personality and Socialization" P. Baltes and K. W. Schaie (eds.), Academic Press, New York.

Bayley, N., 1963, The life-span as a frame of reference in psychological research, *Vita Humana* 6:125.

Bearison, D., 1974, The construct of regression: A Piagetian approach, *Merrill–Palmer Quarterly* 20(1):21.

-Beilin, H., 1971, The training and acquisition of logical operations, *in* "Piagetian Cognitive Development Research and Mathematical Education" M. Rosskopf, L. Steffe, and S. Taback (eds.), National Council of Teachers of Mathematics, Washington, D.C., pp. 81–124.

Bell, C. R., 1954, Additional data on animistic thinking, *Scientific Monthly* 79:67.

Bentler, P., 1973, Assessment of developmental factor change at the individual and group level, *in* "Life-Span Developmental Psychology: Methodological Issues" J. Nesselroade and H. Reese (eds.), Academic Press, New York.

Berzonsky, M., 1971, Interdependence of Inhelder and Piaget's model of logical thinking, *Developmental Psychology* 4:469.

Bielby, D., and Papalia, D., 1975, Moral development and perceptual role-taking egocentrism: Their development and interrelationship across the life-span, *International Journal of Aging and Human Development* 6:293.

Bingham-Newman, A., and Hooper, F., 1975, The search for the Woozle circa 1975: Commentary on Brainerd's observations, *American Educational Research Journal* 12:379.

Birren, J. E., 1959, Principles of research on aging, in "Handbook of Aging and the Individual" J. Birren (ed.), University of Chicago Press, Chicago.

Blasi, A., and Hoeffel, E., 1975, Adolescence and formal operations, Human Development 17:344.

Bondareff, W., 1959, Morphology of the aging nervous system, in "Handbook of Aging and the Individual" J. Birren (ed.), University of Chicago Press, Chicago.

Botwinick, J., 1967, "Cognitive Processes in Maturity and Old Age," Springer, New York.

Brainerd, C., 1973, NeoPiagetian training experiments revisited: Is there any support for the cognitive-developmental stage hypothesis?, Cognition 2:349.

Brainerd, C., 1974, Structures-of-the-whole: Is there any glue to hold the concrete operational "stage" together?, paper presented at the Canadian Psychological Association Meeting, Windsor, Canada.

Brainerd, C., and Allen, T., 1971, Experimental inductions of the conservation of "first-order" quantitative invariants, Psychological Bulletin 75:128.

Campbell, D., and Stanley, J., 1963, Experimental and quasi-experimental designs for research on teaching in "Handbook of Research on Teaching" N. Gage (ed.), Rand McNally and Company, New York.

Chandler, M., 1975, Relativism and the problem of epistemological loneliness. Human Development 18:171.

Chap, J., and Sinnott, J., 1975, Performance of old persons on Piaget's tasks, Unpublished manuscript, The Catholic University of America.

Crannell, C. N., 1954, Responses of college students to a questionnaire on animistic thinking, Scientific Monthly 78:54.

Crowell, D. H., and Dole, A. A., 1957, Animism and college students, Journal of Educational Research 50:391.

Cumming, E., and Henry, W., 1961, "Growing Old: The Process of Disengagement," Basic Books, New York.

Denney, N., 1974a, Evidence for developmental changes in categorization criteria for children and adults, Human Development 17:41.

Denney, N., 1974b, Classification abilities in the elderly, Journal of Gerontology 29:309.

Denney, N., and Cornelius, S., 1975, Class inclusion and multiple classification in middle and old age, Developmental Psychology, 11:521.

Denney, N., and Denney, D., 1974, Modeling effects on the questioning strategies of the elderly, Developmental Psychology 10:458.

Denney, N., and Lennon, M., 1972, Classification: A comparison of middle and old age, Developmental Psychology 7:210.

Dennis, W., 1953, Animistic thinking among college and university students, Science Monthly 76:247.

Dennis, W., 1957, Animistic thinking among college and high school students in the Near East, Journal of Educational Psychology 48:193.

Dennis, W., and Mallinger, B., 1949, Animism and related tendencies in senescence, Journal of Gerontology 4:218.

Eisner, D., 1973, The effect of chronic organic brain syndrome upon concrete and formal operations in elderly men, unpublished manuscript, William Patterson College of New Jersey.

Eisner, H., 1974, Verbal and nonverbal models of development, paper presented at the Meeting of the International Society for the Study of Behavioral Development, Ann Arbor, Michigan.

Elkind, D., 1961, Quantity conceptions in junior and senior high school students, Child Development 32(3):551.

Elkind, D., 1962, Quantity concepts in college students, *Journal of Social Psychology* 57:459.

Flavell, J., 1970a, Cognitive changes in adulthood, *in* "Life-span Developmental Psychology" P. Baltes and R. Goulet (eds.), Academic Press, New York.

Flavell, J., 1970b, Concept development, *in* "Carmichael's Manual of Child Psychology" P. Mussen (ed.), Wiley, New York.

Flavell, J., 1971, Stage-related properties of cognitive development, *Cognitive Psychology* 2:421.

Flavell, J., and Wohlwill, J., 1969, Formal and functional aspects of cognitive development, *in* "Studies in Cognitive Development: Essays in Honor of Jean Piaget" D. Elkind and J. Flavell (eds.), Oxford University Press, New York.

Garber, E., Simmons, H., and Robinson, P., 1974, The effect of task parameters on surface conservation in the elderly, unpublished manuscript, Cornell University.

Goodnow, J., 1962, A test of milieu differences with some of Piaget's tasks, *Psychological Monographs* 76(36, Whole No. 555).

Goodnow, J., 1969, Problems in research on culture and thought, *in* "Studies in Cognitive Development: Essays in Honor of Jean Piaget" D. Elkind and J. Flavell (eds.), Oxford University Press, London.

Goodnow, J., and Bethon, G., 1966, Piaget's tasks: The effects of schooling and intelligence, *Child Development* 37:573.

Goulet, L., and Baltes, P. B., 1970, "Life-Span Developmental Psychology: Theory and Research," Academic Press, New York.

Graves, A., 1972, Attainment of conservation of mass, weight, and volume in minimally educated adults, *Developmental Psychology* 7:223.

Hawley, I., and Kelly, F., 1973, Formal operations as a function of age, education, and fluid and crystallized intelligence, paper presented at the Annual Meeting of the Gerontological Society, Miami, Florida, November.

Higgens-Trenk, A., & Gaite, A., 1971, Elusiveness of formal operational thought in adolescents, *Proceedings of the 79th Annual Convention, American Psychological Association* 6:201.

Hooper, F., 1973a, Cognitive assessment across the life-span: Methodological implications of the organismic approach, *in* "Life-Span Developmental Psychology: Methodological Issues" J. R. Nesselroade and H. W. Reese (eds.), Academic Press, New York.

Hooper, F., 1973b, Life-span analyses of Piagetian concept tasks: The search for nontrivial qualitative change, theoretical Paper No. 46, Wisconsin Center for Cognitive Learning, Madison, Wisconsin.

Hooper, F., Fitzgerald, J., and Papalia, D., 1971, Piagetian theory and the aging process: Extensions and speculations, *Aging and Human Development* 2:3.

Hooper, F., Sipple, T., Goldman, J., and Swinton, S., 1974, A cross-sectional investigation of children's classificatory abilities, Technical Report No. 295, Wisconsin Center for Cognitive Learning, Madison, Wisconsin.

Horn, J., 1967, Intelligence—Why it grows, why it declines, *Transaction* 4:23.

Horn, J., 1970, Organization of data on life-span development of human abilities, *in* "Life-Span Developmental Psychology: Research and Theory" L. R. Goulet and P. B. Baltes (eds.), Academic Press, New York.

Hornblum, J., and Overton, W., 1976, Area and volume conservation among the elderly: Assessment and training, *Developmental Psychology,* 12:68.

Hoyer, W., Labouvie, G., and Baltes, P., 1973, Modification of response speed and intellectual performance in the elderly, *Human Development* 16:233.

Inhelder, B., and Sinclair, H., 1969, Learning cognitive structures, *in* "Trends and Issues in Developmental Psychology" P. Mussen, J. Langer, and M. Covington (eds.), Holt, Rinehart & Winston, New York.

Klausmeier, H., and Hooper, F., 1974, Conceptual development and instruction, *in* "Review of Research in Education" (Vol. II) F. Kerlinger and J. B. Carroll (eds.), Peacock, Itasca, Illinois, pp. 3–54.

Kohlberg, L., 1973, Continuities in childhood and adult moral development revisited, *in* "Life-Span Developmental Psychology: Personality and Socialization" P. B. Baltes and K. W. Schaie (Eds.), Academic Press, New York.

Kominski, C., and Coppinger, N., 1968, The Muller-Lyer illusion and Piaget's test for the conservation of space in a group of older institutionalized veterans, unpublished manuscript, College of William and Mary.

Kvale, S., 1975, Memory and dialectics: Some reflections on Ebbinghaus and Mao Tsetung, *Human Development* 18:205.

Labouvie-Vief, G., Hoyer, W., Baltes, M., and Baltes, P., 1974, Operant analysis of intellectual behavior in old age, *Human Development* 17:259.

Langer, J., 1969, "Theories of Development," Holt, Rinehart & Winston, New York.

Langer, J., 1970, Werner's comparative organismic theory, *in* "Carmichael's Manual of Child Psychology" P. H. Mussen (ed.), Wiley, New York.

Lawton, M., 1972, Assessment of the competence of older people, *in* D. Kent, R. Kastenbaum, and S. Sherwood (eds.), "Research Planning and Action for the Elderly," Behavioral Publications, New York.

Looft, W. R., 1972, Egocentrism and social interaction across the life-span, *Psychological Bulletin* 78:73.

Looft, W. R., 1973, Socialization and personality throughout the life span: An examination of contemporary psychological approaches, *in* "Life-Span Developmental Psychology: Personality and Socialization" P. B. Baltes and K. W. Schaie (eds.), Academic Press, New York.

Looft, W. R., and Bartz, W. H., 1969, Animism revived, *Psychological Bulletin* 71:1.

Looft, W. R., and Charles, D. C., 1971, Egocentrism and social interaction in young and old adults, *Aging and Human Development* 2:21.

Lovell, K., and Ogilvie, E., 1961, The growth of the concept of volume in junior school children, *Journal of Child Psychology and Psychiatry* 2:118.

Magladery, J. W., 1959, Neurophysiology of aging, *in* "Handbook of Aging and the Individual" J. Birren (ed.), University of Chicago Press, Chicago.

Meacham, J. A., 1975, A dialectical approach to moral judgment and self-esteem, *Human Development* 18:159.

Meichenbaum, D., 1974, Self-instructional strategy training: A cognitive prosthesis for the aged, *Human Development* 17:273.

Mikulak, A., 1970, A note on Piaget's animism, *Journal of Experimental Education* 38:59.

Muhs, P. J., Papalia, D. E., and Hooper, F. H., 1976, *An initial analysis of cognitive functioning across the life-span–Final research report.* University of Wisconsin Agricultural Experiment Station Research Project (Hatch) No. 142-1857. Madison, Wisconsin: Child and Family Studies Program, School of Family Resources and Consumer Sciences, September.

Nassefat, M., 1963, "Etude quantitative sur l'évolution des opérations intellectuelles." Neuchatel: Délachaux and Niestlé.

Nesselroade, J., and Reese, H., 1973, Life-span developmental psychology: Methodological issues, Academic Press, New York.

O'Bryan, K., and MacArthur, R. S., 1969, Reversibility, intelligence, and creativity in nine-year-old boys, *Child Development* 40:33.

Overton, W., and Clayton, V., 1972, The role of formal operational thought in the aging process, unpublished manuscript, State University of New York at Buffalo.

Overton, W., and Reese, H., 1973, Models of development: Methodological implications, *in* "Life-Span Developmental Psychology: Methodological Issues" J. R. Nesselroade and H. Reese (Eds.), Academic Press, New York.

Papalia, D., 1971, The status of some conservation abilities across the life-span, unpublished doctoral dissertation, West Virginia University.

Papalia, D., 1972a, The status of several conservation abilities across the life-span, *Human Development* 15:229.

Papalia, D., 1972b, Toward a redefinition of the life concept in young adults, unpublished manuscript, University of Wisconsin.

Papalia, D., and Bielby, D., 1974, Cognitive functioning in middle and old age adults: A review of research based on Piaget's theory, *Human Development* 17:424.

Papalia, D., Kennedy, E., and Sheehan, N. W., 1973a, Conservation of space in noninstitutionalized old people, *Journal of Psychology* 84:75.

Papalia, D., Salverson, S., and True, M., 1973b, An evaluation of quantity conservation performance during old age, *Aging and Human Development* 4:103.

Piaget, J., 1929, "The child's conception of the world," Harcourt, Brace, New York.

Piaget, J., 1933, Children's philosphies, *in* "A Handbook of Child Psychology" C. Murchison (ed.), Clark University Press, Worcester, Mass.

Piaget, J., 1960, The definition of stages of development, *in* "Discussions on Child Development" (Vol. 4) J. Tanner and B. Inhelder (eds.), International University Press, New York.

Piaget, J., 1972a, "Essai de Logique Opératoire," Dunod, Paris.

Piaget, J., 1972b, Intellectual evolution from adolescence to adulthood, *Human Development* 15:1.

Piaget, J., and Inhelder, B., 1969, "The Psychology of the Child," Basic Books, New York.

Reese, H. W., and Overton, W. R., 1970, Models of development and theories of development, *in* "Life-Span Developmental Psychology: Theory and Research" L. R. Goulet and P. B. Baltes (eds.), Academic Press, New York.

Riegel, K., 1973a, Developmental psychology and society: Some historical and ethical considerations, *in* "Life-Span Developmental Psychology: Methodological Issues" J. R. Nesselroade and H. Reese (eds.), Academic Press, New York.

Riegel, K., 1973b, Dialectical operations: The final period of cognitive development, *Human Development* 16:346.

Riegel, K., 1974, From traits and equilibrium toward developmental dialectics, *in* "1974–75 Nebraska Symposium on Motivation" W. Arnold and J. Cole (eds.), University of Nebraska Press, Lincoln, Nebraska.

Riegel, K., and Riegel, R., 1972, Development, drop, and death, *Developmental Psychology* 6:306.

Roberton, M., 1972, Uni-directionality in life-span development: A necessary or unnecessary corollary of organismic theory?, unpublished manuscript, University of Wisconsin.

Rubin, K., 1973a, Decentration skills in institutionalized and noninstitutionalized elderly, Proceedings from the 81st Annual APA Convention.

Rubin, K., 1973b, Egocentrism in childhood: A unitary construct? *Child Development* 44:102–110.

Rubin, K., 1974, The relationship between spatial and communicative egocentrism in children and young and old adults, *Journal of Genetic Psychology* 125:295.

Rubin, K., 1976, Extinction of conservation: A life-span investigation, *Developmental Psychology* 12:51.

Rubin, K., Attewell, P., Tierney, M., and Tumulo, P., 1973, The development of spatial egocentrism and conservation across the life-span, *Developmental Psychology* 9:432.

Sanders, S., Laurendeau, M., and Bergeron, J., 1966, Aging and the concept of space: The conservation of surfaces, *Journal of Gerontology* 21:281.

Schaie, K., 1960, "Manual for the Test of Behavioral Rigidity," Consulting Psychologists Press, Palo Alto, California.

Schaie, K., 1965, A general model for the study of developmental problems, *Psychological Bulletin* 64:92.

Schaie, K. W., 1973, Methodological problems in descriptive developmental research on adulthood and aging, *in* "Life-Span Developmental Psychology: Methodological Issues" J. Nesselroade and H. Reese (eds.), Academic Press, New York.

Schultz, N., and Hoyer, W., 1976, Feedback effects on spatial egocentrism in old age, *Journal of Gerontology* 31:72.

Shantz, C., 1968, Egocentrism in children: Its generality and correlates, unpublished manuscript, Merrill-Palmer Institute, Detroit, Michigan.

Sheehan, N., 1975, An examination of selected performance factors and correlates of Piagetian logical functioning in elderly women, research in progress, University of Wisconsin, Madison.

Sheehan, N., and Papalia, D., 1974, The nature of the life concept across the life-span, paper presented at the Gerontological Society, Portland, Oregon.

Sigel, I., and Mermelstein, E., 1965, Effects of nonschooling on Piagetian tasks of conservation, Paper presented at the American Psychological Association Meeting, September.

Smedslund, J., 1963, The concept of correlation in adults, *Scandinavian Journal of Psychology* 4:165.

Stephens, B., 1972, The development of reasoning, moral judgment, and moral conduct in retardates and normals: Phase II interim project report, H.E.W. Research Grant No. 15-P-5512/3-02, Temple University, Philadephia, Pennsylvania.

Storck, P., 1975, The status of logical thought: Stability or regression? Paper presented at the Society for Research in Child Development Biennial Meeting, Denver, Colorado.

Storck, P., Looft, W., and Hooper, F., 1972, Interrelationships among Piagetian tasks and traditional measures of cognitive abilities in mature and aged adults, *Journal of Gerontology* 27:461.

Tomlinson-Keasey, C., 1972, Formal operations in females from eleven to fifty-four years of age, *Developmental Psychology* 6:364.

Vernon, P., 1965, Environmental handicaps and intellectual development, *British Journal of Educational Psychology* 35:9.

Vief, G., and Gonda, J., 1976, Cognitive strategy training and intellectual performance in the elderly, *Journal of Gerontology* 31:327.

Voeks, V., 1954, Sources of apparent animism in students, *Scientific Monthly* 79:406.

Werner, H., 1948, "Comparative Psychology of Mental Development," International Universities Press, New York.

Werner, H., 1957, The concept of development from a comparative and organismic point of view, *in* "The Concept of Development" D. B. Harris (ed.), University of Minnesota Press, Minneapolis.

Werner, H., and Kaplan, B., 1963, "Symbol Formation," Wiley, New York.

Wohlwill, J., 1963, Piaget's system as a source of empirical research, *Merrill–Palmer Quarterly* 9:253.

Wohlwill, J., 1970, The place of structured experience in early cognitive development, *Interchange* 1:13.

Wohlwill, J., 1973, "The Study of Behavioral Development," Academic Press, New York.

Index